T0375526

SHOWERED BY GOD'S LOVE

IRIS LONG

WESTBOW
PRESS®
A DIVISION OF THOMAS NELSON
& ZONDERVAN

Copyright © 2024 Iris Long.

All rights reserved. No part of this book may be used or reproduced by any means, graphic, electronic, or mechanical, including photocopying, recording, taping or by any information storage retrieval system without the written permission of the author except in the case of brief quotations embodied in critical articles and reviews.

WestBow Press books may be ordered through booksellers or by contacting:

WestBow Press
A Division of Thomas Nelson & Zondervan
1663 Liberty Drive
Bloomington, IN 47403
www.westbowpress.com
844-714-3454

Because of the dynamic nature of the Internet, any web addresses or links contained in this book may have changed since publication and may no longer be valid. The views expressed in this work are solely those of the author and do not necessarily reflect the views of the publisher, and the publisher hereby disclaims any responsibility for them.

Any people depicted in stock imagery provided by Getty Images are models, and such images are being used for illustrative purposes only.
Certain stock imagery © Getty Images.

All Scriptures are taken from the New King James Version. Copyright © 1982 by Thomas Nelson, Inc. Used by permission. All rights reserved.

ISBN: 979-8-3850-1980-9 (sc)
ISBN: 979-8-3850-1981-6 (e)

Library of Congress Control Number: 2024903801

Print information available on the last page.

WestBow Press rev. date: 02/28/2024

DEDICATION

To God, for every step that has brought me where I am with You today.
Luke 1:37 NKJV, "For with God nothing will be impossible."

Hebrews 12:10-11 NKJV, "[10] For they indeed for a few days chastened *us* as seemed *best* to them, but He for *our* profit, that *we* may be partakers of His holiness. [11] Now no chastening seems to be joyful for the present, but painful; nevertheless, afterward it yields the peaceable fruit of righteousness to those who have been trained by it."

Quote by Oswald Chambers, My Utmost for His Highest:
"He comes where He commands us to leave…
He teaches where He instructs us not to teach…
He works where He sends us to wait…"

ACKNOWLEDGEMENTS

In memory of Pastor Robert Hubbard, Jr., and to his wife, Kathy, for their spiritual guidance, prayer coverage, and encouragement. Deeply grateful for opening your heart and your home in love and support.

Sincere appreciation to CME for consistent prayer support over the past 10 years.

Gratitude to Al and Judi for friendship with prayers, laughter, and shelter.

Book Cover courtesy of Dan Amburgey, Memphis, TN

CONTENTS

PROLOGUE

"Is this all there is?" The unexpected words in 2010 broke through my peace of mind, interrupting my progress, while I was dusting the furniture. I stood still, unsure, trying to process the clearly spoken words. I had not uttered them, and they did not reflect my heart. Indeed, I was loving life and marriage with my incredible husband, Scott. We were sharing the housework on this particular Saturday afternoon. He preferred to vacuum and was working in the great room, while I tackled the home office we shared. The dust had collected once again on our desks and various mementos. My collection of candy dispensers and novelties had grown over the past 10 years, prior to my move to Goshen, and now these reminders of fun moments adorned the shelves above my desk. Family photos filled in the spaces. I enjoyed having these memories in view while I worked, and regular cleaning was required to keep the dust to a minimum.

Concerned that the words were prompted by some element of hidden ingratitude, I quickly prayed and thanked God for my blessings and for the amazing love with Scott. I did not share the words with anyone at that time, and the incident moved to the back of my mind as I continued working without further interruption. Scott soon relocated to heaven, life changed dramatically, and time passed.

This same question jogged my memory in July 2016 with profound revelation. The words from 2010 had not come from my mind or my heart; rather, God was posing this question about my life. Understanding came with clarity, correcting my initial misinterpretation. God brought complete healing from the pain of my grief in May of 2016, five years after Scott's move to heaven. A soft suggestion that this simple question would provide the opening for a second book in the future registered vaguely. I was prompted to start writing this book in 2021, and the question from 2010 returned to my mind.

Whenever I read or listened to testimonies by individuals who had experienced amazing adventures in service to God, I wondered what life would look like following Jesus. Some had accomplished major feats for His Glory, and some had lost their lives, with other losses as well. I was unable to imagine the reality of their daily lives. I declared to God many times, after my husband moved to heaven, that I wanted to live for Him and to serve Him, whatever that entailed. The words spoken from my heart came easy. The steps that followed challenged my words and tested my resolve repeatedly.

This book details my trek through a spiritual wilderness that at times proved to be physically, emotionally, and mentally exhausting. When people and circumstances changed around me, affecting my peace and my steps, blessings and love from heaven sustained me, strengthened me, and renewed my focus. The Holy Spirit enabled me to continue one more day after one more day, culminating in another week, another month, another year. I began to understand how King David wrote the Psalms; soaring in victory and praising the Lord of the Battle for victories one day, and then seemingly crying from the depths of despair the next. Traveling through these pages, you may recognize a similar yo-yo pattern in your spiritual journey with Jesus. My story is not a set formula in the quest to reach the heights. I share the steps I traveled as encouragement from a co-laborer in seeking Christlikeness, the ongoing goal in the hearts of believers until we enter eternity.

"Showered By God's Love" reveals the course of events following my departure from Goshen, Indiana, on November 14, 2012, and my subsequent arrival in Knoxville, Tennessee, that evening. The next five and a half years would be foundational in my desire for more of God, to know Him on a deeper level and to better understand myself. The greatest adventure in life has become the ongoing discovery of God.

CHAPTER ONE

NOVEMBER - DECEMBER 2012

The man I hired to drive the large moving truck departed Goshen very early Wednesday morning. Per our arrangement, he would park the truck in front of the townhouse where I would be living in Knoxville, and I would return the vehicle to the local branch after unloading. So many thoughts were tumbling in my mind as I drove out of the driveway that morning. Gratitude rose for God's presence and love through all the chaos of the moving arrangements. My father-in-law actually found the man I hired to drive the truck, which was a huge relief, as I did not believe I could handle the large vehicle over that distance. My son would meet me at the townhouse once I arrived in Knoxville. I marveled that I was moving to East Tennessee to live and looked forward to the beauty of the mountains and the freshness of a new locale. I was hopeful for my future with God's direction, though grief continued over Scott. Discovering God's love for me in the midst of that indescribable pain was transforming. His presence comforted and strengthened me, and I was filled with purpose as I drove south that day.

I stopped only for gas and when I needed to shake off any drowsiness with hot coffee. As I neared the Tennessee State border, the reality hit me of another new beginning. Suddenly I was overwhelmed with the prospect of being in a new place without any friends or connections. My son thankfully would be with me; otherwise, nothing would be familiar.

A rush of questions followed that realization—what was I doing? Why did I leave Goshen? What did I hope would happen in Knoxville? I forced down the panic and confusion that ensued, reminding myself of the answered prayers from the Lord about the timing of the move, trusting His guidance and believing His plans for me would be revealed in due time. My employment would continue once I was settled and connected on the internet, and life would move forward in a new way. My love story with Scott was still just as real and the love we shared had expanded through my relationship with the Lord.

I called my son when I reached Knoxville, and we met at the leasing office. Paperwork was finalized, and then we dashed to the water and utility offices to pay deposits and take those receipts to the leasing office for the keys. We made it with only five minutes to spare. I was relieved and thankful that everything had fallen into place and that my drive had been uneventful. The large truck was parked in front of the townhouse as arranged. Though not unloaded yet, I slept soundly that night, in awe of my new surroundings. I had hired a moving company in advance to unload the truck the next morning. The two young men arrived as scheduled and worked quickly and tirelessly. The furniture downstairs filled the living room to capacity, but it was manageable. One of the movers asked if I would like for them to drive the truck back to the leasing center, and I lifted silent prayers to God in appreciation for their help. I followed them in my vehicle. When we pulled into the lot, the driver let me know the truck was on empty. My dismay must have been displayed on my face because he offered to drive it to a nearby gas station so I could fill the tank before returning the rental. The money I had paid the man in Goshen was to include a full tank of gas per our agreement. Overwhelmed but relieved to have this young man's help, I went inside to pay for the fuel. He drove the truck to the leasing company without incident, and I returned to my new home, eager to start unpacking.

My mind was at rest while I sorted through the boxes to unpack; the kitchen first, then the bedroom and bathroom. The movers had hooked up the washer and dryer, and I used the laundry closet for storage. By the end of the day, the place was functional. Many boxes remained unpacked in the extra bedroom upstairs to be sorted later. The internet provider sent a technician to start service, and I was online that day. My boss was on vacation during the week of my move, and I was ready to resume work next week when he returned. The timing was perfect.

I was prompted to attend church my first Sunday in Knoxville, to maintain that continuity for my spiritual health. Seeking a church similar to Goshen, I searched for contemporary Christian churches. My initial plan was to visit on Sunday the first church that appeared in the search, and then visit other churches subsequently, before choosing my church home. The first listing was a very large nondenominational church located close to my neighborhood. I looked forward to hearing a good word from God following my move, and calm assurance settled on me with this plan.

Sunday morning, I drove to the church in prayer. Regular church attendance was not part of my life as an adult prior to my marriage to Scott in 2008. We had attended church regularly together and enjoyed gathering with fellow worshippers. Now I was approaching a different church alone, and his absence struck me acutely. I had visited churches alone during the dark years of the past, and some of those memories resurfaced as I parked my vehicle. I noticed the families and couples walking towards the entrance of this very large church, and my hopeful spirits began to sink into deep dread. My desire for a word from God, however, overrode my emotional reactions and I walked inside. This was larger than the church in Goshen, and the flutter of uncertainty began to stir. I found a seat in the sanctuary and then was asked to move next to the other people sitting on the same row to make room for late arrivals. I subsequently discovered this was the norm; you had to squeeze in and fill the seats. I made a mental note to visit the restroom first before service because the rows were too close together. If you needed to leave your seat during service, everyone on the row had to stand to let you pass, and they would have to stand again when you returned to your seat.

The praise and worship music was contemporary with cameras, lights, and a band. I had grown accustomed to that style as this was similar to Goshen. The congregation stood and worshipped together. There were announcements, a video promotion of church events, and greetings were exchanged with other attendees. The pastor began his message, and I finally was able to relax. He displayed an obvious love for the Lord and had a powerful testimony to share. He taught on the Word of God, and my spirits were lifted when I left the service. I continued attending this church for several weeks and fed on the spiritual nourishment from the pulpit. There had been an announcement made about a "Next Steps" class, and I signed up. My original plan was to visit several options before deciding on a church home, but God had impressed upon me to stay at this particular church. I was interested to know more about the values and vision of the church, as well as to hopefully connect with other women.

CHAPTER TWO

2013

The "Next Steps" class was scheduled for the end of January 2013, following the morning service, in a smaller sanctuary. The meeting had already begun by the time I located the room, so I chose a table close to the door. A woman noticed my entrance and approached me with an invitation to join her at a table situated closer to the speaker. I felt a rush of appreciation for her kindness and friendly smile, easing my inner tension. She actually sat in the chair next to me throughout the program, and I learned that she served as a table host in this ministry. At the end of the meeting, she reviewed the booklet provided and helped me select an area to serve. I was not prepared for this and was not sure where I would be a good fit. It seemed too soon to make that decision as I had only been attending the church for a few weeks and still did not know anyone. With her encouragement, I tentatively made a selection. Although not clear at the moment, in my spirit I knew this woman was going to play a role in my life in the future. I was silently pondering over this realization when we parted after the meeting.

Stephen Ministries
One Sunday, several weeks later, I noticed various information tables set up in the foyer. One table in particular caught my attention that displayed information about Stephen Ministries. During a coffee visit with Sue in Indiana, following Scott's death in 2011, she had mentioned Stephen

Ministries and had expressed her opinion that I would be a good fit to serve in this ministry. The program was unfamiliar and was not available at the church I had attended at that time. Curious to know more, I stopped to pick up a brochure. One of the women sitting behind the table rose from her chair and came around the table to talk. I shared briefly about my recent move to the area from Goshen, Indiana, following the death of my husband. She encouraged me to fill out a form for a Stephen Minister and explained that someone would contact me soon about this ministry.

I received a call from a woman who served in leadership of the program, and we arranged to meet at a local restaurant. Drawn by her kind demeanor, I shared my story in greater detail. She explained about the ministry and how the program was used to help others. Privacy was protected, and the meetings would be face-to-face with another woman, typically once a week. She suggested this would be helpful as I continued to get acquainted with the area and settled into my new life in Knoxville. I was later contacted by the woman who had been assigned to me through the ministry. She was the same friendly face who had initially greeted me behind the information table at church.

I met with this woman over the course of several weeks. These meetings provided some sense of order to my otherwise unsettled life, and I enjoyed our interaction for a time. I soon reached the point where I no longer felt the need to continue the meetings. I had been helped so much by the Lord and by kind strangers that I decided to enroll in the Stephen Ministries training program to pay it forward. After I signed up for the classes, my books were paid for anonymously. I had not asked for assistance and was surprised and thankful for God's provision through other hands. The classes lasted several months and included hours of instruction, with role playing in the classroom, and reading every week. I prayed for God to help me grasp the teaching in order to apply it with future care receivers. I wanted to be effective and helpful in service through His blessing.

During my initial meeting with the ministry leader, I shared with her my uncertainty about serving in the church. She asked me what I enjoyed doing and was delighted when I responded that I liked to pray for people. She shared that the prayer team wanted to expand, and she would contact the director about my interest. I looked forward to pursuing this opportunity.

The administrative assistant for the director contacted me subsequently, and I shared my testimony and my desire to help others. The prayer team leader sent a message that I would be contacted by the director. A few days later, I received a phone call from this man, who was in an airport out of state. He was in a hurry and asked only a few questions. He was not particularly impressed by what I shared. He did not feel I was ready for the prayer team and did not believe I belonged on the team. The conversation ended shortly thereafter. His dismissive attitude was hurtful and defeating. I did not understand how he could make an accurate assessment over the phone without any previous conversation. My emotions kicked in, and I defaulted to a negative opinion about church people that I had held onto in the past, taking the rejection personally. The two women associated with the prayer team had responded positively about my serving. Had there been a miscommunication somewhere in the dialogue? I resisted the urge to nurse the offense and instead gave the details to God in prayer.

I attended a bible study on Tuesday night, January 29. The leader asked that I help serve in prayer at the Women's Retreat scheduled at the church in February. More details would be provided later for participation. I happily accepted her invitation and remained excited when the class ended for the evening. I stopped at the grocery store on my way home for a few needed items. My heart was light as I mentally reviewed the conversation during bible study, and I was content as I paid for my purchases. As I pushed my shopping cart across the parking lot, I was approached by a young man with prosthetic legs, walking with crutches. He spoke very politely and asked if I could help him with rent money. A quick glance at his appearance revealed clean clothing and white tennis shoes. He was groomed with clean blonde hair and clear bright blue eyes. He looked at me directly when he spoke. He told me how much money he needed for rent and showed me the money in his pocket, fanning out the bills like cards. By his account, I could see he was a few hundred dollars short. I wanted to help him, and a silent battle began inside between my lack and his need. I sighed and told him there was no way I could pay his rent as I did not have that much money. He said any little bit would help but that he needed to pay it soon or face eviction. This was a silent fear of mine, not having a place to live, and I wanted to help but felt powerless. I had just broken my last twenty dollar bill when I paid for my purchases inside the grocery store. I had a ten, a five, and two ones, plus some coins in change, in my purse. This was all I had until my next payday later in the week. I did have enough gas in the car and food at home to last until then. I knew I had to give more than the two singles. I considered the ten, but instead handed him the five-dollar bill and told him I would pray for his needs. He voiced his appreciation with a hearty, "Thank you, ma'am!" and then insisted on returning my empty cart to the corral. My heart was in anguish as I watched him hobble away. I cried as I left the parking lot, because I had the strangest feeling that I had just been divinely tested. I wished I had been more generous and had given him the ten rather than the five. This was the grocery store I shopped at routinely. There were not many people in the store and the parking lot was basically empty as it was now after 10 PM. I had not seen anyone asking for money in the times I had shopped there previously. I wondered if I drove back to the store if he would still be there. The entire episode laid heavy on my heart for many days.

On the last day in January, the leader of the prayer team called. I had sent her a long email earlier in the day sharing some of my story, as we had not been able to speak yet, and she called in response to my message. One of the concerns that the director shared with me during our brief phone conversation previously was my lack of experience with addiction issues. This was an area of need, because the prayer team served with a recovery program at the church. He felt that particular background would be more helpful; however, the team leader explained that most of the team members did not have a history of addiction issues and that was not a requirement for serving. We had a long conversation. I had been burdened since Monday night about communicating with her, and my spirit was lifted before the call ended. God was up to something, and I was on the right track.

Women's Retreat
The special event was scheduled for Friday and Saturday, February 8 and 9. The leader of the Women's Ministries gave the prayer team a homework

assignment in preparation for the conference. Each of us was given a white poster board with instructions. She wanted us to think over our past and remember the most condemning lie we had believed before coming to know Christ. We were to write that on one side of the poster board. On the other side, we were to write the scripture that disproved the lie. We were to complete these at home and bring them to church on Friday night.

I felt a stirring in my spirit as I prepared to work on my project. I looked at the empty poster board and asked the Holy Spirit for guidance. I had believed many lies before coming to Christ. Though I prayed a salvation prayer and was baptized at age 12, my relationship with the Lord began intimately at age 52, a deep chasm across four decades. Lies had hardened into barriers during those years. Which lie to share? I was immediately drawn to Psalm 139. God had spoken to me while reading this passage of scripture one night in Goshen after Scott died. My eyes rested on verse 14, "I praise you because I am fearfully and wonderfully made; your works are wonderful, I know that full well." My heart surged with joy in response to His words! For the majority of my life, I had believed the lie that I would never amount to anything. This was the base lie of all the other lies that had built over the years. I wrote out the words of the lie in large bold letters and drew teardrops around the words. I turned the poster board over and wrote the words from Psalm 139:14 in big bold letters and placed large red heart sequins around these words. Through my relationship with God that began to grow following the death of my husband, I had gained the understanding and assurance that I was forever loved by God and would never be abandoned. He was with me every breath, every step. God ministered to me as I worked on my project, and I rejoiced in our special time of spiritual intimacy.

There were more than 200 women in attendance at the retreat. I served on the prayer team Friday night and Saturday morning. The poster boards were presented on Friday night for a segment in the guest speaker's message. Each of us presented our board with the lie exposed first, then we turned the sign over to reveal the conquering scripture. Flipping that poster board to reveal the truth from God's word was empowering, and I silently prayed for the women in the sanctuary to achieve victory over any lies in their lives through Christ.

The featured speaker had brought a small team to serve with her from her ministry. These ladies performed the foot washing portion of service. This was my first experience and I was not sure what to expect. I made sure my feet were clean and nails trimmed that morning before coming to church in anticipation. A young woman from the speaker's ministry team placed her hands on my feet after sprinkling them with water. She smiled warmly, and I heard her gasp softly in surprise. She spoke some positive words over my life. I was deeply moved and thanked her for sharing. I pictured Jesus washing His disciples' feet, and His love washed over me anew. Tears welled up in response. After putting on my shoes, I moved to the other side of the sanctuary, to help serve the women who would come forward for prayer.

The prayer team wore black tops and pants, and we were given white scarves to place around the neck of the women we prayed with, for them to keep. I was happy to pray with several precious women. The Holy Spirit guided the prayers, and I remained calm and focused during each interaction. I hugged every woman after prayer, draped a scarf around her neck with love, and smiled as we parted. My spirit was soaring with the Holy Spirit, and I believed something incredible was happening.

Later that night at home, as I sat quietly with the Lord, I received a revelation. He wanted me to serve at the event in order to receive His message through the foot washing in response to the poster board I had created. Despite an unhappy childhood and many mistakes as an adult, my life had value and purpose. I basked in His love as I sat with Him quietly in peace, in gratitude, in awe. The depth of His love left me speechless.

One evening, I was sitting at my computer while listening to a sermon on TV feeling somewhat melancholy. My grief family friends from Goshen had called me recently. We were connected through the funeral home in 2011 for grief counseling after losing our spouses that year. There were six of us who had formed a friendship through the meetings, and after the sessions ended, we continued to meet once a month for fellowship and dinner. We had stayed in contact following my move to Knoxville. They had met for fellowship on a Friday night and had called me with the phone on speaker so we could share conversation and laughter together. Hearing their loving voices was a wonderful lift to my heart. I missed their warm friendship, and I was encouraged after our phone visit.

Then, in the midst of the noise from the TV, the distraction of the internet, and my own personal thoughts, I heard these words, "Tell people what I have done for you." I paused for a moment, waiting. I turned everything off and listened. The words came again, "Tell people what I have done for you." I sat quietly with the Lord and understood that I was to write about my love story. Excitement rising, I mentally revisited those delightful details, until my thoughts were interrupted with instructions. I could not solely focus on the love I shared with Scott; I would have to reveal the ugliness in my past. The book would be ineffective unless I included the hurt and the dirt of my life prior to Scott. "Do not preach or interpret. Simply tell your story." I slumped in my chair, deflated, overwhelmed at the prospect of writing a book. I had never even written a short story and had only started a journal following Scott's death, jotting special moments or an occasional thought. My first question was how to start the book. Should I start chronologically with my childhood, or with meeting Scott, or where? The prospect loomed larger than Mt. Everest in my mind, and I was smothering under my own questions. I told myself to calm down and that I would start writing on the weekend. I kept pushing these thoughts to the back of my mind until they faded.

"The Bible" TV Series

On Thursday, February 21, 2013, "The Bible" series premiered on television. The episode featuring the crucifixion touched me profoundly. I have watched that familiar scene in old movies from past decades, as well as the more recent movie in 2004, "The Passion of the Christ." The images depicting the agony and suffering of our Lord and Savior Jesus Christ have always been painful, even unbearable, to watch, as in "The Passion", triggering tears for His unimaginable suffering and ultimate sacrifice for all mankind. Tonight, however, I felt a personal connection with Jesus through the action on the TV screen. In this scene, Christ had just been nailed to the cross. The cross was being hoisted and set in the ground. As the cross was rising upright, in that moment, I experienced the absolute loneliness of Jesus, the rejection, the isolation, the separation. That moment of divine connection by the Holy Spirit caught my breath, and uncontrollable sobs erupted. I sat motionless as the scene progressed on the TV screen, stunned from that divine encounter. Reassurance followed of God's love and presence in my heart. I repeated my resolve to stay the course, to persevere. Jesus had persevered in obedience to the Holy Father all the way to the cross. How could I refuse the Father to share what He has done for me personally?

The next morning my daily devotion included a passage in Hebrews. My eyes read on beyond the biblical reference until the following scripture grabbed and held my attention. The vision of Christ on the cross came to mind, that moment of realization I had experienced returned, and I felt conviction from God. I reread the passage multiple times and highlighted the text for future reference.

Hebrews 10:35-39 NKJV, "[35] Therefore do not cast away your confidence, which has great reward. [36] For you have need of endurance, so that after you have done the will of God, you may receive the promise: [37] "For yet a little while, *And* He who is coming will come and will not tarry. [38] Now the just shall live by faith; But if *anyone* draws back, My soul has no pleasure in him." [39] But we are not of those who draw back to perdition, but of those who believe to the saving of the soul."

JOURNAL ENTRY: *My identity is in Christ, who will supply all my needs. I can do all things through Christ who strengthens me. God equips those He has called. I do not have a vision yet, but God is moving me along towards my destiny.* There would be much to learn between this moment in 2013 and a vision in October 2016 regarding my future.

March 1 was the first class of the Stephen Ministries training. Before arriving at the church that Friday night, I prayed for the Holy Spirit's guidance. I chose a seat next to a woman who smiled in a friendly greeting. We became prayer partners for the remainder of our training, which would continue through the end of May. The training would help me beyond this class in other areas.

The training was interesting and challenging. The skills and techniques taught and practiced through role playing stretched me outside of my comfort zone. My prayer partner and I met for an occasional lunch or dinner, and we shared personal prayer needs throughout the program. The final training class was on Saturday, May 25, 2013. Unexpectedly, my interest in completing this class waned two weeks prior to the conclusion of the training, and I revisited my decision to participate. This had been suggested and encouraged by a few women at church, but God had not prompted me to follow this course. I was impatient to move onto whatever He had planned. I finished the course as scheduled with a more focused mindset.

The leader of the prayer team met with me on Wednesday, May 29. She wanted to explain more about the prayer ministry and to get better acquainted. I liked this woman from the start. She was warm and friendly and encouraging. She talked of the team and the members, giving a brief rundown of their strengths and weaknesses. I shared more about my history and my spiritual growth with the Lord through the love and death of my husband. I recognized that I was still grieving, though not acutely, and I was hopeful for my future. Reassurance returned by the time our meeting ended, and I looked forward to serving again in prayer. Though I had been serving for two months, I remained unsettled in my spirit. The doubts spoken by the director on the phone were triggered every week when I arrived at church on Monday nights. I only saw him occasionally, and he rarely spoke in greeting. The prayer team leader continued to reassure me that I did belong on the team. If a woman requested private prayer, she would usually include me with her in the session. I appreciated these unique opportunities through the prayer ministry, to see a woman who had arrived downcast leaving with a smile on her face and a spring in her step. Those special encounters encouraged me as well, and I thanked God for His work in our combined hearts.

On Sunday, June 9, I attended the second service at church. A woman from Stephen Ministries approached and said she was going upstairs after church for the commissioning of the new Stephen Ministers. I was surprised, as I had not received any notification of this event. She walked away to speak to someone else, and after a few minutes one of the ministry leaders came over and spoke to me, explaining that an email had been sent. I responded that I had not received any message and no one had mentioned this in conversation prior to today. He offered an apology and assured me I was included. I had lost interest before completing the class and that impression had not changed, even with this invitation. I wanted to leave after service, but the Holy Spirit prompted me to attend the commissioning. I asked several people where the ceremony was being held, and by the time I located the room, the program had already started. I quickly scanned the room but did not see my prayer partner. I did recognize some familiar faces and chose a seat at the closest table. The senior pastor delivered a warm message and then one of the leaders announced our names. For each person she had chosen a specific bible verse with a personal note of encouragement. We were presented a certificate for satisfactory completion of the program.

JOURNAL ENTRY, Saturday night, 6/15/2013

I am on the brink of a major breakthrough but do not know when it will happen. I am being tested and wonder if I am passing or failing. If I need more instruction from God, He is patient and will bring me along according to His plan. I trust Him and I will wait upon the Lord. In the past I have tried to jump ahead of Him. His word says in Psalm 27:14 NKJV, "Wait on the Lord; Be of good courage, And He shall strengthen your heart; Wait, I say, on the Lord!" I need and want His direction so that I will receive His best and whatever I am doing will bear Kingdom fruit. I love my heavenly Father, and I am very thankful for His love. He loved me before I was formed in my mother's womb. Amazing love!

One afternoon over the weekend, I shopped for groceries and selected the option for $20 cash back at checkout. I left the store and started my drive home. As I approached a busy intersection, a woman was standing on the raised median holding a cardboard sign. This was a spot frequented by people with signs for help on a regular basis. I had not seen this woman before, and I routinely shopped at this store location. She was attractive, healthy looking, and appeared to be in distress. I felt a twinge as I studied her face while sitting at the red light. I only had the single twenty-dollar bill. Surely I was not supposed to give her the money? That mental battle was raging when the light changed for traffic to turn on the protected green arrow. I drove past her, and as I turned onto the connecting street, I was filled with the assurance that I was supposed to give her that money. I drove down this busy street until I could safely turn around. As I was driving toward the intersection, I saw the woman walking on the sidewalk in my direction, on the same side of the street that I was driving. She was crying and talking on a cell phone. I felt a guilt punch as I pulled over to the curb. I rolled down my window and yelled to get her attention. She approached the car window, distress clearly visible on her face. I handed her the folded money and told her I would pray for her, and she said, "God bless you," in response. I had to move with the traffic at this point, and I started praying as I pulled away from the curb. I never saw this woman again at any intersection in Knoxville during the years I lived there, and I trusted that God was working in her circumstances.

I attended a women's small group meeting later that month and shared my experience. The leader and her two closest friends were critical of my decision and validated their reasons. I listened to their words as they aired their opinions. I did not regret my decision and believed I had obeyed the Lord's desire in that particular situation. I drive past people holding signs around the city almost daily, without being compelled to stop. How does twenty dollars compare to the great love God has revealed to me? I was not in dire financial need, and perhaps this woman needed a touch from God.

On Tuesday, 6/25, the leadership of Stephen Ministries at church approached me about using my story to make a promotional video. They wanted to highlight how the ministry had helped me and why I subsequently chose to go through the training and serve others. A tech team would come to my home to film the short video the following Tuesday evening. I spent the weekend getting my downstairs more organized. I sorted boxes for donation. I called a local thrift store, KARM (Knoxville Area Rescue Ministries), who uses the proceeds from donations to serve the needs of local communities, and arranged for a pick-up on Monday afternoon. I was donating the extra furniture that did not fit in my townhouse as well as the boxes. I worked on a clever regrouping of Scott's large Black & White photos and was very pleased with the result. Next, I hung curtains in my living room. This was a challenge because of the large solid mahogany desk in front of the window and lack of floor space to move it. I prayed for the Lord to help me achieve this successfully. Methodically, I rearranged the desk to have room to stand on it as a ladder. I then measured and correctly placed the anchors for the curtain brackets. The entire process had proceeded smoothly, and I was thankful for His guidance. These simple changes enhanced the room, and I smiled at the results. I then vacuumed and dusted, and the rooms downstairs were clean and in order. I rewarded myself with a pedicure, the first one since Scott's death two years ago. I chose an unusual color for me, a pale shade of teal, and enjoyed the freshness of the experience. Moments like these helped offset the continued grieving process and the adjustment to life in a new area. The Lord revealed His presence on the hardest days with sweet touches from heaven, just enough to strengthen me to keep moving forward. I treasured these bits of progress.

The tech team from church arrived as scheduled. The cameraman videoed my collection of photos arranged on a hutch in the living room and scanned the long sign I had hung above the doorway to the kitchen. Scott and I had bought this sign in 2007 at a local Amish market in Goshen during one of my visits, prior to my move in 2008. I had kept it after his move to heaven because the words had proven to be prophetic, "Give God the pieces and He will patch them together." My life was being rebuilt following Scott's unexpected death. The young pastor who accompanied the videographer performed the interview. He asked me to tell how I had joined Stephen Ministries and what prompted me to want to serve in return. I had prayed for God's guidance before their arrival. I spoke calmly and with my thoughts in order and collected. I felt good about the interview. The pastor asked the cameraman for his opinion, and his response was, "It's perfect and does not need any changes." The pastor asked me to speak again, and I did so with the same confidence. They said the promo would air during church services on the upcoming weekend. I thanked them for the opportunity to share God's story and hoped it would help the ministry.

DREAM, Saturday, 7/6, AM
I have just awakened from a dream. The details remain vivid as I quickly record them on a notepad. *I am sitting on the lawn of a very large house. This neighborhood is familiar, one I have walked or driven through many times*

during my youth in Memphis. These properties are elite in style and cost. This particular house is approximately 3000 square foot. I am sitting on the lawn, with my arms crossed over my bent knees, my head down. I am thinking about someone who is absent, though still alive, and their absence feels like death. The lawn is elevated on a hill above the sidewalk. I raise my head at this point and see a large alligator walking slowly down the sidewalk. A slight shock of fear surges and then hope follows that the creature will not see me or turn around. He ambles by without seeming to notice my presence. The sidewalks and street, and parked cars along the curb, appear as I had seen in the neighborhood in the past. Immediately the view changes, and I am now inside the house. I am standing in a dark hallway. A bathroom door is open to my right, well lit. The alligator is in the bathtub, full of soapy water. Suddenly an oversized python looms up over my head and is towering over me with the head looking down at me. I feel no fear with the python, but the alligator is disturbing. I start running through the house, yelling, "There is an alligator in the bathroom!" I do not mention the snake. I stop when I reach the kitchen. People are seated around a table, hands joined in prayer, apparently unaware of the python or the alligator in the house. They are not aware of my presence. The features of only one person are revealed, and the other faces are not distinguished. He is a thin middle-aged man, sitting in a wheelchair, wearing wire-rimmed glasses with beady brown eyes. His expression is tight and grim. Then I woke up. Was this connected to someone I knew personally, or did the dream hold a more significant message?*

ANGELIC HOST VISITATION, Tuesday morning, 7/9, about 5 AM
I was awakened when the power shut off. The house was still relatively cool since the AC had been running previously. I got out of bed and walked to the window in my bedroom to open the blinds. I looked outside and the entire complex was dark. I laid back down in hopes the power would come back on soon. The weather was calm and not storming. The skies were clear, and it was quiet outside. The ceiling fan started humming about an hour later, indicating the power had been restored, and I fell sleep.

The next morning, Wednesday, 7/10, I woke up, wide awake. Then the power went off. I opened the blinds to look outside. There were no lights shining in the windows or on the lamp posts. The security lights lining the drive into the complex were off. I checked my watch using the flashlight I kept beside my bed, and the time was 5 AM. I laid back down, thinking how strange this was happening two days in a row at the same time in the morning. Suddenly, quietly, the entire window was filled with bright whiteness, solid white, not transparent. My eyes widened in amazement as this white presence moved up and across the ceiling, before retracting to the window and then disappearing. I jumped up from the bed and ran to the window. Incredibly, there were small splashes of this same bright whiteness moving around the complex. I could see several around my vehicle, which was parked outside the front door. Most were moving around the center of the complex, a small park-like setting, across the driveway from my townhouse. These bright white splashes darted sideways, appearing and disappearing in constant movement. They were not high in the sky but rather lower to the ground, under the mature trees that dotted the landscape. I was frozen in awe. What did this mean? Why was I seeing this? No one was outside, and I wondered if anyone could see what was happening. I was not afraid, and I asked the Holy Spirit if this was from the spiritual realm. I did not know how to respond. What was I supposed to do? I began to sing some hymns: "Bless the Lord, O My Soul," "Blessed Assurance," and "Nothing But The Blood", while standing in the window watching these dancing splashes of white. I laid back down. The whiteness passed over my window again, and I returned to the window. Did a vehicle just pass by? No, the white splashes were still present though not as many. As I continued to watch, the moving splashes began to disappear. I turned on a flashlight and stood at the foot of my bed reading the bible, first Psalm 37 and then Psalm 23. I turned off the flashlight and laid back down. The power came back on. I went to the window again. Street lights illuminated the early morning sky. The flashing spots of white were gone. I looked at my watch, and the time was now 5:30. I rested a while before preparing for the workday, unable to think of anything other than what I had just witnessed. Later that morning, when I left my apartment, there was a penny on the step outside my front door. I smiled as I picked it up and tucked it away for safekeeping. I had read stories about pennies from heaven, wondering if they were true, and now I believed.

I shared the encounter with the woman who was appointed as my mentor on the prayer team over dinner that evening. I was hesitant to speak about it, as I was not sure if I should share such an occurrence. I was concerned that the power of the encounter would be diminished if I talked about the details. I told her I thought God was visiting me in some way, but then I thought I was being prideful because who am I that God would give me such a gift? She explained that the first part of what I said was true, but then came the lie. She said that I am special to God, as are all of His children, and He shares Himself with all of us in His own way, in His own time. She encouraged me with her words and offered insight into this heavenly visit. She said her spirit was lifted tremendously when I shared my experience with her and that it blesses others as well to hear about these encounters. She continued to counsel me, and I was at peace when we parted.

Later that evening, I sat in reflection with the Lord. The power went off two consecutive days at the same time both mornings to confirm this was from God, just like the glass shard from the broken measuring cup back in Goshen. That incident occurred in September 2011. While putting away my dishes after dinner one evening, I dropped a glass measuring cup that shattered as it hit the floor. I was standing in front of the counter where my coffee pot was stationed when I dropped the cup. Every morning, I brewed a pot of coffee, and I was usually barefoot when I walked into the kitchen, so I wanted to be sure there were no traces of glass on the floor. I carefully cleaned up the fragments and particles, first using a broom and dustpan, next the vacuum, and then wet paper towels to capture any slivers or glass dust. Two weeks later, I made my way towards the kitchen as usual to start a pot of coffee, stopping in the doorway. A single ray of bright sunshine was streaming through the closed blind above the kitchen sink. My eyes followed this ray of light to the floor, highlighting a large single shard of glass. Joy surged through my heart. Amazed, I walked over and picked up that piece of glass. I knew I had not missed it when I cleaned the floor. I had walked barefoot in that area many times since I had broken the cup and would have stepped on this glass had it been on the floor prior to this morning. Two days later, I went into the kitchen to brew my morning coffee, and again a single ray of sunshine was streaming through the blind, shining on a large single shard of glass in the same spot on the floor. Joy overflowed, and I broke into laughter in the presence of the Holy Spirit. He had repeated the same steps with the piece of glass to confirm His presence and to remove any doubt. Now, two years later, He repeated the power outage on two consecutive mornings to confirm His presence.

We serve a creative God with a sense of humor and imagination. I love Him, and I am in awe of Him.
My Heavenly Father.
My Rock.
My Redeemer.
My Lord and Savior.
My Firm Foundation.
My Strong Tower.
My Everlasting Arms.
Lord of Lords. King of Kings.
Bless the Lord, oh my soul. His love endures forever!

On Saturday, July 20, my daughter and grandson traveled to Nashville, and I met them there to spend the weekend together. It was so good to be with them again. My heart surged with love and pride as I watched her interact with her infant son. He was a happy baby. I was delighted to hold him and love on him, in awe of my status as a grandmother. We drove to the Aquarium Restaurant and enjoyed a wonderful meal, surrounded by walls of glass and water where large fish were swimming by in their natural habitat, seemingly oblivious to the countless eyes watching their every move. We lingered over dessert and then left to return to the hotel. As I entered the interstate, I suddenly started coughing and wheezing. My daughter had an extra bottle of water, which helped some.

Pouring rain pelted the windshield. The wipers on fast speed could not keep the glass clear. Lightning began to flare. Wide jagged streaks of light were continuously flashing all around the traffic. Many cars had pulled over onto the shoulder. Vehicles were stopped under every overpass on both sides of the interstate. Our max speed was 30 mph. The lightning was frantic, sometimes prompting me to duck and touch the brake instinctively. We drove about 15 miles under these conditions. The lightning flashes were so bright that I could still see them after the strike was gone, similar to the old flash bulbs on vintage cameras that produced a ghost flash after the picture was snapped.

I was frightened and silently praying, trying to appear calm, with the wheezing in my throat. I noticed that my gas gauge suddenly dropped to one-eighth of a tank. I had not noticed the gas level when we left the restaurant, and I started praying we would have enough to make it back to the hotel. My precious grandson began to cry, and my daughter was attempting to feed him a bottle from the front seat. Realization dawned that I had not put on my spiritual armor that morning, and I started praying more fervently. The rain and lightning persisted relentlessly even after we arrived safely at the hotel. I was profoundly thankful for God's protection and that we did not run out of gas. The next morning was bright and clear. We enjoyed a wonderful breakfast before she had to leave for home and I began my drive back to Knoxville. I remained thankful for God's hand on us during the weekend and prayed for safe travel for all of us.

JOURNAL ENTRY, Tuesday, 8/6
I received an unexpected phone call from an old friend in Memphis. I had not heard from her since my move from Goshen, Indiana, and I was happily surprised to hear her voice again. We caught up on the events of each other's lives. I shared about moving to Knoxville, and she filled me in on her family updates. She encouraged me at the close of her conversation and said that God is not through with me. He has something planned for me. My spirit quickened at her sweet words.

Monday, September 2, was a difficult day. I woke up late and felt out of sorts throughout the entire day. My backlog had increased, and I could not seem to make any progress with the workload. I was overwhelmed thinking about the book I was supposed to be writing as well. I recognized an element of fear while processing my thoughts. I went to church to serve on the prayer team that evening and was inspired during those few hours. Later at home, while watching TV and checking social media, I received an impression in my spirit that God's promises are mine and to pursue all. I understood that God will bless and provide, and I will not fail when I obey Him. I must get started on the writing.

The next day was dynamic. My entire being surged with strength and stamina and joy. Revelation of the power of love struck my heart, the power of God's love in my life; through Scott, through me, into Scott, into me. During my quiet time with the Lord that evening, I knelt in grateful prayer and meditated on God. He is beyond my comprehension—majestic, powerful, mysterious, loving, faithful, filling my every need. My eyes rested on this scripture from Psalm 106:1 NKJV, "Praise the Lord! Oh, give thanks to the Lord, for *He is* good! For His mercy *endures* forever."

DREAM, Monday, 9/16

I woke up from a dream about Scott. My children's paternal great-grandmother, who had died in 1992, and I are going to see Scott's grave; however, this was not his grave in Indiana. I did not know where we were specifically, but we were in a building in a city, and there was a memorial bench placed over a flat grave marker on the floor. I heard someone say, "This is the only picture we could find." It was a black and white photo, pale coloring, of Scott's face from the side, wearing a felt hat, cowboy style, and he is smiling. I felt a strange sadness looking at the picture. He has a beautiful smile and he looks happy. But why am I with the deceased great-grandmother visiting this strange place that is supposed to be Scott's grave? Scott felt like a distant memory in the dream. I started crying when I woke up.

Sometimes I would experience random physical symptoms that began without warning or obvious cause. One night I was eating dinner with my son at home. Suddenly I began to feel strange. My left eyelid was heavy and my pulse was racing. I wondered if I was having a TIA but did not voice my concerns. I tried to remain calm and act as though nothing was wrong. The strange feelings persisted, and I was praying silently. I remembered a prayer I had read earlier that morning, posted on a ministry social media page. I searched and found the video, but as I started watching the video, it kept pausing. I would praise the Lord, the video would start, and then the video would pause. This continued until I was finally able to finish the prayer. When the symptoms lifted about 9:30 PM, I was exhausted. My strength returned several hours later, and I thanked the Lord for His divine intervention.

Friday 9/27: Wonderful morning. I woke up around 6:30 and enjoyed sweet time with the Lord. I had an urge to be outside and take a walk. A small soccer park was located nearby, and there were no other vehicles in the parking lot when I arrived. A low-lying fog lingered over the field, and the air was crisp and cold. During my walk, I spotted three cardinals and heard many birds singing. So refreshing to be outside in the Lord's creation, and I thanked Him for the surrounding beauty.

Prior to my birthday weekend in October, I noticed that the reinforcement messages I had heard were about obedience and blessing. "Just do it—whatever God has called you to do." That weekend the messages at church, as well as those I heard on television, were focused on serving. I visited a local flea market after church and stopped at a booth filled with books, DVDs, and CDs. I was browsing through a table of Christian books that were priced at $5 each. The vendor picked up a book by a well-known pastor and gave it to me free. He said he was going to throw it away because the binding was broken. I accepted the book, and we spoke about Christ. The book surprisingly, or maybe not surprisingly in view of the earlier messages, was about serving. The first part of the book was called, "Improving Your Serve." Conviction registered as I read the introduction and first chapter. The book challenged me to view myself as a servant for God. This theme would be repeated in the years ahead.

My daughter and grandson arrived in Knoxville as a surprise for my birthday! She and my son had traveled together, as he would be attending the UT football game with their dad. We spent the day together on Saturday and enjoyed a nice dinner that evening. As we were driving home, I said out loud, "Thank You, Lord, for a wonderful day!" My daughter agreed with a hearty "Amen!"

DREAM, Wednesday, 11/20/2013

It seems like I am waiting for Scott with his parents, but I only see his father, and we are in an airport. I see a woman and an older man with a young girl walking by. They have their arms around each other and are smiling. Somehow I know that is Scott's ex-wife. She is with another man. Where is Scott? I follow this woman, and now we are walking into a store. I am asking her questions.

Why isn't she with Scott? Where is he? She explains that she doesn't know and she does not love Scott. She loves this man. I left to find Scott. Now I am in another store ordering something for pick-up, continuing to think about Scott. Where is he? How is he? My order is ready, but when I pick it up, the order is wrong. They gave me a clock. I show my order number, and I am assured a correction will be made. I am waiting, wondering how I will get to Scott. I know at this point something is wrong. I walk outside to find out which direction to go. A man explains the fire department is just ahead. He is going to tell them my situation, and a truck will pick me up and drive me. Next, I am at a house where Scott is staying. There is crime scene tape on the front door. My father-in-law is there with a rifle. Scott is sitting in front of an open window that has no glass, looking straight ahead, head slightly tilted. His chest is bare as he is not wearing a shirt. He looks like himself otherwise, but I sense he is dead. My father-in-law groans out of pain. He extends the rifle into the open window to nudge Scott's shoulder. Scott is sitting in a chair with his arms crossed and elbows resting on a table. I am standing next to my father-in-law. As he nudges Scott's shoulder, the body falls back, and I can see his face as he is falling. His eyes are open, blank, staring without blinking. My father-in-law turns to me and says, "I'm so sorry, Iris." I want to comfort him, and I say, "It's okay." I woke up at this point, disturbed and confused. I immediately wrote down all the details. I prayed for divine interpretation and revelation of the dream. I sensed that God was telling me it was time to let go of Scott, but I did not understand anything else in the dream. Scott's beautiful blue eyes, unsmiling, no longer alive, were shocking.

I was living comfortably in the townhouse my son had found when I relocated to Knoxville. I worked remotely at home at that time. One day in 2013 my sister showed up for a very short visit of only 20 minutes. She had a friend waiting outside in his car while she came in for a quick shower and a few words of conversation. She needed help, a job and a place to live. I was moved in compassion at her apparent distress and told her she could live with me.

We had not seen one another since 2007, and that interaction was only a few minutes. On that day, she had stopped by the office where I worked, with her family, for a quick hello, before continuing on with their travels.

No time for a visit. The few phone calls exchanged in the years prior were mostly updates on life events and our children. We had not been involved in each other's lives or families for decades, and I was unaware of what had transpired leading up to her current needs.

Though I was still going through the grieving/healing process following the unexpected death of my husband in 2011, peace filled my heart and my home. I was growing in my relationship with God, and I held onto passionate hope for my future. I would soon learn that my sister was coming from a world of brokenness, loss, anger, and deep pain. She was driven in managing her own affairs and believed that a person had to make things happen. My walk of faith was in stark contrast to her outlook at that time.

The townhouse where I was living would not be large enough to accommodate our combined needs, and I began praying for God's help. A friend in the widows' group at church spotted a sign advertising a house in the Karns area of Knoxville. She called the number posted for the specifics of the home and then contacted me with the information. I arranged to meet the owners at the house to view the inside. This was a nice home with an attached garage and fenced-in backyard in a residential neighborhood. The rent was below what I would have expected for that area. The owner let his wife do most of the talking. She was a sharp woman who had worked in collections for years, and she was all business. God gave me favor with this elderly couple, and they leased the house to me at that meeting. He had answered prayers in a relatively short time with a perfect solution--a beautiful blessing. I moved in at the end of October and my sister arrived from New Mexico before Christmas. Life was changing once again. My son received a good job offer several months later and subsequently relocated out of state.

One evening in early December, during quiet time with the Lord, I was reading Chapter 9 of the Book of Luke, where Jesus feeds the five thousand. When I read verse 16 (NKJV), the words jumped off the page, "Then He took the five loaves and the two fish, and looking up to heaven, He blessed and broke them, and gave *them* to the disciples to set before the multitude."

God revealed something very important that I had not noticed previously in this passage. When there is a need, take what you have and give thanks to the Lord. He will bless it and surpass the need. I meditated on this scripture for a while.

The following Friday night, while I was driving home, I glanced at the gas gauge, and incredibly the needle had dropped to almost the "E" line. Alarmed, I headed to the nearest gas station in prayer. While I was pumping gas, a young man approached and asked if I could give his car a jump. I readily agreed and pulled over to his car in the parking lot. He attached the battery cables, and his vehicle started easily. I prayed for him, and we went our separate ways. I remembered the young man in the grocery store parking lot who had needed financial help to pay his rent, and I wondered if this was an encounter orchestrated by God.

Reflection

During my first year in Knoxville, I participated in a couple of small groups through a local church, trying to fit in and be accepted. Grief continued as well as my struggle to find my new identity without my husband and our expected future. I lived in a beautiful area, and the mountains became therapeutic for me on the worst days. Driving in the different counties of East Tennessee lifted my spirits and kept hope alive that life would get better and would be different from the past. I tried to receive approval from others in my pain, and this was a failure. I was tolerated but not accepted or understood. I would learn through the next few years that only God could give me what I wanted and needed. I would never find that in another person, group, church, or anything the world offers. It was a painful process but necessary for me to understand my identity in Christ and His love for me forever unconditionally. I needed to connect with others, but I had to learn not to lean on any person or group or expect too much from those relationships. Only God could minister to me deeply, and He would be my source for all needs.

God revealed His presence on the lowest days in sweet, surprising ways. He sang to my heart through different birds many times. I believe they were heaven-sent because each time the singing bird was alone and loud, capturing and holding my attention. I smiled and voiced a hearty "Thank you!" in delighted response as I tilted my head to view the sky. Their songs lifted my spirits and brightened the dreary days of grief. I was functioning in my employment and daily life, but I continued to miss the life and love I shared with Scott. The unexpected singing reminded me of God's presence and that I was not alone.

CHAPTER THREE

2014

DREAM, Saturday, 1/25, 5:30 AM

I am looking down at a generic city street scene. Traffic is moving in both directions, and there are some cars parked along the sidewalks in front of stores and businesses. There are no defining markers or names on the buildings or street signs. People are walking on the sidewalks. I understand this represents routine activity of daily life. Now I am aware of angels hovering over the scene. They are entering the earthly realm as a regular person, walking on the sidewalk, while there is constant activity in the spiritual realm. I do not see the angels in a form; rather, just small blurs of white above the street scene. They leave the scene as unnoticed as they arrive, and the small white blurs rise above the scene below. The angels are constantly entering and exiting life on earth. God is always ready to help us. Call on the Name of Jesus. He watches over us, waiting for a command, a prayer, to activate their help in our daily lives. I was calm and reassured after waking, the images remaining vivid in my mind while I wrote the details in my journal. God's angels are nearby at all times.

Monday night, 1/27: I went downstairs to watch TV after a refreshing conversation with a friend from church. I began wheezing and coughing with heavy mucous production, edema around my eyes, facial flushing, and intense skin itching all over my body, even my scalp. I sat down, but my symptoms were worsening. I went upstairs to my bedroom and used an over-the-counter inhaler. I rebuked the enemy and began praising God with songs and gratitude for my healing. Within 15 minutes, all of my symptoms were completely gone. I went to bed a little later and slept well until the early morning hours when I awakened with intense itching on my forearms and abdomen, and my skin was hot. I could feel bumps on my skin. I turned on the light and saw large whelps on my forearms and abdomen. I applied some lotion and prayed again. I laid down and left off the covers a while until my skin cooled. When I woke up later in the morning, the whelps and itching were completely gone. Praise the Lord.

One Monday night, while serving on the prayer team, a woman came forward for prayer. Following prayer time, we had a conversation. I shared with her that I had received several dreams that I could not understand, though I had prayed for interpretation. She suggested I contact a couple at church, Bob and Kathy, about my dreams and provided their phone number. I was hesitant to call since I was a stranger to them, and she offered to phone first for their permission to give me their contact info. She explained that Bob was retired from ministry and his wife, Kathy, had served with him for many years.

Pastor Hubbard and his wife were both on the landline when I called. I started by sharing about my life and my journey with the Lord. I provided the details of my most recent dream involving Scott, and we talked about the different components. Bob explained the need for detaching and releasing soul ties and then led me through specific prayers. I experienced a lift in my spirit in spite of the tears. He prayed over me and explained that in order to receive what God has in store for me ahead, I cannot hold onto the past. I understood his words and trusted their counsel. The Hubbards would become an important part of my life.

I continued to seek God's guidance concerning the prayer team at church. Every week the same struggle would ensue starting Monday morning. Throughout the day my thoughts would swing like a pendulum, from negative to positive. I continued to pray and seek the Lord about direction, desiring to follow His will. No one prayed with me about this decision; instead, they merely spoke from their own opinion and what sounded reasonable. God does not follow man's methodology. This like-minded thinking without inspiration from the Holy Spirit actually serves in blocking God's work. How much more could be accomplished for the Kingdom of God if pride, arrogance, and self-serving motives were removed from the hearts and minds of the church leaders and decision makers? Since I did not receive an answer at that moment, I continued to serve on Monday nights and to seek the will of God, anticipating His direction.

An internet search of local antique stores led me to visit Harriman and Rockwood one weekend in 2013. Browsing had been enjoyable and interesting, but no specific treasures were found. The next weekend was too beautiful to stay inside and the desire to explore more shops was strong. A woman from the church I attended at that time had recommended visiting Clinton, a short distance north of Knoxville, and I headed there after service.

There were many antique stores in the Downtown area. Most were closed since it was Sunday, but I found a few that were open. One particular shop was filled to the rafters and narrow in structure, so I moved slowly through the store, turning in all directions to see if anything caught my attention. I spotted some old samplers in frames leaning against a counter and carefully made my way to get a closer look. The words of one in particular caught my attention, formed as a question, comparing a person's behavior (perhaps in the past) to their intrinsic worth. I read it several times and wondered about the person who had stitched this piece. These were not the words typically found on a sampler, and I was struck by their intensity.

The stitcher had designed, spaced, and centered the entire text and the border pattern, and then spent countless hours filling in the needlepoint canvas. The message was personal because no one would spend tedious hours on such a project unless it held special meaning. I wondered about the person's heart attitude as they worked to complete the design. Had this person felt condemned or judged? Did they experience forgiveness or love at some point after these words were stitched? What would the trail of this sampler reveal? There were no initials or year noted at the bottom. The canvas was unmounted and lying loosely in a newer frame. Countless questions flooded my mind as I stood there looking at the stitched words, and I felt compelled to snap a photo.

My thoughts kept returning to the sampler as I traveled back home. I prayed for this person and the people affected by their decisions, for God to heal and restore the brokenness, and for purpose and identity through Christ in their life. I hoped and prayed they had found freedom from the past and had discarded the sampler along with the old hurts and negative emotions. I made no purchases that day as I had discovered a greater treasure--a soul to lift in prayer.

I planned to drive to nearby Clinton, Tennessee, for some shopping in the antique shops one Saturday in late January 2014. As I was driving on Pellissippi Parkway towards Oak Ridge, the brake light indicator on the dash began sounding an alarm and lighting up red. This had occurred intermittently over the past two to three weeks, but now it was persistent. I sensed a prompting in my spirit to have this addressed now. The automotive center I typically used for oil changes was just ahead. The technician inspected the brakes and discovered the pads were almost in the red zone of affecting the rotors. He would replace the front brake pads for now and I could return for the back brakes at a convenient time. As I sat in the waiting area, a sense of calm and joy swept over me. Happiness surged in obedience to the Holy Spirit.

While watching a sermon by Dr. Charles Stanley related to obeying God, I was prodded by the Holy Spirit to continue to write. I had begun writing "Showered By Grace" but had not made much progress. I was convicted by Dr. Stanley's words, guilty that I had not already finished the book, since God first called me to write in February 2013. I sensed that many things were on hold until the book was written and published, and I determined once again, in confession, to be faithful in this task.

Saturday 2/22: I woke up around 5:30 AM to go to the restroom. I was struck with severe dizziness and could not walk straight. Perhaps I had gotten up too quickly from the bed. I went downstairs to get some water and noticed a dove just outside the window sitting on the fence. His eye was looking in my direction. God was with me. I went back to sleep until the phone woke me a few hours later. I sat up to talk and the extreme dizziness came again. The room seemed to be jumping. Nausea started. My sister came in the room to check on me and said I needed something to eat and some water. She brought me a banana and a bottle of water. Every time I moved my head, the room would jump. The nausea was worsening, and I vomited multiple times. My sister phoned 9-1-1, and an ambulance transported me to a local hospital. I was given a tentative diagnosis of mastoiditis, after the CT scan showed a collection of fluid behind my ear. The vomiting came again just before the test and the tech was somewhat hesitant to put me in the scanner. Eventually the test was completed. I talked to God silently throughout the scan, and I remained calm without nausea. My son rode with us to the ER, and I was thankful for both of them. My blood pressure was very high in the ER and the EKG strip in the ambulance showed many PVCs. Later that afternoon after arriving home, I remembered the dove. God was reminding me, "I will be with you today." Subsequent follow-up evaluation with a neurologist revealed a different diagnosis, and physical therapy was ordered, with improvement.

Sometime around the end of February, I received an impression in my spirit about the Campbell County Campus, located in Lafollette, Tennessee. The church I attended had several satellite campuses, and this was the smallest, located approximately 35 miles from the main campus in Knoxville. The first time the campus came to mind I was somewhat surprised, but did not pay much attention as it was not a strong unction and more like a soft suggestion. I had never visited this campus and was not familiar with the location. During quiet time with the Lord on March 16, I experienced a definite lead to contact the wife of the Campbell County campus pastor. I had met her previously at the main campus while serving on the prayer team but did not have any contact information. The prodding returned, so I messaged her via social media that I needed to speak to her and provided my phone number. She called me later in the afternoon somewhat surprised at my message. I simply explained that God had impressed upon me to go to the Campbell County campus. She was shocked at my words. Prior to calling, she had told her husband about receiving my message, and his response was, "Maybe God has called her to come to Campbell

County." She experienced a confirmation in her spirit as we spoke. We discussed pertinent information and planned for my visit the next Sunday. The joy of obedience surged through my spirit as I wondered about this new direction.

The widows' group had planned a special event for Sunday evening. A sister of one of our members owned a local "Painting With a Twist" franchise. She had arranged for us to meet after hours for a private party of painting and fellowship. We planned to bring food instead of wine and enjoy this special time together. The leaders had decided in advance that we would paint a decorative cross since we are warrior princesses for our King Jesus. I was excited! I had been wanting to try a class but did not want to go alone, and now I would be able to participate with friends. I arrived a little early and was given a tour of the studio. The larger room in the back displayed a variety of paintings completed by the artists in previous classes. One in particular caught my eye, and I stopped to look at the details. The scene was a tree on a large rock with the moon in the background. Rays of light were emanating from the moon. Still gazing at the picture, I remarked how much I liked it. Unbeknownst to me, the artist was nearby and overheard my words. He picked up the picture and handed it to me and said, "You can have it." Stunned at this unexpected gesture, I asked, "Are you sure?" He said, "Yes!" I hugged him and voiced a hearty "God bless you!" in amazement. My friend asked him to sign the picture. In disbelief, I watched him sign his name, "Scott". I gulped hard and thanked him again. I placed the painting in my vehicle before our class started, thanking God for this surprising gift and asking for His blessing on Artist Scott for his kindness and generosity.

Later that evening, I received a revelation from the Holy Spirit during quiet time. God notices how we treat each other. He sees how the "prize roses" treat the "weeds" in His garden. Am I a prize rose or a weed? Do those roles switch? How do I treat others who are on a different level than I am in a moment? I prayed for deeper relationship with God with wisdom and discernment from the Holy Spirit.

My first Sunday at the Campbell County campus was March 23. The campus pastor and his wife welcomed me, and we had a long conversation with prayer. I began serving with his wife on the prayer team. This was a small campus, and the team was composed of a few faithful servants. I was not familiar with this community or the people in the congregation, but I sensed a connection through the Spirit for His purpose. I enjoyed the drive to and from this campus and used the time to pray and sing to the Lord in preparation for service each week.

On April 27, I drove to Campbell County for church. Too early to arrive at church, I stopped at a fast food restaurant in Lafollette. Two older women came in behind me, and a young couple came in while I was waiting for my order. The younger couple was dressed entirely in black carrying black backpacks. My order was ready, and I carried my tray to a nearby table. I studied the two couples while I ate. Did the older ladies attend church? Did this young couple know God? The desire to invite these people to my church was appealing, but I did not speak to anyone when I emptied my tray and walked out the door. I was now concerned about being on time before church started, because we typically prayed before service. Questions popped into my mind. "Is going to church just attending service and hearing the message, or is it ministering to people in the moment even if you miss the scheduled service? Which would be more serving to God? Which would be more pleasing to God?" Disappointment in myself followed, as well as the realization that I had missed a special opportunity. I was distracted by these thoughts throughout the service.

My daughter had phoned me earlier in the day to tell me of God's intervention. She was driving on a busy street when suddenly, about 15-20 feet in front of her, a very large tree limb fell onto the pavement. She swerved into the other lane to avoid collision, frightened by the immediate danger. Thankfully the other lane was empty of traffic. I praised the Lord for keeping her and my grandson safe. The faces of the strangers in Lafollette came to mind again in the evening during quiet time with the Lord. Humbled by God's grace over my family, I asked for courage and boldness as well as another opportunity.

The following Monday an unexpected surprise arrived in the mailbox. I received a card from the daughter of a sweet lady I had met in Goshen in

2011 after Scott died. The details of our meeting replayed mentally as I read the words in the card. At that time, I had received an email message from the church office, about an elderly member who had recently lost her husband. Her daughter lived out of town and had called the church, concerned about her mother. Her mom was grieving and not doing well with the loss, and the daughter asked if someone could reach out to her mom. After reading the email, I purchased a card and wrote her mother a message including my phone number. She called me when she received the card and we had a nice conversation. She invited me to her home afterwards, and that visit began a pattern of going out to dinner once a week. She lived alone and needed to talk about her loss and her husband. I understood that need. She was a delightful little lady, and I enjoyed her company. This continued for a while until circumstances changed and I began making arrangements to move to Knoxville. After settling into my new address, I had written this special lady and she had responded to my letter.

Following this woman's death, her daughter found my name and address in her mother's belongings and wanted to tell me about her mom. She had written a beautiful note in the card, thanking me for my friendship, and included some sweet words from her mother about our time together. She enclosed her phone number. I called her subsequently, and we talked about her mom's death and her own grief over this loss. We cried some and laughed a little, and I prayed with her before the call ended, particularly with Mother's Day coming up the following weekend. We agreed if I ever returned to Northern Indiana that we would meet. The card was a reminder from heaven that what we do makes an impact on the lives of others, and the Lord notices.

Soon after I started attending the Campbell County campus, God impressed upon me the need to pray at the church one evening during the week, in addition to serving on Sunday. The campus pastor agreed with the plan. A special friend from church, Brenda, joined me every Thursday evening, and we prayed in agreement through the church, for the pastors, staff, worship team, the children and the people in the county, and for all issues as led by the Holy Spirit.

Knife Giveaway

Sunday, May 4, I stopped at the Walmart store in Jacksboro after church to pick up a few things before driving home to Knoxville. A voice announced on the PA system store-wide that a demonstration was going to begin in five minutes next to the shoe department and everyone who attended would receive a free kitchen knife. This store layout was a little different from my local store in Knoxville, and I tilted my head up to read the signs suspended from the ceiling to find that department. I steered my cart towards the gathering of other shoppers, curious to see what was required to receive the free knife. Though I had no need for another kitchen utility knife, the word "free" grabbed my attention. Other shoppers apparently felt the same pull, and I joined the huddle crowded around the podium. We listened to the product demonstrator's pitch and watched him slice everything from paper to pipe with ease, even slicing tomatoes as thin as potato chips. I had not mastered the art of cutting fresh food quickly and efficiently, and I was skeptical this knife would improve my veggie slicing skills in the kitchen; however, I listened and watched hopefully.

At the end of his presentation, he asked that everyone who wanted the free knife to place one hand on the podium he was standing behind. We all moved in closer, nudging to get our hands into position. As he continued pitching a boxed set of matching knives, I noticed the assortment of hands on the table. We all stood there motionless, waiting for our free knife, and I studied the hands and faces around me. One man's hand was burned, and I sensed this was from a drug pipe. My eyes followed the arm up to his face. He was trembling all over and his eyes were fixed on the salesman without blinking. The skin on his face was glistening from perspiration, and I looked at his hand again in silent sadness. Heaviness filled my spirit, and I immediately started praying for rescue of his soul from that darkness with healing and restoration of his life. The hand next to his was bronzed and arthritic, and the woman's face was weathered and set as she waited patiently. There were other arthritic hands and one young hand. The old hands belonged to faces without joy, and I prayed for those dry souls. The young hand had a smile on her face, and I asked God to bless her and keep a smile in her heart throughout her life whatever she faced in the future. I looked at my own hand, dry, in need of some lotion, with a few age spots that have showed up in recent years, and my wedding ring still in place. These hands bore witness to the events of our lives. My attention returned to the pitch man who by now was handing out our free knives as a reward for listening to his entire presentation. We then scattered in different directions carrying our trophies, and I headed home with my free knife sitting in the passenger seat.

While I was driving home from church one Sunday in July 2015, the man with the burned hand popped into my mind and kept returning throughout the afternoon. When a person comes to my mind out of the blue, I lift them up in prayer for God's presence, protection, provision, salvation, or whatever need that prompted the recall. I reviewed that day in Walmart, the awareness of the people around me, and those hands reaching out in expectancy. At the time it had felt like an impulsive whim to participate in the knife giveaway, but perhaps there was a deeper and more intentional purpose.

"Angel Man"

I was not prepared for what happened on Mother's Day, 2014. This particular Sunday morning I was praying and talking to God, with worship music playing on the radio, while driving to church on I-75. I reached the Lafollette exit and turned right. The traffic light after the exit ramp was red as I approached the intersection. I noticed a man standing on the shoulder who appeared to be looking for a ride though he was not holding a sign. The details of his appearance stood out. He was wearing blue jeans, white tennis shoes, a royal blue jacket with white piping trim and black color blocks on the shoulders. He wore a royal blue ball cap with a stripe of black in the middle and white piping trim. In addition, he was carrying matching black duffel bags on his shoulders. His face was without facial hair, and he was very neat and clean in appearance. I thought it strange that he was so well-groomed and his clothes were clean without wrinkles, and yet he was standing next to the highway as in need of a ride. Even the duffel bags were clean. Out of my peripheral vision, I could see that he was looking at me as I drove by. I wondered if I was supposed to offer him a ride, but quickly dismissed that idea because I never offered rides to strange men and I did not believe God would ask me to do something that would put me in danger. I did not see anyone stop and give him a ride in my rear view mirror as I drove away from the intersection when the traffic light turned green.

I followed the local highway to a familiar fast food restaurant in town for a quick breakfast, about three miles from the exit. To my great surprise, the man I had passed standing on the shoulder was now walking across the parking lot, his back to me, towards the Walmart store that was situated next to the restaurant. How did he get here ahead of me? I chose a parking space, wondering what this meant. Was I supposed to speak to this man? If I approached him, what would I say? I was filled with conflicting thoughts as I emptied some trash into a nearby receptacle. I looked out over the parking lot but could not see the man. Puzzled, I went inside for a quick breakfast and then left for church. I was late arriving and missed early prayer before service. My mind kept straying back to the stranger.

When service ended, about two hours later, I went outside to my vehicle to begin the drive home. As I began moving through the parking lot towards the highway, the same man was walking on the sidewalk across the parking lot entrance. There were a few cars ahead of me in line, and I was waiting behind them to turn. The man stopped, turned around, and looked in my direction. I was shocked. Surely I was not supposed to talk to this man. Who was he? He turned back around and continued walking on the sidewalk away from the parking lot, still carrying the identical duffel bags on each shoulder. The distance from the fast food restaurant to our church was about two miles. He could have walked that distance long before our church service ended; how was he crossing the church parking lot entrance at this particular moment in time? I hesitated before turning. Should I turn to the right and pursue this man? Again, questions raged about what I would say. I turned left instead and drove home. My spirit was heavy and my mind was distracted. The fleeting thought to turn around was quickly dismissed. As the distance increased, a proverbial rooster crowed in my mind as the scriptures regarding Peter's denial of Jesus hit my heart. Had I, like Peter, failed in a pivotal moment?

Throughout the afternoon and into the evening my thoughts were absorbed with the details of that day and the man. Why had I not stopped and spoken to him? I saw the man three separate times. That was not a coincidence. Condemnation flooded my thoughts followed by fear that I had missed something significant from the Lord. I was in turmoil. I cried in prayer and my heart felt broken as I talked to God about "angel man". Monday evening I phoned Mrs. Hubbard. She explained that this could have been an angel, a messenger from heaven. My failure to speak to this man was an act of rebellion. She led me through prayers for forgiveness and cleansing of my rebellion, followed by prayers to receive the forgiveness. She advised me strongly to stay in the Word and prayed for God to send the angel again. I was overwhelmed with remorse and sorrow. I had been seeking God in my prayers, desiring to be used by Him in life, and now I had failed to step up. *O Lord, please forgive me.*

This turmoil in my spirit lasted through the next day and into the night. I continued to pray and read the bible, desiring to hear from the Lord. I asked God to resend the messenger. Then on Wednesday, I received an impression in my spirit, while I was watching a video on social media. In the video, a piano had been set up in a train station in London in the middle of a crowded area. There was a handwritten sign on the piano that read, "Play Me, I'm Yours." The video showed the reactions of passersby to the piano and the song. Finally one man hesitantly sat down and began stroking the keys before breaking forth in song. As I read the words on the sign, I heard these words in my spirit, "Take Me, I'm Yours!" Pure joy surged in response. I was laughing and crying, thrilled, after the dreadful events on Mother's Day. I received the revelation from God, "Receive! Take my blessings, my love, ME! Take and receive!" I sat in awe in His presence, soaking in the awareness of His great love. I was afraid that I had failed an important test from God, canceling His plans for my life, and tonight I had received reassurance to continue my journey.

Though I prayed repeatedly for God to send His messenger again, he did not return. Every Thursday night and every Sunday morning when I drove to that church campus, I hoped and prayed that he would be standing on the side of the road. My heart would beat a little faster in hopeful anticipation as I slowed down in the exit ramp off the interstate. The same hope would spring up in my mind when service was over on Sunday mornings as I started the drive home. I served in prayer at this campus until May 2016, and he never reappeared. Indeed, I never saw anyone standing on the shoulder at the traffic light again in the two years I served at that campus. The deep disappointment in myself lessened with time but did not disappear completely. Awareness grew of God's great patience with me as He continued to teach and guide me moving forward.

The following Saturday I was driving in moderate traffic in Knoxville and noticed a woman walking on the sidewalk, uphill, on the opposite side of the street. The temperature had climbed upwards and the sun was shining brightly. I thought to myself that the woman needed a hat to protect her bare head. I had two hats in the car, having just bought a pink ball cap to support a teen ministry. I had the choice to turn around and go back and offer the woman a hat. I recognized this awareness of choice today for the first time at this level. I received a revelation that when we give what we have to help someone, God replaces what we give. We are to be vessels of giving and receiving. The more we give, the more we receive. How do we receive? We give away. I had been asking God about reaping after sowing, and I thanked Him for this illustration today.

The next day, Sunday, I followed the usual route on I-75 to church. During the drive I had been listening to praise music on the radio. I was 12 miles from my exit when I spotted a woman sitting on the side of the interstate with a small black bag. She held no sign but appeared to be looking for a ride. There was no tug in my spirit to stop. Driving past her I was aware of choice, a new awareness of choice. I weighed those options as I drove past her at 70 mph. That seesaw was working in my mind. In view of the revelation yesterday, I decided to take the next exit and turn around. I had no plan past that point and would simply trust the Holy Spirit to lead. I prayed as I drove, which turned out to be 10 miles round trip. She was in the same spot, now standing up with her thumb out and pulling her bag behind her. Her appearance was not typical of a person walking the highway. I had driven to church every Sunday on this route for many months and had not seen anyone hitchhiking in this area, until today.

I exited and turned onto the entrance ramp in the opposite direction, and pulled safely onto the shoulder. She started walking towards my vehicle.

I got out and spoke to her. She said she needed to get to the East Coast. She put her bag in the back seat and sat down in the front seat but did not close her door. As we talked further I sensed that she was becoming very uncomfortable. I was calm and at ease while she was speaking, without fear or internal alarm. She finally asked for some money to buy a bus ticket. I explained to her that I had no cash on me as I had put my last twenty dollars in the gas tank and that I was on my way to church. She hopped out of the car and said, "I can't do this," her voice rising. "This is not going to work." As she opened the back door to retrieve her bag, she added, "The church needs to wake up and help people like me. You're going to hell!" With that she slammed the door and marched angrily down the entrance ramp. Her words bounced off me as I lifted her in prayer and accelerated onto the interstate.

I was a little early when I got to town, so I stopped for a breakfast sandwich and some coffee. I recognized the elderly ladies sitting in a booth enjoying their breakfast. I had seen these women almost every Sunday morning when I stopped at this location and decided to speak. I smiled and asked if they attended church anywhere in the area. They smiled back in recognition, the way strangers who see each other in the same place on a regular basis sometimes do. One of the women explained that she goes to one Methodist church and her friend goes to a different Methodist church in the same town. I laughed and said I was going to invite them to my church up the road. She invited me to her women's group that meets on Tuesday mornings; however, I explained that I was employed full-time and could not attend. After speaking a few minutes, I wished them a good week and said I would look for them next Sunday.

Church was awesome. The praise worship and the message were inspiring, and my soul was overflowing as I headed home on the interstate. My thoughts returned to the woman with the black bag. I did not see her. Perhaps she had found a ride, or maybe she had chosen a different direction. I lifted her in prayer for God to extend His mercy over her and keep her safe. I thanked Him, once again, for rescuing me from the deep pit I had sunk into in the past and for giving me love and life. I prayed for this woman's salvation. Later that night, sitting quietly with the Lord, reviewing the events of the day, I penned these words in my journal, "You choose to be more like Jesus. You are not always prompted. You see a need, you help. You grow, you learn, your relationship with God deepens."

VISION, Thursday, June 19 AM
I received a vision while in prayer and quiet time with the Lord. *I am standing on a dirt road that stretches out before me as far as I can see. The dirt road is white, in color. There is well-manicured grass on both sides of the road and vivid blue sky overhead. I am standing on top of an elevation, a grass covered hillside. I look to the right, and below I see gentle movement of deep blue water lapping on a sand beach. No one is on the road or on the beach. It is beautiful and quiet. Suddenly, the man I saw on Mother's Day is standing on the road facing me, dressed in the same attire with the identical duffel bags, one on each shoulder. My face breaks into a big smile. I am excited to see him! I wonder if he could possibly be Jesus in disguise. I am filled with the urge to hug him and feel his strength and love. He is standing close enough that I can see him smiling at me. I start to cry and apologize again for not stopping that day. I confess any rebellion, disobedience, pride, in surrender to Him. As I am crying and praying, the vision ends.* I love the Lord. I love His tenderness with me.

Tuesday, June 24, brought breakthrough unexpectedly. I had read a weekend devotional by Dr. Charles Stanley titled, "Where the Battle is Won." His teaching spoke strongly to me about coming alone before the Father and surrendering to Him completely. He talked about "wrestling things out with God until you know what He is saying". The word, "wrestle", thudded in my spirit. I thought of Jacob in the bible wrestling with God all night, and I was confused. "I am not wrestling with God about anything. I am surrendered to Him," were my thoughts, but I was troubled in my spirit. I had sensed a barrier over the past several days. I had prayed and asked God, with no answer. I reviewed the recent lessons I had learned about decision and choice, my giving and God replacing. I dwelled on decision and choice especially. I recalled God's command to write the book, "Showered By Grace," over a year ago and admitted only minimal progress because of my employment. Then realization hit—my job. I experienced a hot flash and went downstairs to turn down the thermostat and cool off. I logged onto a social media page in the meantime and saw a post from a ministry about wrestling. He explained that God wrestles with us to bring us to a point of total surrender. I reread that several times and then returned upstairs to pray. God did not give me a spoken answer, but I began to understand the issue was my job. I had originally planned to stop working June 1 of last year, when my employer was going to make a change for his future, but instead I had agreed to finish his work and had been contacted to transcribe dictation for another physician as well and I had continued working. As a result, I had made little progress with the writing.

I understood I had to make a decision, now. This decision was my choice— obey God, or continue on as I am and suffer the consequences. Images from 2000 began to replay in my mind, when I faced a similar situation and made the wrong decision with disastrous results. I could not go through that again. In a sense, God had let me be, so to speak, for five years, before bringing the dream in 2005 that my life was going to change. Scott arrived in 2006. With this new revelation, I determined to trust and obey God. Peace and joy returned. I composed and submitted my letter of resignation to the office administrator. July 4, 2014, would be my last day of employment. God had called me to write in February 2013, and now one year and five months had passed without obeying His call. The time had come to write the book.

During the years following the divorce in 1996, I made my employment the top priority in my life. I had to support myself and pay my bills, so income was very important. Nothing came in front of my job during those dark years because I had nothing and no one to fall back on. I had to work. Then Scott came and life changed for a sweet season. My intensity about work decreased significantly with the love we shared. With his death, work was still necessary; however, God revealed to me how my work, my ability to earn income, had become an idol on the throne of my heart. I was relying on self instead of Him as my Provider.

I started writing on Monday, July 7, 2014. I wrote Monday through Friday, the same hours as my regular work day. I dressed and ate breakfast before starting. Then I sat down at my desk and prayed for the Holy Spirit to guide the writing, according to His purpose. My past would become an open book for all to read, and I would need His daily guidance to share the details.

During this season of writing, which lasted several months, I battled with self-image. Digging into the past and reviewing the disastrous decisions in my story with the Holy Spirit was necessary. One Saturday night I listened to a CD teaching by Dr. Charles Stanley in which he discussed letting go of baggage. He explained there are many hindrances that can affect our walk with God. There were several that applied to me, but I felt the root encumbrance was a poor self-image. I prayed and talked to God. I realized that negative thoughts, criticisms, and my perceived social inadequacies came from this poor self-image. I laid this down that night, surrendering all to God, and there was a definite lift in my spirit after prayer. This would be a process, and giving all to the Lord would be a major first step in His transformation.

DREAM, Tuesday, 7/15/2014, AM

In the first scene, three little girls are dancing around, happy, in frilly dresses. One girl, smiling, spun around to show the ruffles. Innocent. Playful. Running through a large garden with columns. The scene abruptly changes. Now I am standing in what looks like a fast food place with video games and activity in the background. I can hear the sounds of people talking and the game sounds, but no specific faces. I am in front of a white counter with a small modern cash register on the corner. No one is behind the counter. There is an oversized white platter on the counter holding a very large snake, brown with black markings. The snake is coiled in an elongated figure 8 pattern on the platter with the head poised on top of many coils. At first glance it appears to be preserved, not alive. The end of the tail is facing forward with a rattle on the end, and the rattle is red. I see no eyes. The head is mottled red, and red outlines the mouth. No one seems to see the snake though it is situated on a platter on the counter in front of the kitchen. I watched as the snake slowly and deliberately moved the tip of the rattle into its mouth and then removed it. The mouth opened and a red bubble floated out. As the bubble moved out, the mouth appeared to be grinning and it was evil. Suddenly it was very loud around me. People who had been playing video games were now violent and shouting. I heard screaming and yelling. Then I woke up. The images persisted vividly all day with heaviness and dread in my soul. What kind of diabolical evil was this? I prayed for interpretation and discernment.

Later in the month I shared a few paragraphs with a friend in excited anticipation. I had written sincerely and was eager for her feedback. Her response was jolting. She wrote back, "super rough, rough, rough, rough draft." No encouragement. No specifics. She had read my words with technical eyes and not the heart. The arrow of rejection shot through me and the negative emotions registered, but then the Holy Spirit reminded me this was an assignment from Him and not to depend on others for understanding or acceptance. Obedience was key. He would be monitoring everything written and the reactions. My focus was adjusted properly, and the writing continued.

I watched a message on TV by a pastor and then viewed it again several nights later. I jotted down the truths that he spoke and the congregation repeated back to him out loud. I was standing in my living room stating the same declarations. "My children will be blessed because Worthy is the Lamb. I will have supernatural favor and blessings because Worthy is the Lamb." This book will be successful according to God's plan and purpose, not because of me, but because "Worthy is the Lamb. The Lamb is worthy of the Glory." I prayed for the Lord to seal this truth in my spirit.

During the last week of July, I was writing about my mother. The memories triggered sadness, pain, and tears. The Lord revealed that I was angry with Him about my mother, because I did not have a mom while growing up. While my younger sister was still a baby, something happened to our mother. She was institutionalized and diagnosed with a mental illness. We did not live with her after that time. I was about three and have no memories of us living together as a family. We eventually went to live with one of my father's older sisters in Memphis. Many nights as a child, I laid in bed and prayed for God to heal my mother. I could see the glow from the lamppost on the sidewalk from my bedroom window as I prayed in tears. I missed Dad, who had subsequently remarried, expecting our stepmother to care for us and him. Circumstances revealed she did not want to share our father with his family. As a child, I thought if mother was healed, we could be a family again. I was 16 when mother died, and all hope was gone that I would ever have a mom. Now, decades later, I was struck by God's baring of my soul in a split second. We spent time together in prayer. I confessed my anger, resentment, and disappointment, and I asked God for forgiveness. I thanked Him for the love I had received from her and from anyone else in my family. I also thanked God for protecting me. I was surprised at my reaction as I wrote about my mother, but God knew this needed to be addressed and healed. I thanked Him for His wisdom and kind guidance, in quiet awe of His ways.

The next day was Sunday, and I woke with a lift in my spirit. When I went outside to my car to go to church, a single small gray feather was resting on the window edge of my vehicle on the driver's side. The presence of the Lord was tangible in the car as I drove to church in Campbell County. This would be a glorious day filled with joy after yesterday's spiritual and emotional cleansing.

My writing at this point was focused on childhood and the relationships of that time period. The details were a struggle to put into words. I listened to an encouraging message one night on God's provision. The speaker shared that God can provide in four ways: through man's hand; through His hand; through our own hand; through an enemy's hand. He talked about how valuable we are to God in the assignment He has given us. The level of blessing on the other side of the attack equals the level of the attack beforehand. Staying faithful when attacked will bring blessing.

II Corinthians 9:10-11 NKJV, "¹⁰ Now may He who supplies seed to the sower, and bread for food, supply and multiply the seed you have *sown* and increase the fruits of your righteousness, ¹¹ while *you are* enriched in everything for all liberality, which causes thanksgiving through us to God."

I received encouragement from the Lord just when I needed it most to continue this writing assignment.

Tuesday, August 5: I simply could not focus. I was in a blocked mode with the writing, struggling with discouragement and grief. I was trying unsuccessfully to move into a more positive mindset when I suddenly received a vision about Noah. "The ark took many years to build. During that time he was mocked and ridiculed. No doubt this bothered him at first and he may have struggled to stay focused in the face of discouragement from his environment. As time went on and he continued working, the voices were not so dominant. By the time Noah was almost finished with construction, he was solely focused on preparations and instructions for the long journey ahead. There were provisions to store and water to be collected. The space in the ark had to be utilized according to God's specific instructions as every inch of space would be used. While the work continued, God prepared Noah with the knowledge he would need for the journey ahead. When the family boarded and God sealed the ark, Noah was deaf to the critics' voices. He never heard words of affirmation from the people, but by that time he did not need them. He and his family were safe on the ark, spared from the flood. "Do not wait for people's approval. Keep working and moving forward. As you step into your purpose, those voices will no longer be in your mind (not important, of no consequence)." I sat still, soaking in this revelation and wisdom from God. Purpose and focus were reestablished.

The next morning I woke up dreaming of "angel man", the man standing beside the highway on Mother's Day. In the dream, his appearance was exactly the same, and he was walking along a familiar road in the Knoxville area. I cleaned up and drove there in excited anticipation, hoping to see him again. I drove past the area I had seen in the dream, turned around and made another pass, but he was not in sight. I stopped for breakfast and then experienced the encouraging presence of the Holy Spirit in my heart. I returned home and produced many pages of writing.

I stopped to check the mail about 3:30 that afternoon and found a mysterious envelope in the mailbox. My address and return address had been typed and printed on paper, then cut out and taped onto a plain white letter-size envelope. Inside was a cashier's check for a substantial amount. It was noted at the top that the purchaser was "anonymous". On the line labeled, "purchased for," were typed words that read, "go see your grandson," highlighted in pink. A sheet of paper was enclosed with the check and a devotional titled, "Being a Vessel to Bless Others," by Os Hillman, dated 8/1/2014. The first two paragraphs were highlighted in pink. Tears flowed while I thanked God repeatedly. The unspoken desire of my heart had been to visit my daughter and grandson, and He had provided travel funds with margin through very generous hands. I prayed blessings over the giver that day and during my subsequent travel. I was in awe once again of God and how He works.

Lack of adequate finances occurred frequently. One night in 2014 I attempted to purchase a book for $10. The cashier swiped my card and informed me that only $4.76 was approved. I canceled the sale and drove straight home to check my account. The balance showed zero. An unauthorized purchase of $49.95 had been processed from my checking account the day prior with an 888 phone number exchange. I spoke with a representative at my bank and explained the fraudulent charge. My account was blocked, and I was told the amount would be refunded to my account in 7 to 10 business days. I was in a panic. I had zero money and, on top of that, I had mailed my tithe check to the church because I forgot to deposit it into the offering box yesterday. I did not want that check to run through the bank. I removed all the coins from a jar where I kept loose change and spread them out on the bed. Then I prayed over them, as Jesus did over the five loaves and two fish. I checked the balance in my prior account in Indiana, and I could withdraw $40. I took the coins to a vending machine and collected $37. I went into the bank to explain about my debit card, and they invalidated the card and ordered a new one, which would take 7 to 10 business days. I called the church office and explained the hacking of my checking account. The woman I spoke to in the finance department said she had my check in her hand at that moment. I went to the church and retrieved the check, exchanging it for $74 cash to cover my tithe. Relief flooded through me as I drove home from church. That night I prayed for provision, believing His promise to provide. This happened on Monday. Saturday morning, I felt led to check my account, and incredibly the $49.95 had been debited back to my account as well as the $4.76 from the attempted book purchase, which should not have been processed. Additionally, my new debit card arrived in the mail. I would have access to my funds for gas in the morning for church. My needs were covered just in time.

I met a friend from church for lunch the following week. This refreshing interaction provided spiritual fellowship and strengthening. I was battling fear over finances to cover the monthly expenses versus faith that God's provision would arrive on time. He provided in an unusual way for two consecutive months in that the utility bill was much lower than normal. I heard an on-time message from a pastor on television about God's provision. He explained, "God is not going to send more money than you need in a one-time bulk gift because who would get the glory if He did that? Man would. God will send the need, and then when another need arises, you pray and ask for provision again. It keeps us mindful of our dependence on Him and God gets the glory. No matter how large the amount is, He will never send so much that you won't need to come to Him again. This is true for individuals as well as churches and ministries." I needed to hear these words, because I had believed God would send a large amount to cover everything. I also experienced a stirring in my spirit about witnessing to others and talking to people. I felt desire growing in that area.

On September 11, I worked on the last seven pages of "Showered By Grace." The Holy Spirit had guided the writing, and I finished the book with the satisfaction of accomplishing His assignment. I reflected on the sacrifices involved with this commitment, and I thanked God for His help. The entire book had been completed in only two months by the power of the Holy Spirit.

By Tuesday of the following week, my anxiety about finances had escalated almost to despair. I recognized I was in a spiritual battle because the negative thoughts were replaying in my mind like a roller coaster—lack of employment, lack of income, uncertain future, unknown steps after writing the book. I declared, out loud, my trust in God to provide and guide. Every day I went to the mailbox expecting a check but nothing arrived. The weekend passed, and Monday was worse than Friday, with no internet or phone service. I had to borrow my sister's cell phone to call the provider. Needing to be outside, I took a walk in the neighborhood to calm my mind. As I neared the house, I spotted a penny in front of the neighbor's house. I put it in my pocket as I walked to the mailbox.

There was no check. Panic. The rent was due on the first and my landlord had already called once. My car note was two months past due, and that bank was calling me every day. A credit card company was also calling. The water bill was past due. I had not bought groceries in more than two weeks. I had a quarter tank of gas and no cash. Despite multiple phone calls and hours on the phone with the internet provider, my attempts were unsuccessful in restoring internet access and landline phone service.

I was so defeated and weary when I went upstairs for quiet time with the Lord that I could not pray. I sank to my knees in tears, asking God to please help. I had already prayed every prayer that I knew about provision and blessing over finances as well as declarations of faith. I did not understand why God had not answered. What was I doing wrong? Was I saying the wrong words?

I woke up in the morning strong, confident, and encouraged. I called and requested a withdrawal on my 401K. I had received a major breakthrough. I understood all of my money belongs to God including this fund. God is first.

With this breakthrough came a painful revelation about the forty-plus boxes stacked in the garage. These held vintage possessions I had collected over decades, and they were another idol on the throne of my heart. The loss of time with my children in the past had left deep wounds. I had filled the weekends, when I was not working, by hunting for special items at yard sales and estate sales, or staying busy in the flea market, or sitting at an auction, to offset the emptiness from their absence. Instead of seeking God when life fell apart, I had used my time, energy, and resources in the pursuit of fruitless treasures that held no eternal value. The things themselves were not bad, but the devotion I had given to the search for them would not be healthy for me spiritually moving forward.

The sorting was painful because much of this stuff was connected to past events in my life, my thoughts and emotions at that time, my losses and hopelessness. Possessions could not produce the love that I wanted and needed. I had moved many times during the years between the divorce by my first husband in 1996 and Scott's death in 2011. The boxes had moved as well. I received a mental image of pulling on a thick rope tied to an enormous burden that looked like bondage. I could not make any progress struggling with this oversized load. Realization dawned that it was time to be rid of these boxes.

I shared my decision to donate the boxes with my children. My son gave me his view. He felt that stuff represented the worst years of our lives, and he wanted none of it. The impact of his words struck me fully, and I could not deny the truth he spoke. My daughter thought it would be better to sell it because of the increased value. I explained the need to purge it from my life and my heart. Trying to sell it for the best price would drag out the process and allow unnecessary temptation to keep some of the items.

The associated memories were holding me bound to the pain of the past- -old identity, old thoughts, regrets and disappointment. Because of God's grace, I am a new creation in Christ through salvation. I am not who I once was, and I desire the complete freedom that can only come through Jesus. I am eager for what God has planned for me in the future. The boxes and their contents must be removed for my spiritual health. This revelation was delivered with blazing clarity, and I decided to obey.

I donated the first seven boxes to a local Salvation Army center. I donated another load the following day in obedience to God. I received a recurrent theme during prayer that this had been a stumbling block. I reaffirmed my desire to honor and obey God in all things. He is my driving need. Everything I have belongs to God.

The next day I loaded seven more boxes and donated them to KARM (Knox Area Rescue Ministries). Painful conflicting thoughts raced while I was placing the boxes in the car. I was weighing donating versus selling, battling the suggestion to sell all of it and donate the money to charity. I wanted to let go. God cared about what was best for me and not the value of the box contents. Though difficult, I was beginning to thank God for the purging.

One box in the garage was labeled, "Scott", containing funeral mementos, cards, and letters. This was very painful and deflating. I resealed the box. This was not part of the vintage treasures. I found some recent gifts from my sister that I unpacked and displayed in the house. I gave her a vintage bedspread, then packed and mailed some collectible figurines to a special friend in Goshen. I was able to return a large box of vintage salt and pepper shakers to my dear friend in Mississippi. She had given them to me many years prior from her grandmother's kitchen. I believed she and her daughters would appreciate having those returned now for their own homes. I took a long walk that morning and again that evening.

I reflected on the years I had spent collecting. I would find something I liked better than what I had and then sell what I replaced. I maintained a booth in an antique mall for four years until I met Scott. By that time, I had sold off the junk and was keeping the best, my favorites. When I moved to Indiana in 2008 to marry Scott, there was not enough space in the house we were renting to display everything. Most of the packed boxes were stored on shelves in the basement. He was sympathetic to my disappointment. He said we would have a finished basement when we bought our own home, and he would help me get everything displayed to my satisfaction. He died before that could happen. I moved to Knoxville subsequently in November 2012, and these boxes had remained unpacked since my arrival. I desired the love, peace, and joy of God above all else.

The next day I took another load of boxes to KARM. Irritation began to rise again. The process was exhausting emotionally, and I was weary of the mental battle. I had to open some of the boxes as they were unlabeled. Some items were wrapped in newspaper dated 2007 and 2004, hidden away through the years. As I rewrapped the breakables and loaded them in the car, I was filled with the realization that God wants to be First, First, First in all things in my heart and life.

A few nights later I listened to a message about dreams for our lives. I reaffirmed my belief in the images I had received from God concerning my future. I have to cooperate with God for this to happen and follow His leading. My personal circumstances will not affect the dream if I am working towards that goal. I prayed and sat with the Lord later in the evening thinking about my situation. *"Stay focused on the dream. Stay close to Me. Obey Me. No turning back."*

I printed out the typed pages of the book to begin editing. I had read it so many times on my computer that I needed a fresh perspective. Seeing the words on paper would be helpful in reading. I drove to a local fast food restaurant and sat outside, working diligently--making additions, correcting grammatical errors, and deleting redundant words, feeling pleased with my progress. A couple of hours had passed, when a woman came out onto the patio eating an ice cream cone. We smiled in acknowledgement, and she mentioned the weather. A conversation began. She talked about her ex-husband recently dying of prostate cancer. Neither she nor their three sons had known he had been sick for five years. He had left her for another woman many years prior, and she had prayed for him for salvation, healing, and forgiveness. She had also prayed for God to work in his heart and restore their marriage, but that did not happen. The oldest and youngest sons did not attend their father's funeral. Her name was "Rose," and she remarked that we both had flower names, after I shared that my name was "Iris." I told her a little of my story—from Memphis to Indiana to Knoxville, and how my relationship with God changed through the love and loss of my husband, Scott. I explained how God had called me to, "Tell people what I have done for you," and that I was working on the book, pointing to the stack of paper on the table. She invited me to her church, and I told her where I attended. She asked if I came to this fast food location very often and suggested maybe we would see each other again and share a meal. I replied that I would enjoy that very much. I then asked her if she needed prayer for anything, and she requested prayer for an upcoming doctor visit the next week. She asked if I would like for her to pray about my book, and I gave a hearty "Yes!" in response. By this time she had finished her ice cream cone, and we exchanged goodbyes. I returned to reading and editing.

A short time later I heard a bird singing loudly across the parking lot, perched on top of a skimpy bush. I smiled as I turned my head to look and listen. My soul was refreshed by the time I headed home after 7 PM. I had read all the pages and made additions as prompted. I had a lot of work to do on the computer now. I felt like a new woman as I drove home. Awareness dawned that I need God every moment of every day, and I thanked Him for this special time. I prayed for "Rose" and her sons.

Friday, October 10, was a disappointing day. I was distracted by the gray rainy sky. I just could not seem to stay focused. I went out for an early dinner. One table over, I heard the conversation between a middle-age man and a younger man. The young man was sharing how he had given his heart to Jesus! I experienced a lift in my spirit at his words. I silently prayed blessings over his life and for God to guide and protect him in his journey.

Saturday morning, while still in bed, Isaiah 5 popped into my mind. I was not familiar with that passage so I sat up to read my bible. Desolation and judgment are coming. The Holy Spirit must have given me this passage because I would not have thought of it otherwise. He interjected this while I was praying about the day ahead, and I received a reminder to stay focused on spiritual matters and not earthly pastimes.

Later that day I attended a UT football game with my sister, who had been given tickets on the 50 yard line with a parking pass, a very generous gift. While at the game, my attention rested on a couple seated in front of our section. The middle-aged man held a large bottle of Royal Crown that he kept pouring into his cup. I noticed his wife's cup was three-fourths full, and he poured enough alcohol to fill the cup. She used her straw to stir the mixture. He then passed a small bottle of Maker's Mark to the couple seated on his left who also added this to their cups. My eyes traveled from them to the crowds in the stands. Lost empty people were all around us. I felt the pull of the world while sitting at the game—how people get wrapped up in the things and approval of the world, the acknowledgement and acceptance of others. I sensed the emptiness, the loneliness, the desire for things that hold no eternal value in the eyes of the Lord. I lifted a silent prayer for Holy Spirit to sweep across this nation in revival. Isaiah chapter 5 came to mind again. There is a connection to today, the scripture, and the prophetic dreams. Revelation followed that my book is a step towards divine purpose and will allow positioning for what is next. I must listen and follow God only, now and in the future.

My prayer friend offered to contact an English teacher about possibly editing the book. After prayerful consideration, this woman agreed to read the book. I trusted God would direct the editing from her professional perspective.

I listened to a message in November from II Kings 4; the oil in the vessels. The oil is the Holy Spirit. He is seeking a vessel to fill—anoint, bless, give purpose and direction. We do not have to be good looking, talented, connected, et cetera. We just need to be clean and empty. The devil is defeated and does not have the keys to his own house. I asked God to let me be His vessel, to help me understand Him more, and to continue to teach me.

While my book was being edited by the English teacher, I began praying about the publishing. I had no experience or knowledge of how to publish a book, but I believed that God would provide since He had directed the writing. I was doing chores around the house one day and intermittently checking email and social media. I sat down at one point and noticed a suggestion on my social media page. "Hunter Heart Publishing" was advertising a book publishing contest. I skimmed the details and clicked off the page in disbelief. Immediately I was reminded, "Didn't you pray for your book to be published?" I quickly searched the page name and read through the contest details and requirements. I scanned through old posts on the page and the publisher was legitimate. This contest would be open for one month, beginning December 1. The winner would be determined according to the number of votes received for each author who entered the contest. I posted a notice on my page about the contest and asked for my family and friends to vote according to the rules, and I prayed. I reposted reminders through the following weeks and continued to pray.

My daughter and grandson arrived in Knoxville on Wednesday, November 26, for Thanksgiving. We prepared dinner together on the holiday and enjoyed a wonderful meal. A friend had recently given me some toys her grandchildren had outgrown, and my grandson was enjoying those as we relaxed after dinner. Friday we went to the "Fantasy of Trees" in Downtown Knoxville followed by lunch at "Chuy's." Later we drove to "Bass Pro Shops" in Kodak for a photo with Santa and then onto Sevierville and Pigeon Forge to see the Christmas lights. We stopped at "The Island" to look at the lights and do some shopping. Saturday we went to the Children's Museum in Oak Ridge, which was perfect for his young age. There were many rooms and props for him to explore, and we captured special pictures as he played. We stopped for lunch afterwards, and my grandson had the giggles. So delightful to hear him laughing! We attended church and worshipped together. They left the next day to return to Memphis. My face was smiling but my heart was sad as they pulled out of the driveway. With gratitude, I prayed for safe travel. My son had also called over the holiday to talk to all of us, and my heart was filled with joy. Every time we had to say goodbye, I wondered how long I would be out in the "wilderness."

DREAM, 12/1, AM
I woke up on the first of December from a dream early in the morning that was short and strange. In the dream, I am dreaming of a cat. This cat is white with small black spots, almost dot size, scattered all over. Pretty cat with fluffy long hair. In the dream I woke up and discovered the cat was in the house, sitting calmly on the floor next to a wall. I felt no alarm or fear—just surprise. The dream ended that point. I was not sure if the dream held any significance. I prayed while I recorded the details on the bedside notepad.

My friend returned the rough draft of my book on December 12. The teacher had completed the editing. I was eager to see the corrections and suggestions. The Lord had impressed upon me to "plant many seeds" regarding the book.

Bells
I spent some time in the garage going through my Christmas storage totes. My sister and I had already decorated a Christmas tree, and I was looking to see what I had kept from Goshen. I spotted the container containing a special curtain rod and reminisced over the memories. Scott could take my breath away with the stroke of a pen or a simple gesture. Sometimes his ideas surprised me unexpectedly. In 2008 while browsing through Christmas decorations in a local store, he stopped in front of the garland.

I was looking at the ornaments on display, aware of him in my peripheral vision. I heard the soft jingle of bells and turned to look in his direction. He was smiling at me while gently shaking a strand of bead garland with red and green bells attached. He asked me if I would like a jingle bell curtain for the doorway of our home office.

Intrigued by his suggestion, I watched him secure the garland to a small tension rod with red and green cord, allowing the strands to hang in measured lengths. He positioned the bead curtain inside the door frame of our home office and waited for my response. I liked the sound of the bells as I moved through the doorway and shared my appreciation for his efforts. Though playful and fun on the surface, the bells struck a chord deep inside.

As a young child we moved around a lot while living with Dad. During a visit in my 20s, he drove us around Beaumont (Texas) through the neighborhoods where we had lived in the past. I had no memory of some of these places, but I remembered hearing a church bell ringing on Sunday mornings. The jingle bell garland had triggered that memory.

I had not hung the curtain since Scott moved to heaven. Removing the lid, I lifted the rod and allowed the strands to unfurl, the bells jingling easily with movement. Revelation dawned and tears began to fall softly. The church bell had summoned believers to the Lord's house. God had been calling me to Him through Scott's love, words, and kindness. I sat in awe, gently touching the bells, soaking in His love.

My son called and said he was driving up and would arrive later on Christmas Day. I prepared a hearty meal for us to enjoy while we caught up on each other's lives. The next morning I cooked breakfast before he had to leave later that day. He would return to work on Monday. I was blessed to see both of my children and my grandson during this holiday season.

After Christmas, I started working on the corrections I had received from the teacher on my book draft. I received insight from God on different issues to add to the book and incorporated those as well. Excitement was increasing over the book becoming a reality.

CHAPTER FOUR

2015

On January 1, 2015, I was announced the winner of the Hunter Heart publishing contest! God had provided the funds for book publication and He would work through this publisher. I shared the news with all my friends on social media who had voted for me, and they rejoiced with me in God's provision. I was in awe of God's answer to prayer for publication of the book. His ways definitely extend beyond imagination.

DREAM, Monday, 1/5/2015
Woke up from a dream with a sad realization in my spirit. *I am at a bazaar inside a building with two friends. We are looking at the items displayed on the tables while moving along. I see my friends leave without saying goodbye. They did not turn around and look at me as they exited the building. I saw the backs of their heads as they left. I was disappointed and hurt. I had collected some stuff outside on the grass in a small pile to pay for later. I walked around inside the building, and there was a preacher speaking and offering to pray for people. We made eye contact as he was talking, and I walked over towards him. He was strange, and nothing he said made sense. Suddenly it was quiet, and everyone was gone. A large sheet of white paper is now blocking the preacher's face, and he is silent. I went to get my things outside, and they were gone. People were leaving, and someone had taken my stuff. I felt alone, without friends. I see a police car parked on the street with an officer sitting in the car. I look around and notice some stores and a parking lot nearby, but I feel strangely*

isolated and alone, as though everything is unfamiliar around me and I have been abandoned by my friends. I woke up at this point.

Later in the day I received a revelation that the book will move me into position for my purpose. Circumstances will change in my life. I prayed about the dream.

I phoned Pastor Hubbard and his wife the next day. I was able to speak to both of them during the call. I shared the cat dream first that I had received at the beginning of December. Mrs. Hubbard said in ancient times a cat represented a god. God may be warning me that something in my house or life could be creeping into His place. She encouraged me to ask God to reveal anything that I am placing above Him.

Pastor Hubbard spoke about the most recent dream and said it could be warning of future abandonment. Keep the things close that I treasure. The man in the dream sounded good at first, but as I listened to him nothing made sense. White paper could be protection from God against this wrong person. This man represented a leader. Weigh things that are taught. Test the Spirit and ask the Lord to reveal who He is trying to alert me about. We prayed together at the end of our conversation.

Saturday afternoon, my sister and I went to see the movie, "Selma". During the movie, I was elevated in my spirit on a higher level than the scenes in the movie, and the following was downloaded in my spirit: *"Dr. Martin Luther King, Jr., knew his path would lead to an early death, but he drew on the power of God to give him strength to fulfill his purpose. He knew that nothing—no one and no circumstance—could take his assurance of God, nothing could pluck him out of the Father's hand. Though he might lose much on earth, he would gain everything in heaven for God's glory. Mankind has tried to use Dr. King's words and visions for their own agendas, as well as the Word of God has been misused and distorted for the agendas of man. Stay focused on God and His insurmountable power."*

On Monday I was led to look inside my closet, which was a deep rectangle in design. I discovered three boxes in the back of the closet. I set these in the middle of my bedroom floor. Sighing deeply, I remembered that these boxes held my special favorites, carefully padded in bubble wrap and sealed to prevent breakage. The internal struggle began again. I left them sitting there all day and reflected over what God had revealed through the dreams and the donation of the previous boxes. I understood that incomplete obedience was disobedience, rebellion against God, and this would block what God had planned for my life.

The next day I loaded this last load of boxes and drove to KARM. I was mentally calculating the value of the contents, when suddenly I received a revelation from God. I experienced how He felt about the stuff man idolizes. It is all detestable to Him. I was overwhelmed with the insignificance of what I had considered treasure. This held zero value to God. The money I had spent, the time I had used, the priority I had given to this stuff was abhorrent to God. I felt a sad detachment in my spirit, acknowledging God's truth and letting go of the past that these boxes represented. I took a long walk after I arrived back home. He must be God on the throne of my heart. This stuff represented a god in my life in the past, before I knew Jesus in my heart. There was no place for it now. As I processed letting go completely of old stuff, old thoughts, old desires, the old me, I was filled with inexpressible freedom in my soul. The peace, love, and joy of the Lord flooded my heart, and I thanked Him through the rest of the day and evening.

I continued to write while the book was undergoing a second editing. The teacher had returned the book, and my prayer friend had offered to edit it as well. I agreed because I wanted to present the best manuscript I possibly could to the publisher for publication. The publishing deal included editing, but I thought a second set of eyes would be helpful. My friend would send suggestions after reading a set number of pages, and I worked on those through the subsequent days. Reading through some of these, I reflected on the hole left by Scott's death and how only God could fill that emptiness—not another man, not a job, not my vintage items, not anyone or anything. Only God can fill the place created in us for Him.

During this time of waiting, I spent a lot of time in thought and reflection, while continuing to serve at church in prayer. For some reason, I offered to let a couple in leadership at the church campus read my book in draft form.

I soon regretted that decision as suspicions arose that my book had been used by them as a source. I felt physically sick as I realized I had tripped over my ego. I was ashamed for not protecting this beautiful gift from God. As I bared my heart alone with Him, God helped me to understand that everything is for His glory, including someone using anything from the book. My life is for His glory. The book is for His glory. Scott's life is for His glory. If anyone does anything wrong in God's eyes, they are accountable to Him, not me. I had awakened that morning after a terrible night and very little sleep. My prayer friend contacted me later and said she had awakened at 4:30 in the morning feeling physically sick. She sensed it was something connected to me. I repented. I must seek God and His wisdom in all situations.

I was sick Wednesday night with vomiting for the next eight hours, then diarrhea started with intermittent hot and cold spells. I was very weak and stayed in bed most of the day. I would be unable to attend Bible study that night. I spoke with a friend over the phone who prayed for me. Low-grade temperature continued. After-effects of the illness remained Friday and Saturday. I had planned to attend an outing with the widows' group on Saturday evening but had to cancel, and I was unable to attend church Sunday morning. On Monday I was fine. All symptoms were gone, and I was healed. Tuesday night an ice storm struck the area. Thankfully we did not lose power, but plans were canceled through the week due to the weather. I reflected on this down time with the sickness and then the social cancellations. It seemed as though God was flushing toxic thinking and breaking the pull of getting over-involved with people for wrong reasons through this period of isolation. I was refreshed and strengthened.

On Monday, February 23, my friend sent a message that she had finished editing the book, and she sent me a formal review to use on the back book cover. Her words were encouraging, and excited anticipation was increasing about the finished book.

DREAM, Wednesday, 2/25 AM
I had a dream this morning and woke up early, still able to see it clearly in my mind as I recorded the details. *I am in an area like a swamp, and I am stranded here. I do not like this environment. I do not know how I got here or*

any other details. I am thinking about God and His faithfulness. I am aware of the danger of the swamp—snakes, alligators, spiders, dark murky water full of danger, and I am thinking about God. I am reminding myself of His scriptures of victory and triumph over evil and the enemy. I John 4:4, "You, dear children, are from God and have overcome them, because the one who is in you is greater than the one who is in the world." I am standing on a small patch of land and alligators have noticed me. They are crowding in the water and coming closer towards me. I see the danger, and I continue to think on the Lord. I do not know how I am going to get out of this place or how I will be rescued, but I believe God can do anything. Suddenly, Jesus appears in shepherd form and sweeps me up in His arms like a weightless child and carries me out of that area. His feet are not touching the ground. I wake up while I am still in His arms. The alligators and the danger are behind us.

I shared the dream with Mrs. Hubbard the next afternoon, following prayer. She said waters represent people. God is going to remove me from people who are not good for me. This is not of my doing. It is not in my power. This is ALL God. He is showing His protection and deliverance by carrying me. It is His desire for me. He is doing everything. I can ask God if I need to do anything to prepare. She urged me to thank God for what He is doing and what He has shown me. She was very positive and excited about the dream, and she stressed praising God for His gift and loving care.

The atmosphere at church on Sunday was cold and unfriendly. Just prior to the holiday season, the campus pastor's wife had met with me and shared her desire for me to assume leadership of the prayer team. She explained that she was not called for that role and believed that I was suited to take her place on the team. I had insisted on praying first before accepting, and she allowed me time to seek God. I subsequently agreed to lead, and she informed the others on the team about this change. Unfortunately, the others on the prayer team decided they no longer wanted to serve at that point. I was aware of undercurrents and chatter. I spent the afternoon walking with God alone in fellowship.

The next day was amazing with the Lord. I enjoyed a special unexpected visit with my niece for a few hours while her mother was at work. I talked to the Hubbards who prayed over me on the phone. I was thrilled to hear from my father-in-law and catch up on our families. I appreciated this day of heart connections.

I had been seeking God's input regarding the book cover. Today the image of the special picture Scott had given me on my birthday in 2007 came to mind. I was prompted by the Holy Spirit to contact the photographer of the "Oak Arches" photo. I searched many websites for contact info and found one email address. His name was Jim Morris, and he resided in Tuscaloosa, Alabama. I did not know if this email was current, but it was the only information available. I typed a long message to Mr. Morris explaining the role of his photo in my love story and asked if he would grant permission for the publisher to use the image for my book cover. I said a prayer as I pressed "Send".

I had coffee with a friend the next morning, and we spent a few hours chatting. When I arrived home, my answering machine indicated a message. I listened in astonishment as the caller identified himself as Jim Morris. He said he was moved by my email and wanted to talk to me further. He would be out for a while but would call again when he returned home.

We had a long conversation when he phoned later that evening. He explained the details surrounding the "Oak Arches" print. The photo was taken about 20 years prior in the low country of South Carolina, close to Beaufort. He and his youngest son were in the area on school break to visit a friend in a nearby city. He was walking one morning in mid-March and there was a light mist in the air. The road in the photograph once led to an old plantation. The home was long gone, but the road and the canopied oak trees along the road remained. I listened in awe. He was so impressed with my message that he shared the details with some of his retired friends, and they were amazed as well. He said they felt an emotional impact on reading my writing and had never heard such a story. He shared that he was originally from Memphis and grew up in Germantown. He went to medical school at UT. He moved to Alabama in the 1960s and was now retired and 85 years old. Photography had become his second career. His first wife was deceased, and he had remarried a few years ago. They had a cabin in Pigeon Forge and were familiar with East Tennessee. He asked me to keep him informed about the book and for us to stay connected. He said he would give permission to use his photo and would not charge any royalty fee. My spirit was singing! Only God! I shared the book description, the excerpt from the book involving the "Oak Arches" print, and some photos of Scott and me, as well as the framed picture Scott had given me in 2007. God had provided once again as only He can. I notified the publisher of this amazing blessing, and she contacted Mr. Morris with the proper paperwork.

The next day, I met John Edwin May at Pellissippi State Community College in Knoxville for our photo session. He had graciously agreed to take some pictures for my author photo, which was required by the publisher. I was nervous and fretting over my recent haircut. Looking in the mirror today, it seemed too short. I was careful with my makeup and wore solid color clothing. Scott's class ring adorned my neck as well as a necklace and earring set in a love knot design that he had given me for Valentine's Day in 2007.

Mr. May was nice and friendly in greeting and led me to the studio. Two students were in attendance listening and observing his points on portrait lighting and set up. He shot several photos with my glasses on and then I removed them for the next picture. He messaged me with the photos a few days later. To my great delight he posted the last photo taken on my social media page. The picture was beautiful. I kept looking at the image and thinking, "Is that really me?" In the message, Mr. May said the Holy Spirit guided the last photo. This would be the author picture for the back book cover. God had answered my prayers about this session above my expectations and had blessed me with a wonderful picture.

DREAM, Friday, 3/13 AM
I am riding in the car with my husband, Scott, and we are traveling home from somewhere. I want to stop at the mall at the next exit. Scott asks why I want to stop. I want to go to the Christmas store, and I can see it from the interstate. We pull into the parking lot, and I give him some ibuprofen. He is tired. I reassure

him I only want to go in the Christmas store and no other shops. The picture changes. I am standing on a beach. The sky is darker than daylight but not completely dark. I look out across the water. There are black jagged mountains jutting up from the surface, like a long mountain range of bare dark rock. These mountains are glowing red at their base. The red is reflected on the surface of the water. There is no movement of the water, not even a ripple. I look back to the beach. I see Jesus walking in the sand, dressed in a tunic and sandals with brown hair and a beard. He is walking with purpose, not a leisurely stroll. He is alone. He stops and turns towards the black rock mountains in the water, and bends down as though to pick up something. I was awakened from the dream by loud noises, drawers slamming, and heavy footsteps. My sister was getting ready for work. I experienced a sense of foreboding and dread. I began to pray for interpretation.*

Later I shared the dream with the Hubbards. Kathy noted that Christmas is the time we celebrate the birth of Jesus. I wanted to go to that Christmas store. I wanted Jesus. Pastor Hubbard remained silent about the second part of the dream. I sensed he knew the interpretation, but he remained silent.

The finished book was submitted to the publisher on March 16, 2015. Deborah Hunter would schedule the professional editing on her end and keep me updated. I continued in bible study at church and serving in prayer at the Campbell County Campus. There were many changes ongoing with staff and positions, and I shared everything in prayer with God only.

DREAM, Wednesday, 4/8 AM
I am in a flea market type place with a concrete floor and aisles of tables displaying items for sale. People are shuffling along around me. No faces or specific wares for sale—just the awareness of this environment. I look to the right and on the floor are neatly stacked rows of small black alligators with black eyes, in rows of five. The eyes are open, not blinking, round and solid black. Looks odd and creepy. They are not moving and remain in stacked order. I walk on down the aisle a little further. On the left on the floor are four very large brown alligators lying side by side, very still. I feel uneasy as I pass by. I sense they are not asleep and are alive, though they are not moving. I walked

on a little further and suddenly one of the large brown alligators comes after me. I turn around and see his mouth opening. Just as it is about to clamp down on my arm, I cry out, "Help me, Jesus!" I woke up at this point. I thought on this dream and the other alligator dreams. What do these alligators represent? Prayers lifted for the Holy Spirit to reveal the interpretation of these dreams.

DREAM, Friday, 4/17

I see a woman I had worked with from 1992 through 1997. I have not seen her in several years. In the dream I have hung some blankets and bedspreads of different sizes and thickness on a fence at a park. I walked to the park to gather them thinking I would carry them home. But they were too heavy, and I realized I could not carry all of them in my arms. The fence was old. The heavier bedspreads were hanging on large tall pieces of wood fencing, while smaller ones were on chain link or wire fencing. While I am assessing the situation, my friend appears with her vehicle and it looks like an SUV taxi. I do not know why she is here or why she is driving a taxi. I woke up wondering if something was wrong. I tried to call her several times, but the line was busy. I decided to try again the next day and mail a card.

VISION, Friday, 4/17

Later the same day, I had a vision of "angel man." *I am in a grocery store exchanging a few words with an older man in front of me checking out, poor in appearance. I watch him as he walks toward the door to leave the store. He takes a few steps and turns around. It is "angel man!" He is dressed in the same clothing as previously.* I understood that I am going to see him again, but I will not recognize him unless he reveals himself to me. Perhaps I have already encountered him and did not know it. Hope surged that I would see him again and be able to speak to him. I prayed the Lord would help me not to suffer another faith failure.

I attended a birthday party for a friend and later went to our church's main campus for Saturday evening service. During quiet time with the Lord, I saw a closed curtain in my mind. I had believed previously that God was loving me through Scott and loving Scott through me; however, revelation came tonight that God was starting something much bigger when He brought us together. I sat still in silence as He ministered to me. I thanked Him for my life and my family. I praised Him for the present.

Beginning in May, I was aware of a change in attitude and atmosphere at the church campus where I served. There were several incidents that I had shared with God, and His response was, "Can you handle this rejection?" I thought about that question at length and reflected on the words and the actions of others. I allowed myself to experience again my inner reactions to those people and their behavior. I let it move through me and then out of my emotions. I answered the Lord, "Yes, with You, I can."

The first 10 days in May were filled with daily battles about my future, provision, and God's promises. Though weak and scared at moments, I kept reaffirming my trust in God. He loves me. He showed me a contrast between living spiritually minded versus physically minded. Some live day to day based on the next paycheck and that affects their spending. When you know you only have a couple of days before you get paid, there is a sense of security in that paycheck. Spiritually, you do not know when you will receive your next dollar. I recalled the panic I experienced daily in the fall when I was faced with waiting on God to provide. I am still living lean. I watch my spending more closely. I experienced a struggle in my spirit with the adjustment from a definite paycheck to the unknown, but certain, provision of God. When I return to regular employment I will need to stay mindful of wasteful spending. I remembered my past spending habits and realized God is teaching me His way. I prayed God would grant me His wisdom. I asked Him to bless my finances and the work of my hands.

"Jim"
Thursday, May 14, my checking account showed -$2.62 in the red. I found $6.55 in change in my purse. My car had a quarter of a tank of gas, and I was supposed to go to church for the hour of prayer. I liked to call it "Power Hour of Prayer". As I left the house, I prayed for God to extend my gas mileage to and from the church campus. I arrived early to prepare mentally and spiritually. I had spent about 20 minutes praying when I crossed the foyer to the children's area. I glanced through the glass front door and noticed a man sitting across the parking lot on the pavement.

I stopped for a few seconds in observation and then continued into the hallway. I finished my prayers through each section of the building and the sanctuary. I returned to the foyer and the front door. The man was still sitting outside. Many cats were lounging around him on the ground. I pushed open the door and headed across the parking lot, praying silently.

He noticed me about halfway over and stood up. His clothes were a little dirty, and he had a bandana rolled and tied around his forehead. I thought I spotted blood on his left hand as I extended my hand and said, "Hello, my name is Iris." He promptly and firmly grasped my hand and said his name was "Jim." He was missing most of his bottom teeth. He started a conversation talking about the cats. He was amazed that they had all remained in place and at ease as I walked over because "they don't like strangers." He seemed very impressed that the cats had accepted me. With a sweeping glance, I quickly counted 10. He showed me where one of the cats had just scratched him on his left hand. I encouraged him to clean it with soap and water, but he smeared the blood across his t-shirt and said he would be okay.

I invited him to join us for church on Sunday. He asked if I would sit with him on the porch and talk. The porch steps were not large enough for us to both sit comfortably so I stood while he sat. He rolled a cigarette and asked if I did any writing, specifically any poems. I was surprised by his question and explained that I wrote but had no gift for poetry. He wanted to know about my writing. I shared my testimony and the amazing love God had brought into my life. I told him how I discovered God in the pain and loss of my husband. He had not expected my response or passion as I spoke. Reaction flickered across his face with moisture in his eyes. He spoke of the bible and doctrine. He wanted to "go deep" in theology, and I explained that I was not a bible scholar. I said, "My relationship with Jesus is based on what He has done for me."

He talked indirectly about relationships. I shared that I did not find love and that God had brought love into my life. I had tried for years and never found it in my search. With the loss of my husband, I discovered God, and I was sure of His love for me. He told me that he was 47 and had never been married. He said that there were women in the church who were marriageable, but they were not interested in him. I encouraged him to get close to God and to let God bring love into his life. At this point a tiny caterpillar was hanging down from a web close to my head. He got up and removed it. He asked me if I believed in miracles. "Oh Yes," I responded. He extended his hand, and I held it firmly in mine. We talked about healing. Moist eyes again. I mentioned faith. He said, "No, not by faith, but by truth."

He let go of my hand and sat back down. He explained that he worked as a welder and how welding uses a material to bond metal to metal. "You have to use something that will bond two different metals so they will hold." We had been talking about relationships, so I told him that Christ is the bonding agent in a marriage. I shared that my husband had stated it takes three to make a marriage—a man, a woman, and God. He was silent with moist eyes as I spoke.

I asked him if he had ever prayed the sinner's prayer. He shook his head no. I spoke a simple prayer out loud. Again the moisture. I told him Jesus is here at this moment. He is interested in the present and what we are going to do with Him. We talked about God and heaven.

It was close to 8 pm at this point and time for me to leave. He rose from the porch and walked over to me. He said, "Before you go, let me share two poems." He recited two sweet poems on the spot with a little effort but completed them, and I suggested that he write them down. He said he had recorded all of his poetry and motioned towards his house. I asked him if I could pray for him. He just kind of stood there, so I placed my hand in the center of his back. I prayed simply for God to minister to "Jim" and to bless him. He then hugged me slightly. This was an emotionally charged moment. I could feel the brokenness in him. I told him to come over to the church on Sunday.

As I walked back towards the church building, I sensed he was going to follow me in a few minutes. I gathered my things and walked outside, locking the door behind me. "Jim" was crossing the parking lot. He came over to my vehicle and stood there looking sort of lost and uncertain. He said, "I need your left hand." I extended my hand, and he clasped it and knelt down on one knee. I bent over with him. He prayed out loud, asking for mercy and forgiveness for the wrong things we do. He said, "We don't mean to do the things we do, but we do them anyway over and over." He asked for mercy again. He then stood up and hugged me from the side and kissed my hair on the side of my head. I smiled and told him to take care of himself, and he walked back towards his house. The home was older and almost completely hidden by overgrown trees and bushes. A lawnmower was parked in the tall grass. I started praying for God to set him free and to give him life—life far and above what he had known. When I returned home, I had used less than one-eighth of a tank of gas, and I thanked God for His blessings.

On May 18, the book publisher emailed three book cover designs to choose from. As I studied the images I was struck anew by the reality of a published book. I reflected on the loss of Scott and how his departure had triggered my salvation and the writing of our love story. God led me to read Joseph's story in the Bible in response to my battle for His provision. I spent time out on the deck gazing at a sycamore tree and allowing my spirit to respond to God's creation. Peace and assurance were restored. I prayed, "Lord, may I serve You with boldness and humility, aware of my constant need for You. Thank You, God, for blessing my family and me. I love You, Lord!"

DREAM, Sunday, 6/7, 6 AM
I am sitting at a table at a famous comedian's performance in an event venue with round dinner tables and white tablecloths. The comedian is entertaining the crowd with a skit. A man in the audience is trying to talk to him personally, out loud from his seat, while the comedian is on stage. I look down at my plate, and there is a clean solid white feather resting on the rim of my empty plate on the right side. The comedian is aware of what the man said but is ignoring him and continues in character. The man in the audience blurts out, "He won't talk to me." The comedian speaks to the other players in the skit and ends the performance. I look down at my plate again, and there are now three solid white feathers on the rim of my plate. I woke up at this point. I saw no other

faces in the dream except the comedian's face on stage, and he was dressed in a
white tunic. I could only see his upper body.

After receiving no response to my prayers, I called the Hubbards to share
the details. Pastor Hubbard explained that most people are entertained at
church; it makes them happy and they laugh. A lot of people go because of
that. Some people will have questions or problems that are not addressed
because "the show must go on," so to speak. He advised me to continue
praying and ask God if He is saying something to me specifically. He
suggested that maybe I am not getting what I need. There is no food on
my plate. Perhaps a change is coming. Be willing to follow Him.

Later in the month I began searching for work, looking at employment
and volunteer websites. During quiet time at night, I realized my desire
for God had intensified during this time of waiting. I wondered if this was
preparation for the next step. There had been no further communication
from the publisher, and I trusted God to guide the editing and the
development of the final copy. One night, after confessing my heart
towards a family member, I thanked God for this trial. Immediately I felt
a burden lift off my spirit. I had read in a "Jesus Calling" devotional that
we are to thank God for our trials, and this was a new revelation for me.

My daughter and grandson arrived on July 9 in the evening. The next day
we drove to Chattanooga to visit the Children's Museum and the TN
Aquarium. We finished the day with a nice dinner at a local restaurant
on the Tennessee River. Fun day with lots of pictures. Saturday we drove
to "The Island" in Pigeon Forge and had a great time in spite of the rain.
Later that evening at home, I held my grandson while my daughter lit
fireworks. He was fascinated by the bright colors bursting in the sky. His
eyes wide with wonder, his small fingers pointing to the sky, he ooohed and
ahhhed at each display. The next day my daughter painted a canvas using
my grandson's foot and hand to spell LOVE and gave me this special gift
to keep. I cherished these precious moments with my family.

The Hubbards invited me to their home to meet in person and to learn
more about me and my walk with God. I met them on August 4, 2015.

They lived in the mountains of East Tennessee in Morgan County, north of Knoxville. I was not familiar with this area. We met on the main highway, and then I followed Mrs. Hubbard up the mountain to their home on a narrow winding road, only wide enough for one vehicle in places. I had been talking to the Hubbards on the phone for months and did not know if I would ever meet them. Today, I would match the faces to the voices from our numerous phone calls over the past year.

We parked in front of the house, and I noticed a large garden and a small orchard nearby. She had birdfeeders and many flowers and plants. Pastor Hubbard was sitting in his chair, and he rose to greet me when we entered the home. I immediately felt welcome and at ease. I shared about my life, my marriage, and meeting God following my husband's death. Kathy served fresh coffee and homemade cake as we talked. The Holy Spirit confirmed to her that I was there to share dream revelations, to tell them about myself, and to connect with them on a deeper level. They prayed over me. She said there may be more reasons for our connection that would be revealed in the future. Then they took me to lunch in town. By the time we parted it was 2:30 in the afternoon. Driving home, I reflected on the events of the day. I was in awe once again of God and His ways. My time with the Hubbards was nourishing and inspiring, filled with significance.

DREAM, Monday, 8/17 AM
I am walking outside on a gentle sloping hillside with sparse green grass. Someone is walking with me. I cannot see them, but I sense their presence. I turn around and a wild looking dog is behind us. The face has a hostile expression. The legs are black similar to a red fox. One of the hind legs is broken and turned outwards. The person with me pushes the dog away and it is gone. But immediately there is another dog, just like the first one, but this one is normal with no broken leg. The dog appears menacing. The person with me removes the dog. I walk into a village street alone. I see a woman moving around; she appears to be getting ready to begin her day at a market. There are open air stalls in the middle of the street. It is early and not many people. I see debris in the street. I notice a broom leaning on a building nearby, so I walk over to it. I am going to sweep the curbs. Then I woke up.

On Friday night, the Campbell County church campus held an evening of praise and worship. There had been struggles to bring this night to fruition, first with gaining approval from the home campus and then with finding musical talent to lead the worship. I celebrated this opportunity for our campus to honor God with music and scripture reading. Our campus pastor opened the evening in prayer. Danny Bright ushered in an atmosphere of worship and reverence with beautifully soft music. The congregation then read bible passages out loud in unison. We started with scriptures of praise, followed by scriptures of commitment to God, and closed with Psalm 23. The pastor led in prayer and announced the Lord's Supper. Several women kneeled in tears at the altar. We had gathered to worship and to glorify God, and He had blessed us with the presence of the Holy Spirit.

Sunday morning I drove to church, taking the familiar Lafollette exit. As I rounded a curve on the highway, a brilliant rainbow was over Cove Lake. I was so moved that I stopped on the shoulder to take some pictures. The colors were vibrant even at the ground. I stood still for a few moments in appreciation of this beauty from the Master Artist.

Tuesday morning was gloriously beautiful with low humidity and cooler air. I wanted to be outside for a while and drove to a local fast food restaurant. I sat on the patio for a few hours, reading the bible and praying. I read several passages including I Kings 13. I received a revelation in my spirit, *"Do not give praise to man for what God has done."*

Later in the afternoon I spoke with Mrs. Hubbard on the phone about the most recent dream. The dogs represent something I need to be aware of but not to fear; just be aware. She advised me to be careful in associating with people. Not all church people are what they appear. Be cautious of what I say and with whom I share. She reminded me that the Holy Spirit will lead me. Let Him guide. I saw the debris and wanted to clean it up, and I had the tool I needed, the broom. Keep praying and asking God for further interpretation. As she was speaking, she received a revelation from Holy Spirit that something big was going to happen for me. She gasped two separate times in happy surprise. She did not know if it was material (earthly) or if it was spiritual (a higher level maybe), but that it was big and it was already done—not released to me yet.

She was excited and prayed for me right then. My spirit was soaring when the conversation ended, and then I remembered God's warning from the morning.

I had reached the point where I needed to work to earn income. My sister shared with me that the office where she worked was going to need a medical transcriptionist as their employee had given her notice. I met the administrator and the office manager in September. I had actually interviewed with them a few months ago, but at that time I could not hear the dictation. We had turned the volume all the way up and had tried with and without the headset on speaker. The sound remained very low and not clear enough to discern the words. They had purchased new equipment in the interim. Their transcriptionist received a better job offer and submitted her notice. The administrator asked my sister to contact me about the position.

This was a very pleasant meeting. We discussed responsibilities and the salary. The founding physician of the practice joined the meeting. I was kindly asked about my book, and I enjoyed sharing with them the details. Next, I transcribed some dictation, and the sound quality was excellent. I could hear their voices perfectly. I silently thanked God for this blessing. I was confident that He wanted me to work in this office. I praised God for taking care of me.

I received an email from the publisher on September 1 outlining the total printing cost of almost seven hundred dollars. The minimal order was 100 books, since this was a first-time printing, and there were additional related fees. I refused to worry or panic. I believed that God would provide. He had given me the love story to experience and to write; He had provided the publisher free of cost to me; He had provided the book cover free of cost to me; and I had no doubt He would provide the printing cost so the book could be released. I lifted the need to God in prayer. "Heavenly Father, You provided the publisher who has edited and prepared the book for printing. You provided the book cover photo as well with no royalty charge. Now it is time to print the book, and I am looking to You for that provision. You have met every need for Your love story, and You do complete work. This is the next step, Lord, and I thank You for this journey. I do not know where we are going, but I trust You in all things."

The next day the office administrator called and offered the job at one dollar more an hour than I had hoped for secretly! I was stunned at God's movement on my behalf. I remembered words I had heard spoken previously that where God leads, He provides. I was on the right track with Him, and I rejoiced in that awareness. My children were happy for me and offered to help me if I needed anything before I was established in my employment. Their love and concern flooded my heart. I thanked God in tears during quiet time with Him later in the evening.

DREAM, Friday, 9/11, 5 AM

I see a large house in an isolated area that looks like the desert. "Jesus man" lives there and people go there to meet with him. The term, "Jesus man", was given in the dream. I go there with someone, but cannot see the person, and we are talking about what we see. This dwelling is an open door structure, like a shrine or meditation house. Bright sunshine and blue sky with white fluffy clouds. It is cool inside the dwelling. Dim light in the hallway, which is open and wide. I am standing in this hallway and looking towards the doorway opening. I can see the sky and clouds outside. I have no fear. It is quiet. We enter a room of rose colored marble. There are two benches, hand carved, with rounded edges. There is a partial wall of marble flanked by glass and the other two walls are glass. I have the impression that the "Jesus man" is somewhere in this dwelling walking softly. As we are in this marble room, we see the "Jesus man" through the glass. This man has a fair complexion, light brown hair and beard with green or blue eyes, and thin. He is descending the steps into the water. We walk outside the room. Around the corner is a large pool of water with steps leading down into the water. The water is clear. We see the "Jesus man" sitting on the steps. His appearance has changed. This man has dark hair and beard with brown eyes and a stockier build. His body is underwater and the water line is just below his neck. There is a large gold dagger sticking in his chest and there is blood around the large blade. His eyes and mouth are open. A young girl, maybe 12 years old, has come looking for the "Jesus man." She starts descending the steps into the water. She is almost submersed when she sees the apparently dead "Jesus man." She gasps in shock and goes under the water with her mouth open. She appears to drown, as though hopeless with no reason to live. I woke at this point. The time on the clock display was 5 AM. The images remained vivid as I recorded the details on my bedside notepad. The first "Jesus man" resembled a Hollywood movie version of Jesus in older films. He was wearing a white tunic with a simple brown belt at the waist in the water.

I could not sleep after this dream and prayed for interpretation. The images remained on my mind all day, and I called the Hubbards that evening. Pastor Hubbard said that I was hearing from God in this dream. "Jesus man" is the anti-Christ. He will look and act like Jesus. He will deceive the very elect, the church. He will be killed and come back to life. The Western World/ America has substituted intimate relationship with being in a church, being religious. The spirit of anti-Christ is leading many people astray. Some will fall and be overcome. We talked about the symbolism in the dream. He said God was showing me prophecy. We also discussed the dream with the dogs. He explained that the Holy Spirit was taking care of me and protecting me. I wanted to clean things that need cleaning with the broom. He reminded me to continue to pray about all my dreams and said God is showing me many things. The dreams and our conversation remained in my thoughts.

Saturday, 9/19, was a mental battle that began Friday night. I was fighting to keep peace. Concern had begun again over my financial needs. My phone was out until I could pay for a phone card. Checking account balance was in the red. Most of my money continued to be used for gas. I was working and would be back on my feet soon, but in the meantime there was lack once again. I talked to God about this recurring situation. I was following Him in obedience and keeping Him first in my heart and my life, but I continued to be financially challenged. Scott and I had tithed during our short marriage, and I had continued to tithe faithfully following his death, in Indiana and now in Tennessee. I had used most of my savings during the writing of the book. I would have funds on Monday, but the weekend would be lean. Sunday morning I was slightly anxious about my gas driving to Campbell County. I had about half of a quarter tank of gas. I prayed that God would supernaturally extend my gas mileage and trusted He would take care of me if I ran short. I talked to Him in prayer during the drive, listening to praise music on the radio and singing along.

Monday arrived with glorious colors in the sky. I had enough gas in the car to go to the bank and then directly to the gas station. I had worked almost 37 hours for the pay period, which ended the next day. The publisher contacted me to check on the printing funds and said currently there were 63 pre-orders on amazon. I was blown away and prayed again about the printing provision.

First Baptist Concord in Knoxville was advertising an evening with Dennis Swanberg on Sunday night, September 27, with music by Legacy Five. I needed to laugh. The sound of my own laughter at times sounded unfamiliar, and I wanted to laugh and be at ease for a while. I arrived at the church just before the program started. He shared many stories invoking laughter across the sanctuary. One story in particular about the loss of his father and how much his mother missed him triggered tears. I could relate to her words about her husband's absence. My spirits were lifted through the praise and worship music as well as the laughter. I drove home in peaceful gratitude.

On Friday, October 2, the publisher received the funds for the exact amount needed. She explained that someone had contacted her, who wished to remain anonymous, and had sent the money to her directly. The person did not want to be identified. The publisher would contact the printer and let me know when the books would be available. I sat still with God in praise and in amazement of His creative provision for every stage of the book. Jeremiah 32:27 NKJV came to mind, "Behold, I am the LORD, the God of all flesh. Is anything too hard for me?" and Luke 1:37 NKJV, which is my life verse, "For with God nothing will be impossible." I worshipped God for a while that night.

REVELATION, Monday, 10/12
God is doing a great thing! I am blessed!

Thursday evening, I drove to Campbell County for the usual weekly power hour of prayer at the church campus. I had not stopped praying for "Jim" since that lone encounter. During this interval of time, I had not seen him on Sundays or Thursday nights. Occasionally I would see one or two cats in the yard but no sign of him. He still lived there because his car was in the parking lot and not always in the same spot. Recently my prayers had intensified and persisted. I viewed him as a picture of the area, and my prayers included bringing him out of that house, deliverance from the darkness, out of hiding for salvation, healing, and life. I was shocked when I turned into the parking lot. Every large tree in his yard that was close to the house had been cut down. The overgrown bush next to the house, which had hidden a window from view, had been cut down to the ground. All the limbs and brush had been removed, and the grass was mowed. The house was EXPOSED. A surge flooded my spirit as I sat in my car looking at the house and the grounds. There was no sign of "Jim" or the cats, but a light was visible through a now uncovered window.

I entered the church singing praise to the Lord. I did not know what had happened with "Jim", but I believed God had been working in his heart and mind. I thought he might come over to the church and even checked the front door a few times between prayers to see if he was sitting outside. I did not see him that evening. God seemed to be moving. Turmoil had increased lately at this campus, and I trusted God's will to prevail.

I shared all these details with the Hubbards a few days later. Pastor Hubbard said that God is letting in the light and things are being revealed that have been hidden. Secret things are coming out. This is for the entire body of Christ, not a specific church. God is showing what He wants to do, what He is ready to do. He added that God births in the Spirit and we serve Him faithfully and consistently. We may not be one of those who gets recognition or benefit of the fruit. If I do things for Jesus and receive recognition here, that is all of the reward. If I do things for Jesus and receive no earthly recognition, I will earn a greater reward in heaven.

I shared with Pastor Hubbard that God had asked me a few months ago if I could serve Him anonymously. I had answered, "Yes, if that is what it takes to release people from every form of bondage." I had been thinking of Campbell County, but he was speaking on a much larger scale. Bob said I was a blessing to him and to Kathy. I replied that I do not see myself as a blessing to others and that I was very thankful for both of them in my life. He asked about my book, "Showered By Grace," and I promised him a signed copy once the books were printed. I told them about God's provision for the printing costs, and they shared my gratitude and joy.

The next Thursday, I had no work for the day. I was thinking about the day ahead when the idea popped into my head to contact a young woman about seeing her at lunch. I had met her initially at the main campus of the church and had not seen her in many months. I did not act on the idea at that moment, and soon the idea came again. I messaged her on social media and she invited me to join her for lunch at her job at one o'clock. We talked for a time, and I prayed for her concerns. She then shared that she had asked God to send someone today to speak into her. Her heart was burdened about a past relationship, and she had been considering reconciliation. As I prayed for her and for him, I received a soft impression that God wanted her to pray for this man for healing, repentance, and his relationship with Jesus. I was not sure they would be reconciled, but she was to continue praying for him. She understood and agreed.

Later that afternoon, a friend from the widows' group dropped by for a short visit. She had traveled to Israel with the church tour recently and wanted to give me something from her trip. She brought me a bottle of anointing oil that smelled divine, like a slice of heaven, and a beautiful prayer shawl (a tallit). I was surprised and asked if women could wear them. She assured me that women do wear the shawls in prayer in Israel. I loved this special gift and carried it with me to Campbell County that evening for prayer hour.

I finished my work on Friday in the early afternoon. I bought a phone card and thought of a woman I had met at church in 2013. We had continued to exchange messages and meet occasionally since that time, sharing prayer needs as well as blessings. I considered her a prayer friend. I received an email from her just before I left work, and I was burdened as I read her words. I was driving towards home when I received an impression to stop at the restaurant where she was working part-time to give her a hug. I prayed for God's blessing over our greeting.

The hostess confirmed that my friend was working, and I explained that I only wanted to speak to her for a moment. She told me which section my friend was working. I walked through the dining area and found her clearing a table. She looked up in shock as I approached, and I reached out for a hug. She held me tightly and said she was so glad to see me. I was concerned for the stress in her message. My heart hurt for her pain and struggle. Her eyes were moist, and I was thankful that I had followed God's impromptu visit to the restaurant. I prayed over her during my drive home. God had only sent me there to give her a hug. He would do whatever else was needed.

I wore a favorite pair of earrings to work one day the next week. They were part of a set that Scott had given to me as a gift for a special occasion. Late in the afternoon, just before I left work for the day, I went to the restroom. As I washed my hands, I noticed one of my earrings was hanging out of my earlobe and the back was missing. My dismay quickly turned to gratitude and surprise that I had not lost the earring. When I arrived home, I placed the earrings in the drawer with the matching necklace and bracelet. As I was hanging my purse on the doorknob, I glanced down at the floor. The missing earring back was in front of the jewelry cabinet. I picked it up, grateful and delightfully amazed at God's compassion in small things.

I had received a message in October through social media from a dear lady in Louisiana, who was interested in reading my book. She shared that she would soon be 84 and explained that she "loved to read, but only true things and especially about others' lives." She messaged me after reading "Showered By Grace" and shared her thoughts. Her words touched my heart and encouraged me tremendously.

11/07/2015 10:39AM, *"I feel like I know you so personally now..... And I understood about your life so much! I read your book mostly straight through ... Only put it down when I had to! I am so glad to be your friend on Facebook. I pray that you are tremendously blessed the rest of your life and I know that there are great days ahead because of the path that you have taken! God is love! And you are filled with God and he will send those to you that need that "LOVE!"*

(On Saturday, 4/14/2018, an update was posted on her page by a grandson that this precious lady had moved to heaven. I shared on her page how I had met his grandmother. I read many posts of family and friends who loved this woman, and gratitude swelled in my heart that I had been given the opportunity to "meet" her through my story. Prayers were lifted for the family and friends.) Her generosity of love and kindness during her life on earth would continue to bless those whose lives she had touched. Love expressed inspires me to be an encourager and to plant seeds of kindness into others, to continue to pay forward from so much that I have received.

DREAM, Tuesday, 11/24, 6 AM

I am standing in line, as though I am waiting to check out, but I am not holding anything to buy. Ahead of me are many rows of people that weave back and forth following a roped path. The line is moving forward slowly. We are in a large room, well lit, with many windows, hardwood floors, and painted walls. I can see an open doorway ahead. To the left of the doorway a man is sitting in a chair against the wall, positioned so that the people in line pass by him. He is bald and clean shaven, physically fit, with large dark eyes, dressed in a black t-shirt, black pants, and black shoes. His arms are crossed over his chest, and one leg is crossed over the other with the left ankle resting on the right knee. His head is turned to the left, watching each person as they move past. His expression does not change, and he does not speak.

Next to him, on the floor, is a small alligator. This is not a regular alligator. The hide is black and smooth with a multicolor hue of green, blue, and purple washed over the hide. There are a few shallow treads down the back, like you see on a tire, not the typical hide of an alligator. This creature has small eyes, a small mouth, and small teeth, not the typical features. The eyes are looking at people as they pass and the mouth is constantly moving. This movement of the mouth enabled me to see the small teeth. I can hear no words. The head and the body do not move, but the eyes and teeth move continually.

I am moving closer to where the man and the small alligator are positioned. I still cannot see clearly ahead, but it appears they are sitting at the doorway opening. Once the people pass them, they seem to enter a dark room or connecting hallway. Nothing is visible beyond this point. People are continuing to move along past this man and the alligator. I notice an elderly couple at the door opening with arms linked and one is using a cane. I can only see their backs.

Directly in front of me is a beautiful peacock, and I can see the head. At my side is a baby toddler in a wagon. I am not pulling the wagon. The wagon is moving next to me as we continue in the line. As we get closer to the man in black and the alligator, this creature starts nipping at the peacock and pulling at some feathers. I feel the need to pick up the child and hold it in my arms for protection. The man is watching and says nothing. This is when I see that his eyes are dark. He allows the alligator to continue nipping at the peacock. He remains sitting in the chair, looking at us as we move closer. I am concerned for the peacock, the child, and myself. I woke up at this point and prayed.

This dream weighed heavily on my mind and my spirit. I talked to the Hubbards, and we discussed the details at length. Pastor Hubbard began by saying that the Holy Spirit is leading me and going before me. God has chosen me to serve Him. Stay close to Him. Follow Him. Pray. These visions are a gift, showing me what others do not see. He said I may be writing my next book about all these visions and dreams. God may be showing me these things as part of my next book. He said there are other people like me in the world and my book would encourage them.

The peacock represents the Holy Spirit. I cannot change things in front of the peacock, but I can take up the little ones and they are safe from the enemy. The alligator can hurt the baby but cannot destroy the baby. The baby can represent new believers or Christians who were saved years ago but have not grown spiritually.

I am being led towards something. Not sure what is on the other side. There may be some things that could potentially hurt me or the baby Christians. The guy dressed in black with darkness overseeing what is going on could be a principality in the spirit realm. He is overseeing what is happening. He appears unconcerned, so things are going his way. Every area has different spirits that control them. People do not realize they are headed to darkness and just assume that is the way it is supposed to be. I am trying to protect baby Christians. The Holy Spirit is with me. The peacock is leading me. Peacocks kill snakes. The alligator could be a woman, a jezebel spirit, who goes after pastors and ministers. Pray to keep the baby Christians safe. Pray to keep the Body of Christ safe.

DREAM, Monday, 12/7
I am standing outside, alone, on the ground. I hear a loud "whoosh", and suddenly I am transported up into what I suppose is the night sky, but there

are no stars visible. I am alone and it is dark all around me. In front of me is a solid white round orb, extremely large in size. I am suspended in this blackness, facing this very large white sphere. I feel limp like a rag doll. I have no fear. I do not sense that anything is wrong. I am still looking at this when I wake up. This was incredible.

I shared all of this with the Hubbards later in the evening after work. I could not get that image out of my mind and did not want to. I wanted to know more. What had I seen and what did it mean? Pastor Hubbard called me a daughter of destiny. The "whoosh"/breath is Wind of God. Jesus is Light of the world (bright star). He explained some personal specifics. I am outside of the normal. Holy Spirit is breathing life onto me. Clears all else away. Nothing but His Light is showing. He is drawing me closer to Him. The dreams and visions are part of a complete picture; I am getting pieces of it now. He told me to continue walking with Him. Be careful of others' interpretations and prophecies. Ask the Spirit. Keep praying.

Norris Dam

I then shared with him several incidents involving the Norris Dam area in Anderson County. The first one occurred on December 13, 2014. A sweet friend from the widows' group had invited me to attend the Norris Dam Holiday Homecoming. The location was unfamiliar to me, so we agreed to meet in Clinton in a grocery store parking lot, and we rode together to the park. The dam was built in 1936, and there were cabins scattered in the surrounding woods where the workers had stayed during construction of the dam. The cabins had continued to be maintained and rented out in summer months to campers since that time. For the Holiday Homecoming, several cabins were furnished according to the era. Park workers were dressed in attire of the 1930s and sat in the cabins that were open for the tour. Lighted luminarias lined the drive and walkways to each cabin that was open. The tour ended back at the tea room. We had a fun time walking the tour and talking. A Santa dressed in rustic attire was sitting in the last open cabin, and he gave us some treats as we snapped a group photo.

We made our way to the tea room in eager anticipation of the hot food posted on the menu. The building was adorned with bright lights, and several decorated Christmas trees were positioned in the large room. The wood walls reflected the light beautifully, and a roaring fire was being tended in the old stone fireplace. The welcoming atmosphere exuded warmth, coziness, and peace. The park was offering beef stew and cornbread as well as peach cobbler cooked fresh over hot coals outside in large cast iron covered pots. Several long tables were situated where live music was playing. We sat down and enjoyed the delicious food and the lively tunes. My spirit was soaring in the joy of the season. Two men brought their food over to our table and sat down. One was a widow of three years who lived in the same area of Knoxville where I was located. He was originally from California and retired from the service. He and his wife had moved to Tennessee so she could be close to her mother. I shared with him that my husband had died three years ago (at that time) and that was how I met Jesus. He jerked his head up from eating and looked at me directly in surprise. He was shocked that I said I had found God through the death of my husband. He shared enough that I knew he was still grieving. He was carrying guilt about not moving back to Tennessee sooner at his wife's request. He could not have known at that time that his wife would pass away and now he was focused on that one fact. Grief has that effect. We start looking at past events and dwelling on them to try to make sense of our loss. We blame ourselves in error in an attempt to understand what has happened. As soon as I started talking about God, his friend next to him piped up and stated that everyone goes to heaven when they die. I looked at him in disbelief shaking my head. My friend and I then looked at each other in surprise at what he had just said, knowing he was not speaking truth. I tried to talk to the widower again, but his friend had finished eating and was ready to leave the building. I prayed silently for the grieving man. My friend and I stayed for all of the music. We especially enjoyed a super talented young man named Ethan Ferguson playing "Ole Joe Clark" on the violin, the banjo on his lap, and the autoharp. We noticed the two men coming back into the building a little later, but they did not sit with us and chose a different table closer to the musicians. I prayed for that man many times through the following months after that night. Every time he came to mind, I lifted him in prayer.

The second instance occurred in the fall of 2015. I received an impression to check on the date for the annual Holiday Homecoming in December and to attend the event. I tried to dismiss it as just my imagination, but the idea recurred intermittently over several days. I realized I needed to obey this prompting. I talked to my prayer partner about this occasion and asked her to pray for God's guidance. She messaged me a few days later and said that I was to be there before the program started. Her impression was that I needed to be there no later than 4:40 PM. I checked the website for the park and found that the Homecoming was scheduled for December 12 at 5 PM. Pastor Hubbard confirmed my decision in our subsequent conversation. He agreed with my decision to go the Homecoming and advised me to be open to the Spirit's leading. Seek His guidance. The man may or may not be there, but the Spirit will be there.

Saturday morning the women's small group at the Campbell County campus met at one of the member's homes for a cookie swap and luncheon. Our friend had a beautiful home and every room was decorated for Christmas. The atmosphere was festive as we celebrated our time together. We left in the afternoon, and I drove towards Norris Dam for the Annual Homecoming that would begin at 5 pm. Anticipation rose as I exited the interstate. I did not remember exactly where the tearoom and cabins were located, as I was entering the park from a different direction and it was daylight, whereas it was dark when I attended the Homecoming the previous year. I followed a sign that read "Cabins and Campground". Though a paved surface, the road had steep grades and sharp curves. Surprisingly as I was driving towards the camping area, a single young deer was standing on the edge of the paved road, head up, chewing. I slowed down when I saw the deer. His large brown eyes met mine as I drove by. I reached that campground, but this was not the place. The cabins were newer and the camping sites were empty. I had to return the same way I came in, and as I retraced my route, the young deer was standing in the same spot next to the paved road, still chewing, and again our eyes met as I slowly passed by. Spurred by the clock, I went back to the main road and turned left. I crossed over the dam, and then I saw vehicles turning onto the road I needed to follow. Now I could see the familiar cabins and large tearoom. I parked and walked hurriedly into the main building. The time on my phone was 4:40 when I sat down. I remained in the tearoom for the entire program. I enjoyed the hot chili that was served while listening to the live music. The fireplace hosted a roaring fire, and beautiful Christmas trees with clear lights decorated the main room. I did not see the widower or his friend from the previous year. Nothing significant happened that I could see with my physical eyes, but I was aware of a consistent deep calm in my spirit. I was not involved in any conversation beyond polite greetings with a smile. The program ended, and I drove home covered in peace.

In February of 2016, there were lane closures on I-75 due to a rockslide, so I chose an alternate route to travel back and forth from the church in Campbell County. I drove through the Norris State Park, which was very scenic, and this brought me back to the interstate past the area of the rockslide. I continued to use this route until the interstate reopened many weeks later. The third time I took this route, physical symptoms developed while I was driving in the park. I became nauseated, sick at my stomach, dizzy, lightheaded, and sweaty. A heavy sense of dread washed over me as I drove across the dam and on towards the interstate. The symptoms disappeared as soon as I left the area. Was there a connection? What did it mean? When I left church, I traveled back through the area, and the symptoms recurred until I reached the outskirts of the park.

One Sunday after church I decided to take a walk. I needed to be outside with the Lord. I drove through the park across the dam and came to an area along the lake with a paved walking path that was in the open and not in the woods. I put on my spiritual armor from scripture as I parked my car. The sky was bright blue with sunshine reflecting off the nearby lake casting shadows through the tall trees. I breathed in the fresh air, thankful for this time with God; however, there was a thread of uneasiness in my spirit as I walked. There were no people close around me. I saw one woman across the way walking in the opposite direction and then an older man at another point on the path. I began to notice many butterflies around me as I walked. They did not come all at once. The yellow monarchs appeared intermittently. I thanked the Lord for this sweet reminder of His presence. The uneasiness did not disappear completely, and I shortened my walk. I continued to thank God for His protection as I drove away, and peace was restored when I left the park.

Many months passed before I drove through the park again. I was driving back to Knoxville through the park in the late afternoon. Most of the trees had shed their leaves, carpeting the forest floor, but I spotted one young tree fairly close to the road with bright red leaves and wanted to take a picture. I parked on the shoulder and walked a short distance to snap a few photos. Satisfied with the images, I returned to my car and prepared to drive home. When I pressed on the accelerator, my vehicle slid backwards. Apparently the leaves were hiding a muddy shoulder. I tried again and slid a little further. This time I felt a thud as my vehicle made contact with some type of barrier that prevented further movement. I got out to assess the situation and discovered I had slid into a guardrail, which had prevented me from sliding down a steep ravine. Stunned and dismayed, I sat down on the guardrail to pray and think. My cell phone had no signal. The park was empty of traffic. One vehicle passed by, and after a while a pick-up truck drove by. Neither stopped to ask if I needed any help. As I was praying, I remembered my vehicle was equipped with 4-wheel drive. I had completely forgotten in the angst of the situation. With the four wheel drive engaged, my vehicle left the mud and moved onto the asphalt without any trouble. Hallelujah! Gratitude for that reminder poured out of me to the Father for His loving guidance during the drive home.

Pastor Hubbard explained the physical reactions I had experienced could have been because of a spiritual presence, a principality, in this region. He asked me how I had responded. I explained that I was anxious to get away and had left the park. He advised me if it happened again to ask the Holy Spirit, "Why am I feeling this way?" "What do you want me to do?" "What do I need to understand?"

Just before Christmas, I received a letter from the home office for Stephen Ministries. I had submitted my book, "Showered By Grace", with a letter for their consideration to be used as a resource. They appreciated my service as a Stephen Minister and sent blessings in their letter but declined the use of my book. I was somewhat disappointed but trusted God would open doors according to His purpose and timing.

Christmas Eve, Thursday night, I drove to Campbell County for prayer and fellowship with a young woman I had met recently. She had started attending church with her parents at our campus, and she was interested to know more about my story. When I drove into the parking lot, the front door of "Jim's" house was open and the curtains were pulled back. A TV and a floor lamp were turned on. There was light in the living room. This once dark house, hidden behind overgrown shrubbery, tall grass, and large trees, was now open with debris cleared away and lights shining inside. I praised God for this incredible transformation.

The next day was my sister's birthday. She had invited some friends and her son over for dinner, and I was looking forward to the celebration. My friends, Sue and her husband, from Goshen, were in Pigeon Forge for the holiday, and I planned to drive over after dinner for a visit. While my sister was placing the food on the table, I decided to carry the garbage out to the receptacle. I dropped the bag into the trash can. I was walking barefoot through the garage towards the back door when suddenly I fell. I laid on the concrete floor stunned, not sure how I fell. It had been raining and the garage floor was wet. I did not trip but somehow landed on my left side. The toenail on my left little toe was knocked off in the fall, but there was no pain or bleeding. I asked Jesus to help me as I struggled to stand. I thanked Him that I was not injured. It happened so quickly that I could not recall how I fell. I was walking one minute and on the garage floor in the next instant.

I tried to eat the special dinner my sister had prepared, but I was nauseated and dizzy. I sort of felt like I was in shock. Everyone at the table said it was because of pain. I only felt pain when I put weight on my left ankle, but I did not let that keep me home. I left at 4:15 to drive to Pigeon Forge, as planned, to meet Sue and her husband at their hotel. Walking was painful, and I moved slowly after I arrived. We exchanged gifts and visited over coffee for the next few hours. It was wonderful to see her again after several years, and we took pictures and shared hugs. Heavy rain was falling as she walked me to my car. I arrived safely at home around 10:30 by the grace of God. The torrential rain was relentless while driving. I was thankful for the time spent with my special friend and also excited that my children were coming soon for a visit.

Monday morning I was not able to go to work. My left ankle and lower leg were purple. I texted a picture to my sister who worked for orthopedic surgeons. The doctor insisted that I come into the office for x-rays after viewing the photo. My knee was ok. My ankle showed a fracture of the fibula that was very minimally displaced. He warned me to stay off of it as much as possible to avoid the need for surgery. Full leg walking boot was fitted. I was to wear it at all times. I could work and drive, but I was to keep the leg elevated at work. A recheck at the doctor's office with x-rays the following week confirmed no further displacement of the fracture; therefore, surgery was not required. A friend from the widows' group loaned me her knee scooter, and this was a huge help in ambulation for the next eight weeks.

The first shipment of printed books arrived on December 30, 2015. In surreal wonder I opened the oversized heavy cardboard box and gazed at the stacks of books inside. My name printed in red on the front cover captured my attention as I removed a book from the box. I thumbed through the pages, reading the familiar words on the back cover in delight. Gazing at the image on the front, I recalled the photographer, Jim Morris, and events preceding publication, in deep reverence of God. I read through the acknowledgements and prologue, in humbled awareness, once again, of being showered by His grace. I thumbed the pages, reliving events from the past years that had culminated in this moment. I was officially an author with a published book, glory to God, and a broken leg. Tears flowed as I reflected on the power of God to bring this to pass in a mixture of joy and humility. Everything had fallen into place under the guidance of God. I shouted, "Hallelujah!" from the knee scooter.

My friend, Sue, in Goshen informed me that she had been in contact with people she knew personally at "The Electric Brew" coffee house in Goshen and at "Das Dutchman Essenhaus" in Middlebury about book signings on my behalf. I received email messages from each business on December 30 about the possibility of hosting an event later in 2016 in warmer weather. They would need to read a copy of the book before making a final decision. I would send each a signed copy!

DREAM, Tuesday, 12/29, 6 AM:
There is one single image in the dream, and I see it clearly. I am looking at the face or mask of a man with shoulder length brown hair. I can see only the

head and upper shoulders. The image resembles a typical depiction of the face of Jesus, except the eyes are empty. There are cut out openings where the eyes would typically be situated. Suddenly the eyes start changing. It is as though the eyes are painted on a band that is moving across the opening behind the face. The eye colors change. The shape of the eyes change. Some eyes appear larger than others. The facial expression remains the same and only the eyes change. They are changing continuously.

I had received many dreams and visions since arriving in Knoxville. I prayed earnestly for interpretation, to understand what God was saying through these night messages. He chose to speak to me through the Hubbards, and I accepted this as His divine plan. I treasured my conversations with this special couple, whom I considered my spiritual parents, and deeply appreciated their prayers and support.

CHAPTER FIVE

2016

The first time I spoke to the Hubbards in January, I shared the details of the dream on December 29. We had a long discussion. The face is a presentation. The organized church crucified Christ. He cautioned me to obey the leading of the Holy Spirit. I continued to seek God in prayer concerning deeper revelation.

I spent the next few nights reading my book, different sections at a time, and remembering what God revealed, remembering where I came from, recognizing His power at work in my life. I realized anew how much time had passed since I met Scott initially on the question & answer forum in 2006. God purposefully orchestrated our meeting, then lovingly and patiently guided me through the love and fun of Scott, the agony of his departure, the healing through grief, and the other revelations/lessons/corrections while writing my first book. I am now standing at the threshold of "Next." The pain of my life is connected to my destiny, and the book is a tool for use by God to bring Him glory and serve a Kingdom purpose. Rereading the printed words in my book, I reflected with clarity on my past, and the wonder of God escalated. What God has done for me is almost indescribable; yet, much more is to come beyond what I can imagine. The blessings in our lives are not limited by how we use them in the present. They will provide future openings and opportunities for greater service and increased blessing in different ways. We are not to measure or compare and try to justify what He gives or does for us; rather, we are to be grateful and praise Him.

The church campus in Campbell County was closed on Sunday, January 24, due to heavy snowfall and weather warnings to stay off the roads. I attended the third service at the main campus in Knoxville instead and found a seat where I could prop my leg on the knee scooter without obstructing the flow of people entering or exiting the sanctuary. After service, someone I recognized from the men's prayer team approached and asked how I was doing. We had been in the same Stephen Ministries peer supervision group and I had not seen him in many months. I started talking about my book, and I sensed the presence of the Holy Spirit. I said, "Remember how I said I was going to write a book? Well, now the book has been written, published, and printed, and is available on Amazon!" I explained how God had directed the writing and had provided the book cover, the publisher, and the printing fees. He asked about Scott's class ring. I shared the details of that story and showed him the ring around my neck on a chain. He was smiling as I was talking, and he said he could see the Spirit in me, in my face, in my eyes, and in my voice. He said he was lifted just listening to me talk about the book. I told him that my passion is to tell my story. He put his arm on my shoulder and asked if he could pray for me. He prayed so beautifully over me that I began to cry—for the book, for God to bless me and my family, to bless those who would hear my story, and to work through those people in turn to develop their stories to share. My heart was about to burst at his words. I smiled at him in wonder and whispered, "Thank you." There were tears in his eyes. He walked me out of the sanctuary and held open the doors for me as I rolled on the knee scooter out to my car in awe of the Holy Spirit.

I wanted to remain outside a while in God's presence. I took a long drive and parked close to the river in Clinton. This was the special place I came to whenever I desired to be with Him alone. I sat in my car in quiet conversation with God, gazing out the window at the placid water and the bright blue sky. The water was so still you could see the reflection of the bare trees on the opposite bank. A friend called that I had not heard from in a while. While we are talking, tiny bright lights started sparkling just above the surface of the water, like diamonds, dancing and moving across the water, in front of where I was parked. There were too many to count, mesmerizing. I listened to my friend's conversation, fixated on the movement on the water, until it disappeared as suddenly as it appeared. Tears flowed as I recalled the prayer after church, aware of His presence, my heart surging with joy and gratitude.

DREAM, Wednesday, 2/17

I am standing on a paved street with a sidewalk and green grass on the other side of the sidewalk. The sidewalk looks like new concrete. The grass is very green. The asphalt is a dark gray. The colors stand out boldly. Up ahead I see a car turning from the left onto the street where I am standing. The car is heading straight towards me, fast. I move onto the sidewalk and watch the car swerve and stop across the road. The driver is looking at me. I see his face clearly as the car window is down and his arm is resting on the open window. He is a White male, clean shaven, middle age, gray suit coat, serious expression with sort of a long face, very short blonde or gray hair, and well groomed. He shakes his head back and forth, in a "No" motion, and then drives off. The car is a small sports car. There is no other traffic, and there are no other people. I do not feel it is safe to walk on the street anymore. The next block has no sidewalk. This appears to be a large undeveloped block with green grass and uneven ground. I start walking towards this grass, not at the edge where it meets the paved street, but further away from the edge. I am thinking the car may return and the driver will not be able to drive his car on this uneven grassy ground. I woke up.

I prayed about the dream for interpretation. I sensed a warning of some type but needed divine revelation. After several days without any insight, I prayed and called the Hubbards for their impression. Bob felt that God was giving me a warning that He needs to change something in my life to make it safer for me. The street was broad, an easy way to travel, and a comfortable place. It was safer to go the rough way, which is not an easy path. He could be calling me to a new place or to a deeper spiritual relationship. I could be affected by something that may not be about me, but God has a safe place for me. Keep seeking Him and trusting Him. Our conversation ended in prayer.

Tuesday, 2/23: Today was my final follow-up appointment with the orthopedic surgeon in Knoxville, including repeat x-rays. These views showed no fracture, and I was able to discontinue the walking boot cast. I thanked the doctor for the good news and praised God for complete healing!

Tuesday night I stayed up until midnight. I had watched the political caucuses and spent time in prayer over the nation. I woke up around 3 AM after a dream from the enemy. Bound him and cast him out, spoke some prayers, and asked God for restful sleep. I woke up at 6:40 AM from a phenomenal dream. I quickly recorded all the details on my bedside notepad.

DREAM, Wednesday, 2/24/2016, 6:40 AM

I am standing outside at some type of gathering. I am dressed more formal than usual, and I notice I am wearing dress shoes. I am looking around to see if I recognize anyone. A woman from the church campus in Campbell County comes hurrying over, calling my name. I know her, but she is not a friend. It is starting to rain, and she asks where I am parked. I said, "Over there," while pointing to a cluster of vehicles in the parking lot. I start walking in the direction of my car. I am stepping in water puddles from the heavy downpour, and my feet are soaked. My shoes are full of water. I am calm and not upset about the rain. The picture changes.

I am inside what appears to be a grand old plantation house in a formal dining room. The room is the size of a grand ballroom with high ceilings and tall windows. The room is filled with dinner tables covered in white tablecloths with formal place settings. Waiters are busy serving the many people seated at these tables. I see no specific faces, but I hear the tinkling of stemware and silverware, and murmured conversations. I am seated at a large table near a glass paneled door that is open leading to the veranda. I can see outdoors from my chair, and I am looking at the well-manicured grounds of an estate. Suddenly, a cylinder of crosses begins to rise from the ground. The surface of the grass is not disturbed and there are no breaks in the ground, but this cylinder of rotating crosses is moving up out of the ground. The crosses are in rows and stacks of three, forming a large cylinder that rises like a tower, slowly rotating.

There is a large solid white puffy cloud at the base that seems to be propelling this cylinder upward. The crosses are in countless rows of three and number three in depth. The space is symmetric between each cross and in depth. In each set of three, the crosses are white and perfectly symmetric in size and shape. The rows form a massive cylinder that is lifting out of the ground and rotating. It is slowly beginning to move. The other people at the table have noticed my expression and are following my gaze. Quickly the response spreads across the room, and people are moving over to the veranda doors. They are taking photos with their phones. I want a picture, too. I am watching this cylinder of crosses begin to rise while I fumble with my phone, but I cannot get a picture. I hear people around me saying, "Ahhhh" or "Ohh look!" They snap pictures and then move away. It seems the cylinder is getting ready to move or separate but is still holding the same shape, rising and spinning. The dimensions of the crosses and the cylindrical shape are out of proportion to the surroundings. This is from God. Stunning and exhilarating. I can sense the power of the movement of this cylindrical shape, formed by rows and stacks of crosses in threes, spaced evenly apart, turning and rising up from the ground. I continue watching the tower rotate, while trying to find the camera button on my phone. In my frustration, I woke up.

The week of March 7-11 was a battleground week. Thursday was the peak of the attack. That day I felt totally alone in a spiritual sense. Mouths had been speaking against me behind my back, and I could literally feel the attack physically. These verbal assaults released confusion, chaos, criticism, and judgment aimed at me personally. I had inner peace and reassurance that God was with me, but I was basically without friend support. A Stephen Ministries promo that had been discussed and approved was suddenly canceled. The locks on the front door at the church campus where I had been praying for more than a year were changed without my knowledge. I discovered this after driving to the campus on Thursday night and was unable to enter the building. The enemy was working through others. The janitor had opened the door for two women in the church who had arrived earlier, and we were able to meet subsequently, but I could not contain my frustration. I closed the meeting in prayer about our service to God and our role in the Body of Christ. Something had definitely shifted, and I sensed change on the horizon.

My friend received a vision about me earlier on that Thursday and prayed over what was revealed. She saw me in a plain fishing boat being knocked around in the water, and things were banging into the boat. I had no paddle or help. She told me later that she had lifted me and covered me in prayer at that time. On Sunday at the beginning of the week, I had spent an extended amount of time alone with God, aware of heaviness in my spirit with turmoil. I cried in sadness, yet I was aware of His constant love and reassurance. He would continue to hold me through the following days. My toddler grandson was very sick through this time and had been to the doctor. On Thursday night my daughter had to take him to the hospital. By Friday night he was much better. Many, many prayers had been lifted for my grandson and my daughter. I praised God for His healing and victory in these battles that lasted all week.

I watched a sermon on TV Saturday night, and I felt convicted and enlightened. The pastor taught about speaking judgment on people and releasing judgment on ourselves. This tied into a message I had watched recently on another program. The topic was winning battles in the throne room of heaven instead of engaging on the spiritual battlefield. I listened to the pastor's message again, and I was moved to confess all the wrong words from my mouth over others. I was thankful the Holy Spirit had guided me to watch those programs. I had cried to the Lord the previous evening in distress, and these message provided divine help.

I walked outside to leave for work on Good Friday, March 25, and my car would not start. The radio was playing so I did not think the battery was an issue. I prayed and claimed scripture that God sustains the fatherless and the widow. After praying, my car started. I praised God while driving to work. When I walked out to the car after work, it would not start. I understood that I needed more than prayer this time. I called roadside assistance with my insurance company about 5:20. Text message indicated ETA would be 45 minutes, but the mechanic arrived in 15 minutes. He just happened to be in the area when he received the call from the insurance company. He tried to crank the engine and said I had a dead battery. He used a battery pack to start the car and advised me to drive to an auto center and get a new battery installed. An auto parts store was only half a mile away. The assistant checked the battery, confirmed that I needed a replacement, and installed a new one. Unbelievably I was on my way home by 6:15. I thanked God for watching over me and my vehicle. I was grateful for the help I received in a safe place and not stranded on an isolated road or the interstate.

The widows' group met on Saturday morning, April 9. After serving breakfast, the leader of the group opened the meeting with prayer. Typically she would read a devotional from the book, "His Princess Bride" by Sheri Rose Shepherd. Today, she unexpectedly placed the book in front of me and asked me to read. I was surprised, as she had not done this previously. I started reading the day's devotional and I felt the presence of the Holy Spirit moving in the room while I was reading. Tears began to flow while I read, overwhelmed by Him. Several ladies had teared up, also, and there was a "sacred silence" when I finished reading the passage. He seemed to be ministering to each of us individually. Our meeting was unscripted and extra special that day.

DREAM, Monday, 4/11, 4:30 AM

I am sitting in the back of a large van with clear windows. I am riding on an interstate, though I do not know where I am going. I am sitting in the back seat. The front seats and the bench seat in front of me are empty. I notice vehicles passing by and a train moving over an overpass. I am calm and at peace. A larger van is in the lane to the left of my vehicle, and the name of a security company is displayed on the side of the van. I cannot see any people in the van as the windows are dark. One window is open on the right side and I see clothing hanging on a rack that is moving somewhat in the wind. Suddenly I realize no one is driving my van. I ask myself, "Shouldn't I move up to the front to control the steering wheel?" As I begin to think about that, concern starts growing. I woke up.

As usual, I prayed for interpretation. Subsequent discussion with Kathy was revealing. The security van was a distraction so I would continue to be carried along without leadership. I am riding in the back of the van, and no one is driving. There is no leadership, no direction. She said God may be preparing to move me. She advised me to ask God, to pray, and to stay alert spiritually. I shared that I sensed my time was up at the church campus where I had served for two years, but I would wait on the Lord for His guidance. She prayed with me, laying my ministry and me on the altar, asking for God's plan and leading. She encouraged me to keep talking to God, to keep praying, and to keep reading the Word until I received direction from Him. Deep gratitude filled my heart for God's connection to the Hubbards.

On Saturday night, while I was in quiet time with the Lord, I asked Him about the church campus and if it was time to leave. I shared many situations in the church, and I prayed, "Lord, I need to hear from You. I want the spirit of obedience to rule in my life. I am listening, and I want to obey You." A few nights prior, I had received a profound vision while reading in the Word. *His Presence loomed out from His throne and peered down through the atmosphere, the clouds, the night sky, into my room, as though He was just checking on me. I wanted to shout, "I'm here Lord!," but I was overwhelmed by the reality of God Almighty looking down at me. I remember learning about the omniscience, omnipotence, and omnipresence of God as a young teen, and I believed these attributes of God, but to actually sense His presence up close and personal was uncanny and I experienced a profound reverential fear of the Lord. I dared not speak or move for those few moments.*

Days passed without any word from the Lord. I battled to maintain my peace and combat restlessness about my future. *Where am I going? What is life going to hold for me? What is God doing in me and through me as the days and nights pass, month after month, year after year? Am I doing anything of value for the Kingdom?*

On Tuesday, April 26, my car would not start. Shocked surprise. I sat and cried out for God to help me. I felt utterly defeated and helpless. I texted my job to explain the situation, and my boss offered to give me a ride. My sister brought me home after work. She mowed the backyard, and we shared a pizza for supper while watching TV. I went outside three separate times, and my car started every time. Peace returned to my soul, and I thanked the Lord.

I stopped at the local Walmart after church on May 1 for a few things before driving home to Knoxville. The man in front of me in the checkout lane kept turning around and looking at me. He looked at me directly in the face each time before turning back around. Then he turned around and spoke of the weather and mentioned his garden. I smiled and spoke in response. He introduced himself while extending his hand and said his name was "Billy Joe." I gave my name and shook his hand. I felt prodded to invite him to church, and this was more than a passing thought. I asked him if he attended church anywhere in the area. His face registered slight regret or perhaps disappointment as he shook his head "no." I invited him to the church I attended and explained the campus was located behind a local diner. His eyes widened in recognition of the location, and he said he would consider attending. He gathered his purchases and walked towards the door. I finished my transaction and walked out to the parking lot. I spotted him several rows over getting on a motorcycle and putting on his helmet. I prayed for the man as I drove home. I was not sure of the significance of this encounter, but I do not believe in coincidences in a believer's life. I had wondered at first why the man was talking to me. God revealed that He was working in this man and had caused him to notice me so that I would speak to him about church. I was reminded not to be afraid to engage when God directs.

The following Saturday, I met some ladies from the church campus for a prayer walk in town. We stopped at various points and stood on the ground to read prayers aloud reclaiming territory for the Kingdom of God. We parted after closing prayer, and I chose the long route home to think over our words from the morning. As I drove through Clinton, I noticed a car wash sign in a grocery store parking lot to support a mission trip. I talked to a young man who was going on a nine month mission trip to several countries, and he told me the amount of money required. I gave him a small donation and asked if I could pray for him. His name was "Austin." His face registered surprise at my request. He agreed and asked that I also pray for his older brother's safe return from the mission field. When I finished praying, he gave me a hug, and his mother hugged me as well. I enjoyed our conversation and talking to some of the others in the group who were also trying to raise funds for their travel costs. I prayed over the needs of these young people and for everlasting Kingdom fruit as a result of their service.

Church the next day was a melancholy day emotionally. I wondered if this negativity was me or could it be sensitivity to someone else's pain. After praying for anyone who might be hurting, it seemed that my own spirit was lifted.

I finished work early on Tuesday and was drawn to my special place in Clinton. I sat in the car with the windows down, soaking in the beauty of the river and the partly cloudy sky with a cool breeze. An image came to mind to retrieve my folding chair from the back of my vehicle and sit outside. I did not have any sunscreen and did not want to get a sunburn so I stayed inside my car. The image persisted through the evening and all the next day.

When work was finished for the day on Thursday, I drove to my spot in Clinton. I sat outside in the folding chair next to my vehicle. During this hour, I was visited by butterflies, birds, and ducks. My thoughts drifted to the man on Mother's Day in 2014. I sang out loud with the worship music playing on my phone. I prayed and read scriptures. I was encouraged and strengthened by this special time with the Lord. A bird nearby started singing just as I was putting my chair away in preparation to leave. A large crow landed in the tree closest to where I had been sitting. He appeared to be bullying a smaller bird. I could not see through the leaves, but the smaller bird was hopping and flying to different branches and the crow was following his moves.

I drove to Lafollette in anticipation of prayer later in the evening. I stopped for gas and then went to a sandwich shop to eat. Dark storm clouds were moving in quickly. I chose a booth facing the front door watching the sky. The front edge of the system was changing shape. For several seconds the image of a gargoyle type creature formed in the clouds and was facing the direction of the sandwich shop. I immediately said out loud, "God reigns in Campbell County." I prayed protection over the population and myself. The clouds separated and moved away, and the storm ended quickly.

Before I sat down to eat, I checked the tables. Most were dirty, and I chose the cleanest one. As I started to eat, I noticed two pennies on a table in the seating area in front of me, one on the left and one on the right side of the table. I could not recall seeing those before I sat down. No one had come in behind me and left them on the table. I looked at the pennies in wonder. Should I pick them up? I was impressed to pick them up, as they were here for me in some way that I did not understand. The revelation that my time was up at this campus flooded through my heart and mind.

I drove to the church campus for our power hour of prayer that evening, and my faithful friend met me at the building. We prayed over specific needs, the church, and the Body of Christ globally. This would be my last night of prayer at this campus, and I seemed to be saying goodbye. I told my friend I would be leaving the church soon but did not share the details.

Sunday, May 15, 2016, was my last day at the Campbell County campus. I met with the campus pastor prior to service and shared my direction from God. I explained how God had revealed to me in my spirit that it was time to leave. I shared the revelation I had received; "If you stay, you will be in the way." The pastor nodded as though he understood in acceptance of my words. We prayed together, and then I made my way to the sanctuary. After service, I said goodbye to a few people, sharing hugs and tears. One precious woman prophesied over me that I was going to be very successful for God. I thanked her and her husband for their support and encouragement. I would miss these faces, but I was eager to move onto what God had planned for me next.

I stopped at my special place in Clinton on my return to Knoxville. While I was sitting in my vehicle, looking at the river, suddenly a bald eagle appeared. He seemed to appear from nowhere. The eagle was flying above the water surface and zoomed down the river. I watched his movement until he was no longer in sight. The focus and the strength of the eagle gripped my attention. He moved so quickly in and out of my field of vision that I almost questioned the sighting. While he was moving downriver, he never turned his head to the right or the left. The steadfast focus of that eagle would reappear in my mind many times in the following years.

Thursday afternoon I visited my special place. I positioned my folding chair on a grassy spot close to the river bank. My senses soaked in the sights and sounds of nature around me, cleansing toxic thoughts. I read some passages out loud from my bible, seeking God's guidance on where I was to attend church on Sunday. I received the image of a billboard displaying the words, "Redemption Church". A pair of ducks were flying across the river towards the bank and landed on the water about 20 feet from where I was sitting. I watched as they groomed while standing on a rock jutting above the surface of the water. The mallard scratched his head and continued grooming. Together they bobbed for food. I delighted in watching their movements. They were carefree and unconcerned while doing their activities of daily living. They had water, food, companionship, and could function normally as ducks. The pleasure of a simple life registered in my heart.

Redemption Church

Sunday, 5/22/2016: Today I attended Redemption Church in Knoxville for the first time. I had attended the Perry Stone Conference at this church in 2015, but I was not familiar with the pastor and had not heard him preach. I parked and got out of my car. A woman driving a golf cart stopped and offered to take me to the front entrance. She explained this service was offered on Sunday mornings. There were several golf carts moving through the parking lot carrying riders to the entrance. I enjoyed a nice conversation with the driver, and she shared that her name was "Jane". This seemed significant, and I made a mental note for future reference.

The praise and worship team was excellent with fire and passion. Prayers and offering followed, before Pastor King approached the pulpit. He announced that he was not going to speak on his planned message that he had prepared all week, and explained that God had strongly impressed upon him in the early morning hours to teach on "Destiny." I experienced a thud in my spirit at his words. From the moment the pastor started teaching, it was as though God was speaking to me directly. I was profoundly moved by the wisdom and truth explained through the Word, starting in Psalm 16. I tried to take notes, but I could not write fast enough. Sometimes the pastor would make a powerful statement that left me almost breathless. He could not know I needed him to repeat what he had just said, and I silently prayed the Holy Spirit would seal these truths in my spirit.

At the end of the message, Pastor King said he felt the need to bless the scribes. I came to understand this pastor moved in the Holy Spirit and whenever prompted, he would give a word of knowledge or prophesy according to the Spirit. This was different from my previous experiences at other churches, and I was listening and watching attentively. He explained that scribes wrote the scriptures and hand penned the words. He then asked anyone who was a scribe to stand. I had worked as a medical transcriptionist for 35 years and had written a published book, but this was my first Sunday in this church and did not know anyone here. I did not think I would be included and remained seated. The Holy Spirit immediately impressed upon me to stand up. Somewhat shocked, I rose to my feet, relieved to see a few others standing across the congregation. The pastor prayed a blessing of anointing over the scribes. I wondered what God was doing.

When the service was dismissed, Pastor King requested that anyone who had the ability to write, to transcribe, or to edit, to stop in the foyer and volunteer for the "Legacy Project." I gathered my things and slowly made my way out of the sanctuary, stopping to shake hands with the Pastor and his wife, thanking him for the powerful message. My thoughts were racing as I moved into the foyer from the sanctuary. There was no way I would be allowed to help in this project, because I was a total stranger and could not be validated by anyone at the church, but the invisible Hand of God guided me to a group of people gathered at the blue desk. A leader was explaining the project and the work involved. No one questioned me, and I marveled at this. We were each given an application to complete and instructed that someone would be in touch by phone later in the week. As I completed the form, I prayed for God's will to be done.

A woman in the church office contacted me later in the week, and we had a lengthy conversation. I shared my story of love and salvation and explained how I came to Redemption Church. I was subsequently contacted by the assistant to the director responsible for the project with details for our first meeting as a group. This began a two-year journey at Redemption with the Legacy Project. As volunteers, we transcribed or edited Dr. King's messages that were recorded on tapes in the past. We completed the work at home on our own time and communicated via email or text. The messages would be used by the church in printed form. I was astounded at this move of God. Not only was I being fed every Sunday morning and evening in church, but I was also being taught through the older teachings while I edited the Legacy files. Only God.

During the same week as the initial phone call from the church office, I experienced a startling morning with the Lord, a power session of intercessory prayer, guided by the Holy Spirit, unexpected and strong. Leaving late for work, I walked through the garage to my vehicle. I noticed several gray feathers on the driveway in front of my vehicle and both garage doors, and I stopped to inspect them closer. Most were shorter than typical tail feathers with a few soft downy feathers. Some were lying in the grass next to the driveway, and a single feather was resting on the downspout. I counted more than 30 and took several photos. I discovered more feathers on the other side of the house. There were no doves in sight, but I could hear cooing when I walked around the yard after work later that day. I wondered about these feathers and prayed for understanding.

I shared the details with my spiritual parents. They provided guidance and prayed with me on the phone, reminding me to wear my armor (Ephesians 6) and to pray for the Holy Spirit to reveal what He wants me to know. They both believed the Lord was making me aware that there are predators around. I was advised to ask the Holy Spirit to show me specifically those things that come to deceive and to destroy. They reminded me to be alert, watching and listening. Keep my guard and my shield of faith up, and I will not be hit unaware. They also shared that the Father is showing His love and protection for me. I listened to a short message that night about words and speaking carefully. The speaker warned the enemy will work through someone to start an argument to trip us up by losing our temper. I recognized that this had happened to me previously. I had received much to ponder and pray with the Lord.

Pastor King's message on Sunday, May 30, provided further teaching on "Destiny" and correlated with the story of Abraham in Genesis. Again, it was as though God was preaching to me. He began in Genesis, chapter 12. I noted some key points in my journal. When you step into the plan of God for your life, He initiates it. You cannot do it. What you do with the lot you have been given is very important. When God called Abram, He did not reveal everything at the beginning, and He will not for us, because we could not handle it correctly. God told Abram: 1) Go out of the country you are in. 2) Leave your relatives. 3) Leave your father's house. 4) Go to the land where I will show you. Abram did not know where he was going. He just knew he could not stay. God will tell you what He is going to do when He calls you in life changes. God began to give Abram a big promise. You are under God's protection when you obey. Age does not stop you from hearing and obeying God. When God's destiny is starting to be realized in life, this brings energy and enthusiasm. Abram disobeyed God by taking his nephew, Lot. God's promise of "a land that I will show thee" requires future revelation. Stay in prayer. Continue to seek His guidance. The right thing, the right way, the right place = destiny fulfilled. All three have to be in alignment. God had showed Abram the place, but in verse 9 it says, "He journeyed south." STOP when God says this is the place. When Abram kept on moving, things began to happen. Verse 10: famine, conflict with Lot, plagues on Pharoah's house. In scripture, "down to Egypt" equals world and sin. Up to Jerusalem. Down to Egypt. Stepping out of the will of God affects those around you. Stepping out of the will of God does not always bring poverty. Satan will use the lure of riches to pull you away from the will of God. Money will get in the way if you let it. Be smart enough to see that. After Abram was separated from Lot (family), God showed Abraham all the land (the promise). Abraham tithed. Then God spoke to Abraham and made a covenant, after complete obedience.

I jotted these notes for my review later. This is not verbatim from Dr. King's message.

1. Abram heard from the Lord and left where he lived.
2. He was not fully obedient—learned obedience through suffering in Egypt. God showed him the place, but Abram continued to move—disobedience.
3. You must continue to ask God.
4. Do not become presumptuous.
5. Keep inquiring of the LORD. Keep inquiring of the LORD.

6. Obey instruction fully.
7. You must realize God is working greater plan than you see.
8. Finances are not the guide. Money is the world system and enemy uses as a trap. You can be prosperous and be outside of God's will.

I received much spiritual nourishment to study and review. Every message in this powerful series over the next several weeks was filled with information I had not heard previously. I was a sponge soaking up these biblical teachings, totally in awe of God leading me to this church at this time to learn and grow in understanding.

One night while listening to music, I was struck by the wisdom and tolerance, the patience and love Jesus had for the people. He knew the hearts of everyone around Him. He knew who considered themselves superior to Him. He displayed focus of mind and words in dealing and speaking with people from different walks of life, responding powerfully to the provocative questions thrown at Him by the religious leaders. He possessed tremendous strength in His humility. He loved His disciples even while they were attempting to establish position in His kingdom. I noted in my journal that night, *Revelation and clarity came after His death and resurrection, always after, so that reflection reveals truth. The moment now is important for what will be revealed later.*

I met my friends, Brenda and Diann, at Redemption on Friday night, 6/3, for the first service of the Perry Stone Conference. It was wonderful to see my prayer friend again from Campbell County and to spend time with Diann, whom I had not seen in a couple of years. The praise and worship were powerful, and the message was an on-time word. Another friend from Campbell County had come with a woman who attended Redemption regularly. I was very happy to see this special friend. We met again for the Saturday night service, and the sanctuary was almost at capacity.

My friends did not return Sunday evening for the last night of the conference. I decided to sit in the same area where I had attended the morning service, choosing the seat at the end of a row. An usher seated a younger woman and two children next to me. At the end of the message, an altar call was given to receive the baptism of the Holy Spirit. I went down to the altar and was there quite a while, as many other people had also gone forward. When I finally returned to my seat, most of the congregation was gone. The young woman and her children had stayed and watched my purse and belongings. I was touched by her kindness. While we gathered our things to leave, I introduced myself and shared some of my story including Scott's class ring, which I was wearing that night. She was very interested in my book. Her name was "Ronda." Her smile was warm and friendly, and I sensed a spiritual connection while we talked. I hoped I would see her again, and she said she would look for me next Sunday.

The assistant to the director of the Legacy Project had messaged me about an information meeting following service at church the following week. I was instructed to bring my laptop so the program could be downloaded. There were several volunteers in attendance, and I enjoyed meeting the others involved with this project. We were given information on accessing the files for transcription or editing. I relaxed as I listened and read through the notes. God had led me to participate in this project, and I trusted Him to help me with the work.

My friend, Sue, in Goshen, had been busy arranging two book signings scheduled for the 4th of July weekend in 2016. The first one was scheduled for Friday night at "The Electric Brew" in Goshen, the coffee shop where Sue and I had met once a week following Scott's death in 2011. The second book signing would take place on Saturday at Das Dutchman Essenhaus in Middlebury, where Scott and I had married in 2008. I had mailed a copy of the book to each contact person in advance for their approval prior to scheduling these events. There were many messages exchanged with the contact person in Middlebury. Books were ordered, and flyers were printed to share. "Cindy", the woman who had returned Scott's class ring in 2012, contacted me about the book signings after seeing my post on social media. She had a background in marketing and was able to get a notice printed in the local newspaper about these events. Several of her friends had shared the post on their social media pages as well. The details fell into place, and my excitement grew as the time neared to travel.

Wednesday night I came home from work and planned to start my first file. I could not get the sound on my computer to work. I spent the next hour searching for info on my software and sound, but I could not hear the videos for instruction. I could not remember how to find the project files on the computer. Frustration skyrocketed when I could not locate my notes from Sunday. I needed to take a break.

I had planned to bake a pineapple surprise cake that evening and now seemed like a good time to start. The recipe called for an 8-ounce can of crushed pineapple, drained. I was not focused, still simmering over the lack of sound, and emptied a 20-ounce can, with the juice, into the batter. As soon as the pineapple fell out of the can, I knew I had made a huge mistake. I turned off the oven, discarded the bowl contents, and put away the recipe. It was now 10:45 PM, too late to go to the grocery store and then come home and bake a cake. Ugly thoughts and anger about the computer and the project started playing in my mind. I stopped myself and rebuked that spirit, declaring victory and obedience to God. *This project is important in my journey and will require the same, if not more, attention than my job.* Later that night updates started on my computer. Once they were installed and the computer restarted, the audio was restored. I praised the Lord, and peace and calm were restored as well.

Pastor King continued the "Destiny" series on Sunday, June 12. He spoke of how God wants to covenant with us over our destiny. At one point, he spoke to the congregation and said he had spent hours on this series and that he did not receive the information from books. I understood the teaching was of revelation through the Holy Spirit.

The next Sunday, a woman was seated behind me at church who was friends with the people I had joined, and they talked for a bit. Today was her last Sunday at Redemption as she was moving out of state for a job. She had been attending this church about a year and a half. We talked and shared some personal information in introduction before service started.

Pastor King prayed several different prayers at the end of his message. During one of those prayers, I received a spiritual nudge to pray for this woman behind me before we left the church. Between prayers, I turned around and quickly told her I wanted to pray for her before she left, and she was agreeable. When service ended, our friends spoke to her and shared goodbyes and hugs. I waited quietly. She told them that I wanted to pray for her and asked them to join hands with us. I prayed for this woman at length, as led by the Holy Spirit. She immediately followed with a prayer over me and her friends. She was in tears and trembling slightly. She was grateful and said the prayer was exactly what she needed. We exchanged contact info to stay in touch.

As I headed out to my car, I was thanking God for the opportunity to pray for this lady and continuing in conversation with Him. I was ready to leave when suddenly I remembered there were a few books in the backseat. The idea came to give her a book. In response, I prayed, "Lord, bring her into view so I can give her this book." When I reached into the backseat to retrieve a copy, I saw her walking across the parking lot. I shouted her name and waved. I told her I had a few books in the car and wanted her to have a copy.

We talked further about her life after divorce. She had suffered many losses and changes in those years. There were some similarities in our stories, and I listened as she spoke. She had received a recent job offer out of state and felt this was the direction she should follow. She thanked me again for the prayer. She said people had prayed over her before but that prayer really filled in the gaps, and she felt reassured and solid about her decision to move. We were both amazed and believed God had brought us together for this moment of connection.

DREAM, Tuesday, 6/21 (Three separate scenes)
First scene: I am sitting in a posh theater. I am with a small group of people, all dressed more formal than casual, and we are settling into our seats on the front row. The man sitting in the first seat next to the aisle tells me to sit next to him. He says he is working on getting me into someplace where I do not have access. He is holding a roll of what looks like brown floral tape and says he is going to use it to try to get me in. He is speaking low in my ear and seems serious.

Second scene: Now I am following a well-dressed Black woman into a very large kitchen with a stainless steel double wall fridge. I sense the same people are here from the theater. No distinct faces. The woman is dancing and gliding as she walks. She is swirling a long scarf around her as she moves in the room. The scarf is very light and sheer. The scene seems happy and carefree, but I do not understand. In the dream I am thinking, "What does this mean?" I am puzzled but not afraid.

Third scene: I am alone in a vast open area, solid white. There are no dimensions for sizing. No walls or ceiling, just solid white. I am walking and dancing or gliding along on a white surface while twirling a very long scarf around me. The texture is heavier like fur but moves easily. I am aware of six people standing at a far distance across this empty expanse of white. There are male and female adults, well dressed in business attire. They are standing still with solemn faces turned to the side with chins tilted up. I recognize two former presidents and their wives. There are two other people in suits as well. They do not look in my direction and do not seem to be aware of my movement. I am not moving towards them. I feel free. I am dancing with the scarf. There is nothing else in the scene. No buildings or structures, no nature, no other people, no sounds. There does seem to be a Presence over to my right, but I cannot see any evidence of this, simply an impression. I could only see myself dancing with the scarf in this white place and the solemn faced people in suits far across the space.

Prayer and discussion with the Hubbards a few days later on the phone revealed that I will be moving soon. The kitchen represented supply. They both felt an opportunity was imminent. I would continue to pray and to seek God for deeper revelation.

DREAM, Sunday, 6/26
I see a single image of Scott in my dream. He looks so good, so handsome. He is wearing a white mock turtleneck. I feel a very strong desire to hug him. No words are spoken. Nothing happens. I see him and I feel a reaction to him. He is not looking at me.

I texted the Hubbards about this image of Scott in my dream. I wondered if it was because I was returning to Goshen soon for the book signings, and this would be my first trip back to Indiana since his death. They believed that because Scott was looking away from me, this symbolized my freedom, release from my commitment to him. White symbolizes purity, reassuring me where he is. They did not believe this was a test. Kathy said the Lord was letting me know my return to Goshen will not be sad. I will feel my release, signifying my own inner healing. She gave me two scriptures, Psalm 73:24 and Psalm 32:8. There was a powerful reaction in my spirit at her words, and I rejoiced in the Lord.

Psalm 73:24 NKJV, "You will guide me with Your counsel, And afterward receive me *to* glory."

Psalm 32:8 NKJV, "I will instruct you and teach you in the way you should go; I will guide you with My eye."

I shared the upcoming book events with everyone including my friend, "Christina." She had been a part of my journey since our initial meeting in 2013. Many steps, many changes, a few cups of coffee later, our communication had grown into more of a prayer connection, and I believed our association was of God. We faithfully covered our families and each other in prayer. Grief had continued up to this point.

The communication with my friend was primarily via email, and on a rare occasion we scheduled a phone call. We had never called each other while at work, so I was very surprised when she phoned Wednesday afternoon on June 29. She asked if I could meet her downstairs in the building lobby where I worked and explained she only needed a few minutes. I hurried down to meet her, and to my great surprise she was holding a basket by the handle in one hand and her granddaughter's hand in the other. She smiled brightly and hugged me in greeting, and I was introduced to the sweet young lady by her side. She explained that they had been grocery shopping in anticipation of my trip to Indiana and wanted to bring me a special love basket for my drive the next day.

I listened in amazement as she showed me the contents. A handwritten note was attached to each item in the basket. The contents on top hid more delights underneath, each with its own note of love. She had included a cup of plastic utensils, napkins, and a devotional book--food for the body as well as the spirit. Tears welled as she spoke. Mere words were inadequate to express my shocked gratitude at this degree of thoughtfulness. She then added a sealed envelope with instructions to open later. In stunned disbelief, I said good-bye to her granddaughter and hugged my friend, and returned to the office. I marveled at the basket while I worked during the remainder of the afternoon, incredulous at her unexpected generosity of heart.

That evening I opened the special sealed envelope in the basket. There was cash to cover the cost of gas and incidentals for my trip. God had provided for every need. I felt like an official author as I prepared for the momentous weekend ahead. I packed my "FUN" bag with table props for the book signings, including the tablecloth, a runner, wooden coffee box to hold some books, and a crafted paper garland to attach to the tablecloth with the words, "When Love Comes Knocking", a creative gift of love from Sue.

The next morning I arose early and loaded everything in my vehicle that I would need for the trip. The love basket was placed in the front seat within reach, and I left the notes attached. Her handwriting with the smiley faces lifted me during the long drive to Northern Indiana. I did not stop for food, choosing instead the healthy snacks provided that were covered by my friend's prayers. The love expressed through the notes traveled with me, and I arrived awake, alert, and refreshed. Sue and her husband welcomed me into their home for the few days I would be in town. We shared good food, hot coffee, and conversation in between the events. Their gracious hospitality anchored me in the midst of this emotional return to Goshen.

"Patricia" and I met for lunch on Friday at a local eatery. We had met in 2011 at the funeral home during grief sessions and she was a part of my grief family. We had discovered that we only lived a few blocks apart and during the summer of 2012, we enjoyed long walks most evenings through the neighborhood. Our conversations were fun and healing as we shared memories of our husbands and our lives. We had continued to communicate through messages, with an occasional phone call, after I moved to East Tennessee.

I was thrilled to see my friend again. After lunch, we sat outside at her home and caught up on our latest news. She had been busy with many projects updating her home, and I complimented the improvements. We discussed her plans to retire in a few years. She accompanied me to the coffee shop for the book signing. After helping with the setup, she decided to remain for the evening. I was touched that Scott's employer and his wife, as well as several employees and their spouses, came to the event and bought books. I signed each copy. There was no pain of grief or tears, and I enjoyed seeing them again. They had been connected to Scott in the years prior to our meeting, and each person held a place in his life. The representative from Yoder-Culp Funeral Home who had assisted with Scott's arrangements surprised me when he came into the coffee shop. He shared that he had recently lost his wife, and he bought a book to read about my grief. I silently prayed for God's comfort, peace, and strength, with healing from the loss, for him and the family. My friend, "Cindy", who had placed a notice in the local newspaper, brought some friends to the coffee shop and made the introductions. We explained how we met through the return of Scott's class ring. I was wearing the ring and showed it to them as I shared more about my love story. They were intrigued to know more and bought a book as well. I discovered that talking about my love story with Scott and the greater love story with Jesus filled me with joy. To my great surprise, the couple who had led our grief counseling sessions at the funeral home also came. I was delighted to see them again! We spoke briefly while I signed their book. This event had turned into a special evening, and I thanked God for these blessings. I rode to Sue's home that night in awe, reflecting on the faces and the hugs.

Sue and I rode together Saturday morning to Das Dutchman Essenhaus in Middlebury. The staff had a table already placed, covered with white linens, and a nice flower arrangement with a small pottery vase of pens adorning one corner of the table. A framed color flyer of the book signing event stood on display as well. The table was positioned so that we would be visible to everyone walking through the restaurant and the gift shop. A nearby free-standing floor display held a quantity of books as well.

In addition, the large digital sign situated on the busy highway leading through town advertised the event. The manager, whom I had communicated with prior to this weekend, had placed a handwritten note with a gift card from the restaurant on the table. An announcement was repeated over the intercom intermittently regarding the book signing event. The staff were very thoughtful. They brought us ice water and later in the afternoon provided cups of fresh coffee. Sue took several photos of the outdoor sign and was able to capture good images in spite of the constantly changing screen.

A woman in a wheelchair accompanied by her two sisters came over to the table to ask about my book. As I shared my story, I sensed deep sadness in this lady. At the end of our conversation I asked her if I could pray for her. She agreed, and I walked around to her wheelchair. Squatting down, I put my arm around her shoulders and prayed. She began to cry, and her sisters placed their hands on her arms. When the prayer ended, she was smiling. In some way I was helped by praying for her, and silently I thanked God. My dear friend, "Monica", came and visited during the event. She was a young woman I met at church a few months after Scott's death in 2011. We had remained connected after I left Goshen, and it was wonderful to share this sweet time together. She had previously purchased her book and brought it to be signed. I talked to a woman from Canada who bought a book. One woman sent her husband over to the table for a book while she stood at a distance. I was happy to see another one of Scott's coworkers and his wife, who purchased a book. My father-in-law brought his book that he had purchased previously online for me to sign, and we planned to visit later in the evening. A delightful surprise was meeting the woman who was a babysitter for Scott when he was a young child. She had also bought her book online and brought it in for me to sign. She was interested in reading our story as she had remained friends with the family through the years long after Scott was grown. An older couple approached the table at one point. While the wife was looking at the book cover, her husband asked me if I was on TV. Laughingly I replied, "Not yet!"

Sue arrived at the end of the event, and we walked across the property to the covered bridge where Scott and I were married in 2008. Bittersweet memories swept over me as we neared the area where Scott and I had exchanged vows with our families in attendance and the pastor and his wife. She snapped a few pictures, and we returned to the restaurant. We enjoyed a delicious dinner of home-cooked Amish food in the pleasant atmosphere of the dining room.

Sue drove us later in the afternoon to meet my father-in-law at the cemetery in Bristol. The familiar roads that had filled me with incredible pain following Scott's death now were without sorrow. We spoke as we started walking, and the conversation dropped to soft silence as we approached his son's grave. I looked up at the sky peeking through the canopy of graceful tree limbs and marveled at how God had taken away the pain of that loss. There were a few tears as I stood silently remembering, but no pain, and my memories quickly brought me back to the present. We returned to Jerry's home where we enjoyed fresh coffee, fruit, and cookies. We talked quite a while. This was a momentous time of reminiscing and sharing, exchanging warm hugs and words, before returning to Sue's home.

I left Sue's house the next morning at 7:30 for first service at the church where Scott and I had attended together, and where I had continued alone after his death, until I moved in November 2012. I sat with "Monica" and her family during service. The music and message provided spiritual nourishment that fed my soul. I went to the fast food restaurant that I had sometimes visited after church in previous years and enjoyed my meal in sweet peace. I stopped for gas at the station we had frequented most often when Scott was alive, and then drove through the neighborhood where we had lived. As I drove past the familiar houses, remembering the good memories and the neighbors, there was no pain. I crossed the city limit sign, and awareness dawned that all my grief was gone. God had healed my broken heart, and all heaviness was lifted. I understood that was the primary reason for my return to Goshen over the weekend. The book signings were the avenue He used to bring me back to this area for His purpose.

The Hubbards had accurately interpreted God's message through my dream of Scott. My spirit surged with the joy of freedom, and I was aware of being strengthened with this closure. I could feel the healing physically from God, tender and energizing. This was necessary for me to move forward and to continue on the path He has planned for my future. I marveled over the precious moments from the weekend and this divine revelation during the long drive back to Knoxville. I drove away from Goshen in profound gratitude to God. These pieces of my previous life were part of my journey but not part of my present. I was released from the wounds of the past and the grief with my own inner healing. Only God.

Some treats remained in the special basket from my friend and her granddaughter for the return trip, and those carried me back to Knoxville. In spite of constant rain during most of the trip, the handwritten notes reminded me of the great love contained in the basket. I saved the paper notes and placed them in my special memory box once I arrived home, to serve as a physical reminder of God's amazing love.

My sister had texted me one morning in May that she was going to look for another place to live. Reading her reasons vented in the message, I was not surprised by her announcement. That night I had started praying and asking God for His direction; would I remain in the house, or would I live elsewhere?

Memories from the past two years of living with my sister flooded my mind as I reread her abrupt message. Several weeks passed from that initial text message, and then she informed me that she had been unable to find another place to live that was comparable in amenities, location, and rent. I had continued in prayer, and then I received these words in my spirit, "You will not be living in this house in August." I received no further impressions and no answers to specific prayers about the situation. I shared with my sister that I would be leaving the home on July 31. I then discovered she had already talked to a friend about sharing the house with her as a roommate.

On Tuesday, I received an impression in my spirit from the Lord about my "Next". I quickly wrote what I received. *I believe I need to pray and thank God for His plan and ask for His direction, favor, and guidance. Everything is going to change; job, location, work, income. I will be learning as I work. Someone is going to help me move up to the next level. God will bring this to pass. I am to seek and ask continuously with a spirit of expectancy in faith. I believe this will start before the end of the month.*

The rest of the week was uneven with some turbulence. I stayed focused on the profound blessings from the weekend, though I was keenly aware of the trouble around me and the source. I remembered a warning from God previously; *sometimes a predator comes without claws or teeth and is very destructive.* I prayed for God's protection. I reviewed my notes from church about "Destiny" and continued conversation with God in prayer.

Sunday's message at church in the Destiny series was "God is My Source". Once again, I sensed God speaking to me directly through the teaching from Pastor King.

DREAM, Sunday, 7/17
First Scene: I am driving in a vehicle, going to church some distance away. Feels like a regular day. There are vehicles and people typical of a city street intersection. Detour signs with an arrow and road barriers are positioned in the street, blocking the street ahead, redirecting traffic to turn left. The road ahead is completely blocked and the sign reads "Road Closed". I have no choice but to turn left.

Second Scene: I am in a large open room. People are milling around. The room seems empty except for some folding tables and chairs for a gathering or meeting. The only face I see is a man who resembles a pastor from the past, though his lips are a different shape. He is looking at me intently, directly. I am surprised that he is talking to me. I walk into another room.

Third Scene: I walk into an area that looks like a boiler room in a basement, where someone would work in the maintenance or engineering department of a large building. A small luncheon has been set up on a table. A man is standing there. He is in his late 40s, thin, wearing jeans and his shirt tucked in, reddish blonde hair, thinning on top and long in length, with blue eyes. I sense I have seen him or know him from the past. He does not look familiar, but I feel like I know him. I am trying to figure out who he is. I glance to the left and see a small table in the adjoining room with maybe three people around it. One is a woman in a wheelchair. A large overhead light fixture is hanging from the ceiling. Extending more than halfway down, the walls are light green. The top portion of the walls are flat pale yellow. These are the same colors the hallways were painted in school when I was a kid. I smile and speak to him. He says he is happy for me. He hugs me and says again, "I'm so happy for you. I really am." I hug him back and he holds onto me. He starts crying, and I continue in the embrace while he is crying. He says, "I'm sorry for all the things I said about her." He has turned his head and is looking up towards the ceiling. His face is agonizingly sad as he is looking up, while holding onto me. I sense he has lost someone in death. He continues to hold onto me, still crying, and I feel his pain. Silently, as he is crying, I am praying for him, for God to release him from his pain and give him healing, like He did for me in Goshen. I physically felt his anguish in my dream and I prayed in tears still holding onto him. I woke up at that point. I could feel the pain of that man after awakening. I asked God about the man's identity. Does he represent something or someone? There was no immediate answer.

A guest pastor spoke at church on Sunday. His message was on roots and being rooted in Christ, like a palm tree, bending but not breaking, and being useful in this world as a Christian. His words were inspiring and encouraging. The woman I had met previously, who was moving out of state for a job change, was at church. We talked at length after the service about my ill-fated attempt to move to Knoxville following Scott's death in 2011 and my abrupt return to Goshen the same weekend. It was a costly and exhausting experience, as I had not prayed or consulted God in my decision. The lease on the house where Scott and I lived had expired the month he died, and I was not offered a renewal. I had to move soon after his death. I shared those details and how God worked through the situation to teach me valuable lessons. I sensed that God was ministering to this woman in a powerful and reassuring way through the message and my experience in the book. Awareness of God expanded while I talked.

Later that evening, I sent a message to the Hubbards with the details of the dream with the three scenes. They prayed and waited a few days before responding. *"The man in the first scene probably represents someone with an abundant word from the Lord for you; don't go trying to find him. He may not look exactly as you saw him, but you will recognize something in him as he speaks. The road bearing left represents a change in direction; I believe there is still something in Goshen for you, but the Lord may take you in another direction at some point. You may be in Goshen for a while but not forever. The last scene speaks strongly of intercession. I am not physically holding the man and feeling his pain, but in the spirit in intercession. This is Great!! One of the most important things is where this is happening!!! It is NOT in a church building!!! Again, I believe you are traveling to Goshen; there is unfinished business there. You may live there a short time. The Lord will reveal; the interpretation belongs to Him. I find I get many answers as I leave things in His wonderful Hands and sings praises to Him. All Glory and praise to The Father, to The Son, and to The Blessed Holy Ghost!!!"* I listened without speaking, awestruck.

While I was making arrangements for the trip to Goshen for the book signings, I rented a storage unit to begin the process of moving my personal items out of the house. On the days when I was not working, I sorted, packed, and transferred boxes to storage. I worked at home all day Tuesday, as there was no work at the office for me that day, and made great progress.

Pastor King was going to speak on prophecy Wednesday night, and I was eager to hear his words. The evening service opened with praise and worship and prayer. The ushers came forward as usual to collect the offering. I was not thinking about an offering, as I always tithed on the Sunday morning after payday. Suddenly an image appeared in my mind. I saw my wallet with a single dollar bill and much loose change inside. I was stunned, and silently I prayed, "God, it's only a dollar and a bunch of loose change. Surely, You don't want that!" The image remained. I quickly unzipped my purse and retrieved my wallet. I removed an offering envelope from the back of the seat in front of me. I tried to fold the dollar bill so no one would see the number one in the corner. I was hurrying in order to have the offering envelope sealed and ready to drop in the bucket before the usher reached my row. I was awkwardly trying to get all the change out of my wallet quietly. I hastily placed all of it in the envelope, hoping no one heard the coins clinking together. The sanctuary was so quiet you could hear a pin drop. To my ears, the coins sounded like loud cymbals, and I dared not look around. I barely got the envelope sealed before a bucket was handed to me. I tried to set it quietly in the bucket but the heavy coins in the envelope landed with a thud. Flustered by the whole incident, I felt the warmth of embarrassment hit my face and a sweat broke out. I tucked the empty wallet back in my purse and prayed for God to bless that piddly amount, thankful that the bucket was now being passed on a different row. I did not understand why God wanted that dollar bill and loose change. I did not mind giving it, but I wanted to understand. If I needed to give it, I could have had it ready before service started and placed it quietly in the bucket, but instead I was prompted at the moment just prior to collection.

I turned my attention to the pastor and allowed the tension to fade. The message was very interesting, and I took many notes from Ezekiel 37 and 38 primarily. He ended by speaking about transhumanism and the days of Noah. I left the church building revisiting the pastor's words. He described how Jesus stood on Mt. Hermon and declared the gates of hell would not prevail against His church. I was walking to my car when suddenly I experienced a momentary inner explosion of tremendous power and awareness that the same God is in His followers. We have victory over the enemy and darkness. I drove home soaking in that revelation, praising God and declaring His Glory and His Sovereignty. The sky was beautiful with streaks of pink banded by the blue gray of the coming night. I thanked the Lord for the beauty.

When I started driving home, my thoughts focused on the need to refill the minutes on my phone and the lack of funds in my checking account to cover the cost of the phone card. I was close to home when I received an instruction in my spirit regarding my need. I understood and planned to do it tomorrow, as I had arrived home at this point. I checked messages and took care of a few minor needs. My mind was continuing to process the message at church and the revelation afterwards. The phone card had remained in the back of my mind since arriving home. Suddenly I stood up and asked God out loud, "Am I supposed to do that now?" No answer, but I sensed that I was supposed to have obeyed when I received the instruction. I drove to the store in prayer. I was disappointed in myself. *Lord, help me to learn Your Kingdom principles and to obey promptly.* Later that night, during quiet time with the Lord, He revealed that this instruction regarding my checking account and the phone card was related to my offering earlier at church. I had a need, and my obedience in giving provided. It is important to obey whatever He instructs in the moment, because we do not know what that obedience is attached to in the future.

When I arrived at church on Sunday, 7/24, the young woman who had contacted me initially from the office about serving on the Legacy project came over to speak. She had finished reading my book and wanted to share her thoughts. She said it brought her to tears, and she loved the love story. I shared how God had brought me to Redemption Church for the teachings by Pastor King. I talked about the first Sunday when he had asked for scribes to stand and then volunteer for the Legacy Project. She encouraged me to continue serving in this area, and I was blessed by our conversation.

I received a message from the woman I had met at church who was moving out of state for a new job. She had sold or donated everything that would not fit in her SUV and relocated for the job that had been confirmed prior to her move, according to her understanding. Upon arriving in this new location, she discovered the job was no longer available and was offered a part-time position at a significantly lower hourly wage. She was crushed, devastated, and angry. She said she drove back to Knoxville shattered. She emailed all the details, and we continued to communicate through email after her return.

Tuesday night, 7/26, we talked on the phone, and I prayed on her behalf. She said she read my book after returning to Tennessee. She talked about the book and how it spoke to her in many ways. She said she cried through it and was stunned that I was not bitter and angry over the losses in my life. I heard raw pain in her words throughout the conversation. I sensed several issues in her heart, and I was burdened for her suffering.

After the call ended, I continued in prayer with God about this woman, and an image appeared in my mind. I was asking God to soften her heart and chip away any hard edges, and I received the image of a heart in my hand. God impressed upon me in the spirit, not words, to start massaging it in a circular motion, gently. I went through those motions visualizing the heart warming and softening, becoming pliable, with hard pieces falling off, revealing fresh tissue. As I continued praying and massaging this virtual heart, my hand became warm and I asked God to flood her heart with His love. This was a totally different experience in prayer with God. I was overwhelmed with joy and wonder and tears. I did not share this experience with her or anyone else at the time. She did not wish to continue communication with me after the exchange of further messages. I honored her request and did not contact her again, but I continued to lift her in prayer for many weeks.

The following days were filled with frustration. I had boxes in my car to put in storage and a large box to drop off for donation. Lightning had knocked out the gate system at the storage facility, and a new system was installed with new codes. I could not get the gate to open with the new codes on Monday or Tuesday. I stopped at the office after work, and the manager checked the codes. The gate was working, but the gates would be closed for three days for resealing of the driveway. The end of the month was fast approaching, and I would have to wait until the weekend to bring the remainder of the boxes to storage. Funds were low, and I could not afford the gas for extra driving before payday on Thursday. My prayer friend messaged me with a word from God, "Look for Me in the waves of the storms". He is present.

Friday evening after work I was able to open the gate with the new code, and I unloaded the boxes that had been in my car all week. Saturday I worked on packing, loading my car, and transferring to the storage unit. I went to church on Sunday and then worked all afternoon to empty the house of my stuff. I would leave the furniture for my sister and her new roommate. I told her the furniture now belonged to her, to sell or to use. If she decided to sell it, the money was hers to keep. This was from divine instruction of the Lord. When I was concerned about how to move it into storage, the Lord led me to give the furniture to my sister. I understood I could replace it later and trusted that He would provide whatever was needed.

I carried the last three loads to storage and prayed for the Holy Spirit to show me how to fit it all in the unit. I had many items that would not fit in a box, and these were piled up somewhat precariously on top of boxes and storage totes. He answered with His guidance and somehow it all fit. I thanked Him for His strength and wisdom. I was exhausted by Sunday night, and I still had to load my clothes in the car. I was thinking silently about having no one to call that might help me, as I started downstairs with the first load of clothing. I left my clothes on hangers and laid them flat on a blanket in the back of my vehicle to keep them clean and minimize wrinkling. At that moment, the neighbor across the street walked over and offered to help. She said she was getting ready to go to her small group meeting and God had impressed upon her heart to come and help. I was so happy and humbled at God's care for me that tears were triggered. Exhaustion must have been evident in my face, because she insisted on carrying all the clothes downstairs and loading them into the car. She brought down the hats and accessories from the closet shelves as well. I hugged her and thanked her profusely. I could not have done this work on my own. I simply did not have the strength for multiple trips up and down the stairs. Glory to God. I was refreshed and strengthened.

The next day, Monday morning, after getting ready for work, I carried out my toiletries and a few miscellaneous items. I placed the garage door opener on the kitchen counter and gave the house keys to my sister later in the office. I left this house for the last time and drove to work. God had impressed upon me that I would not be in this house in August, so I would not return here at the end of this day, August 1, 2016. He had carried me to this point, and I trusted Him to lead me onward.

I went to work, not knowing where I would be that night. I had been praying and asking God for my next step without receiving an answer. I was in alignment with His instruction and did not fear the unknown. After work I had something to eat and then rented a room at a local hotel. I spent the evening with the Lord in prayer. I went to work the next day at peace. When my work day ended, I stopped at a café with Wi-Fi and checked emails. I sat outside on the patio for a while, listening and praying. I did not receive any definite leading, so I returned to the same hotel. I was given a nicer room with a better AC unit, and breakfast was provided the next morning. I went to work, again not knowing where I would be that night. There was a soft impression to text the Hubbards about my situation and ask for prayer. I followed His instruction and asked them to let me know if they received any word in the spirit. They texted me later in the afternoon. They had prayed together and believed God was leading them to open their door to me. I prayed about their invitation and received a rush of warm reassurance in response. They instructed me to come to their home after work.

Scott had purchased a Garmin back in 2009 to help me find my way around on the county roads in Northern Indiana. The Garmin proved to be a prophetic gift following his death and very helpful. Tonight, as I was driving to the Hubbards' home in Morgan County, I was especially thankful. They lived in an unfamiliar area of East Tennessee, and I would not have found my way without the GPS. I followed the road that turned off the highway and climbed the mountain to reach their house. The first road branched off, and I followed Kathy's directions. This was a single lane road, only room for one vehicle, and the same road was used to drive up and down the mountain. I wondered what God would reveal and teach with this new living situation and the new driving route to work.

The Hubbards welcomed me warmly when I arrived. We talked for a while before I unloaded my clothes and personal items. I was concerned about being an imposition, but they explained this was not unusual as they had hosted many people in their home, including missionaries and exchange students, during their years of ministry. I was reassured that they were not inconvenienced by the situation. They had prepared the larger of their extra bedrooms for my stay, and I settled in for the night, thankful and in awe of this sudden change in my life. There were many questions with no answers, and I spent time thanking God before drifting off to sleep.

The next morning I left for work at 8:30. I had decided to wear a pair of post earrings with flat disc backs to hold them securely in my ears. I was working at my desk when suddenly my left earring rolled down my blouse and off my lap onto the floor under my desk. I moved my chair and crawled under to retrieve it, surprised to see the back still attached. I wondered how the earring had fallen out of my ear. I checked in the mirror to make sure the earlobe had not torn and then I chuckled. I had been working since arriving at work that morning and it was now 2:30 PM. I had not lost the earring or the back. The incident felt like a soft reminder of God's presence, and I smiled to myself.

VISION, Sunday, August 7
Pastor King had been teaching on *Identity* in the "Destiny" series. During the message today, I received a vision with revelation. A large black banner was suspended above me, with white block letters that spelled, "AUTHOR." I understood God was giving me a new identity. I am now an author. I may work as a medical transcriptionist, but that is not who I am. The Apostle Paul came to mind. He was an apostle who sometimes worked as a tentmaker. I am an author that may work in other roles. My new identity was impressed so strong in my spirit that when I left church, I drove to Morgan County practicing out loud. "Hello, my name is Iris Long, and I am an author." I wondered how this would impact my future. My first book had been published, by the power of the Holy Spirit, and I was only writing an occasional blog currently.

There was no internet available where the Hubbards lived. After work the next day, I went downstairs to the café in the building where I worked and used their Wi-Fi to upload the Legacy files I had finished editing. The project coordinator at church then sent two more files to be edited within the next week. The sky was overcast when I left the building, in shades of gray, following the recent thunderstorms. Later when I turned off the highway onto the mountain road, there was a break in the clouds, and a spot of moonlight shone through. I could see the moon at the top of my windshield. This sliver of light remained in view as I rounded the curves up the mountain. I sang in praise as I drove.

DREAM, Friday, 8/19
I woke up from this dream, and the details were trying to fade as I was fighting to retain those while writing the notes. I asked the Holy Spirit to help me remember. *I am looking at the open trunk of a car. It appears to be a 1940s style, burgundy in color. Nothing is visible in the trunk except a black metal box with the back side facing me. There is a large brass plate across the back of the box and a name is stamped in the metal in all capital block letters. I see the name clearly. I then see a letter from a pastor addressed to a real estate company and to me. My name is written in capital letters. The letter is written on a sheet of notebook paper with writing sideways in the margin, and the paper is folded in an unusual manner. I glanced across the writing and saw my name in the letter. This letter covered a full sheet of paper plus a half sheet. I did not get to read all of it. The letter starts by congratulating a real estate company on*

sales of 4+ million dollars. A young boy appears with a piece of chalk. He wants to write on the wall to the left of me. The wall is black. I scold him and tell him not to. He puts his hand on the wall full of chalk dust, and I tell him he has to clean it up. I turn back to the letter wanting to read the rest of it, and I woke up. I am frustrated even as I am waking up that I did not get to read the letter.

The rest of the day was filled with tense moments. I was restless in the afternoon and irritable. I struggled to get internet connection in the café downstairs to post my latest writing. When I arrived back in the mountains, I shared the dream with the Hubbards. They joined hands and prayed for interpretation. They said the little boy was a distraction in my dream, and the enemy continued through the rest of the day to keep me distracted and disrupted. I also shared with them a recent dream of horses. We prayed again for interpretation and trusted God to bring revelation.

Saturday morning I went to a fast food place and used the Wi-Fi to work on a Legacy file. I wanted to bless the Hubbards in some way and decided on barbecue for dinner. I arrived home a little after 5, and we enjoyed a pleasant evening. Gratitude filled my heart.

The pastor delivered an encouraging message on Nehemiah the next morning at church. God truly has all the answers, and He is our go-to for everything in life, all questions and all situations. I prayed for interpretation of my dreams. Once I left church, the spirit of irritability and restlessness came upon me, and I began thinking about the negative aspects of this change in my living situation—longer driving time, extra gas, mileage on my vehicle, no internet at the house. I stopped at the Wi-Fi café and worked on the second file. I was very tired by the time I finished, and I had to lie down after I arrived home. I napped a long time. I repented for my negative thoughts when I woke up and determined I would be thankful in all circumstances.

VISION, Tuesday, 8/23

I was in my room, having quiet time with the Lord, on my knees reading I John 5, asking God if I should renew my storage unit. I had been feeling weary, intrusive in the Hubbards' home, and impatient about my life in general. I was losing focus. I turned off the overhead light and became still. Then I received a vision. I saw myself sitting at my desk in the office in Memphis, where I had worked as a medical transcriptionist for many years. I was looking at the small thumbnail picture of the "Oak Arches" print while I was typing. (This print was used as the cover for "Showered By Grace.") Words had come to my mind as I was looking at the image, and I had hastily written them on a piece of paper. At that time, in 2006, I thought the words had come from my imagination, though they sounded poetic and I had no gift for writing poetry.

Tonight, I received revelation that those words were from the Holy Spirit. *The road in the picture transforms into a life-size image, and I am standing on that road. Jesus is standing there, too. He is wearing a white tunic and sandals with shoulder length hair. I "see" the words spoken in 2006. Jesus extends His hand. He smiles warmly at me with a big smile. I place my hand in His and move close to Him. I feel safe, reassured, loved. I am happy next to Him.* The vision ends at this point, but the image of Jesus taking my hand remains. Tears are falling with the realization of His great love for me. I am walking forward with Jesus on the road, not knowing where. I continued to hold the vision in my mind. Ten years ago, God had been calling me. I had not known those words were from Him, until now. More tears from this powerful revelation. I am overwhelmed and overjoyed in my soul. His warm reassuring smile. My hand safe in His. I feel a sense of excited freedom!

The words from the Holy Spirit replayed in my mind:

"take my hand

walk with me

down the road

not knowing where

smile at me

kiss me

whisper my name

bliss"

I sat in wonder as questions came to mind. Did I fully grasp the weight of this gift? Was I sufficiently grateful? Did I understand the significance of this invitation? I did not think I could answer "Yes" to any of my questions. What would my future hold? Only God could answer that question, but He was telling me to trust Him because He loves me. I had come too far to turn back. What would I turn back to? There was nothing behind me to sustain me. I wanted to continue onward with Jesus.

I received a profound revelation from God unexpectedly Saturday night during quiet time with Him. *"You do not want to give your heart away."* The words shot through me like a blazing arrow. I cried at that piercing truth. A few moments later, I prayed to the Lord. *"You're right. I do not want to give it to another man, but I give it all to You, Lord. I want You to have all of my heart and to reign in every area of my life."* Tenderness and peace descended over me and through me. I repeated my words several times and determined I would keep declaring His Lordship in my life.

Tuesday morning I had to drag myself out of bed and get to work. We had stayed up later than usual talking, sharing, and laughing. The evening had been fun and refreshing, but I struggled through the work day. Kathy texted after lunch to update me on her nephew following a major car wreck on Friday night. Prayers were lifted. Later that afternoon she messaged that she and Bob were at her brother's house to sit with him for a while. I asked her if she wanted me to go to the hospital and pray with the family. I had experienced a familiar spiritual nudge and asked the Lord in prayer about His desire. There was no answer, but I recognized the option of choice. I considered the situation. This would be a long drive, further away from Morgan County, and I had been looking forward to getting off work and going home to rest. I noted how I felt when I decided not to go, compared to how I felt when I decided to go. The peace I experienced with my decision was confirmation in my spirit.

I found the address for the hospital and typed it into the Garmin. There were no problems in traffic as I headed toward the hospital. I entered the parking garage and found a space on the second floor next to the elevator. One other woman was on the elevator, and I asked her if she was familiar with the hospital. She led me into the entrance, and the info desk was straight ahead.

I became aware of the Lord's presence at that moment. I located the ICU waiting room and the family members. They were surprised, to say the least, as we had never met. Our only connection was the Hubbards, and I spoke about our relationship in explanation. I had prayed before I entered for God to guide me in conversation. I talked to the nephew's mother, sister-in-law, and his young adult son. This was a nice young man who had served as a Marine and was going to school. I shared some of my story and how I had met God. I asked them if I could pray with them, if they were comfortable. They looked at each other and then back at me and said "Yes" in agreement. When I finished praying, the older lady had tears in her eyes. I told them I would continue to pray, and I spoke to the young man as well. As I left the room and retraced my steps out of the hospital, joy surged through my heart. I was happy that I had come.

DREAM, Sunday, 8/28

I have received an invitation to attend an event. I am standing at the door outside a mansion. There are large windows across the front of the home. A man dressed as a butler opens the door and ushers me inside. I am standing in an open foyer that flows into the adjoining larger room. There is a grand wooden staircase against the far wall of the larger room. I am vaguely aware of rich furnishings and decor. There is a figure at the foot of the staircase clad in a long black robe with a black sash draped across his arm. He seems to be hovering as I do not see any legs or feet, and he is above the floor. I cannot distinguish the facial features as I am at a distance from the staircase. I stand in the same spot and do not move further into the room.

The man who seems to be a butler says something about the planned activity. I sense this is evil or will celebrate evil. I firmly say, "I serve the Lord Jesus Christ." The man standing in front of me becomes very agitated. The figure in black swooshes up the staircase out of sight. The dream ends at this point. I woke up mad at the enemy, binding and rebuking him, not understanding how he got in my dream. I had put on my spiritual armor from Ephesians 6 and prayed Psalm 91 before bedtime.

The Hubbards invited me to attend a local Pentecostal church on Sunday for the church's homecoming celebration. Kathy had prepared several dishes for the dinner that would be served after service. I enjoyed the music and the songs. The pastor gave a message on God's grace. I was able to speak to him afterwards and asked about waiting on breakthrough. He said to continue to be faithful and keep doing what I am doing. He reminded me of Joseph's story and highlighted the part that most people overlook when the baker forgot to mention Joseph to Pharaoh upon his release from prison. The Word says, "two years later." He said during that time Joseph remained faithful to God and continued serving in prison. He advised me to stay faithful until God moves. I was encouraged by his words and the fellowship with other believers.

The Hubbards and I discussed my latest dream during the drive home. Pastor Bob believed God could be warning me of deception, as the enemy works through people. He suggested that I continue everyday to declare Jesus as Lord of my life and stand on that. He said, "We know God has something big for you to do and He is preparing you." His words were reassuring. I prayed, "Lord, show me what comes to deceive and to destroy."

VISION, Thursday, 9/1, 2 PM
I am sitting at my desk at work, transcribing dictation, and I am thinking about a social event that I was not invited to with the office staff. This was the third time I was not informed about a social gathering, and I marveled that this time I was not hurt or embarrassed as I had been previously. Out of the blue, I receive a vision. *Jesus is looking down on me, protective from anything that would hurt me, with strength and tenderness. He loves me, and I am precious to Him. Then for a moment, I see Him looking down over a street view of Downtown Goshen.* Silently I thanked God for the precious gift of His presence, constant, everywhere.

The Hubbards invited me to attend a family picnic and cookout at the Nemo Campground in Wartburg on Saturday. This was a scenic area of historical interest, the site of the Nemo Bridge over the Emory River, and old train tunnels. The original bridge with iron framework constructed in 1929 was closed to motor vehicles with the construction of a modern concrete bridge in 1999 and now is open only to foot traffic. The weather was perfect on this fall day with a vivid blue sky and white puffy clouds. I enjoyed meeting everyone and listening to their family stories. One guest in particular, JW, asked me to walk with him across the old bridge. We joined other walkers crossing the bridge over the gently moving water below. JW was in his mid-90s, and he stepped carefully with the use of a cane. We crossed the bridge in conversation and then sat on a section of guardrail next to the road while he talked about the history of this area. He shared some highlights of his busy life with his wife whom he married in 1951. He worked as a coal miner as a young man and then later as an electrician at a nearby nuclear plant in Oak Ridge. During the 1970s he became concerned and involved on behalf of the coal miners. He traveled to Washington, DC and appeared before a Senate oversight committee hearing on specific issues. His wife was active in supporting his work and travel. He met with many influential people at that time and often was gone from home in travel due to political causes. They lived in the community where Brushy Mountain State Prison was located and both had wanted to give back to the area. His wife obtained land to open a local health clinic. She ministered at the prison and in the community. She was a strong woman who stood in staunch support of her husband and their town. She faced some scary moments because of her husband's work, but she suffered no physical harm. They both had a bold faith in God. I loved hearing his stories and hoped that I would be able to meet his wife in the future. We made our way back across the bridge and down to the picnic tables where the food was being served.

Later in the evening, I spent some time in prayer. The penitentiary was used for over one hundred years. This was Tennessee's first maximum-security prison holding the state's most violent criminals. Most of the men who walked into its gates never walked out. I thought about all of the people and families affected by the crimes and the prison sentences, and by the presence of this prison in the area for over a century. I considered the spiritual activity associated with the criminals housed in that prison. I thought about JW's wife ministering many years in the prison and the community with compassion and the truth of Jesus. Light in the midst of darkness.

During the month of September, I became aware of the first indication that I would be changing employment at some point in the future. God would be moving me into another position on this faith journey. I was reflecting on my steps with Jesus since the death of Scott as I worked on a Legacy file after work. I reread the message I had just edited and realized I needed to read more of the Word of God. I wanted to hear from God and was looking for a physical messenger, but I understood that God often speaks while we are reading His Word. I prayed for direction from the Holy Spirit. The drive home from the café was uneventful. A bright crescent moon shone above my windshield as I climbed the familiar mountain road in peace. *"Thank You, Father, for safety and protection during the day and while driving. Thank You for the truths I read in Pastor King's past message today."*

September 11 was the 65th wedding anniversary of JW and his wife. The Hubbards had been invited to their home for a celebration, and I was happy to be included. We enjoyed a delicious dinner with their family while JW and his wife shared some amazing stories of their marriage. I was privileged to hear of their work in the community through the years and their struggles and challenges in serving. They told of the dangerous threats against them during the coal mining legislative battles from years past. They brought out photos of JW with prominent political figures of those days. His wife had remained at home protecting their children and property. I was fascinated as I listened and hoped someone in the family would record their stories.

I returned to church later that afternoon for evening service. Evangelist Dwight Thompson had preached an encouraging message that morning. After his sermon, Pastor King spoke a prophetic word. I was moved profoundly as I wrote his words and tucked them into my Bible. *"You have been waiting for God to move. God is healing you, restoring you, moving you very soon. Your life is going to change completely. It is going to happen."* Tears flowed as I listened. Silently I told the Lord, *"Thank You. I receive these words. I claim everything from You with my name on it. Praise You, Lord."* My spirit was overflowing when I left the church.

I started editing new Legacy files after work. I received three instead of the typical two, related to dreams and their interpretation. My laptop was not charged and I needed to go to a Wi-Fi café. The truth that spoke to me the loudest was that God sometimes reveals things in our dreams that can be avoided. I need to pray against what He is warning about—deception in the Body of Christ, the enemy's plans against the church to be confused and canceled, and all evil to be exposed. I was surprised to learn that what is revealed in a vision or dream is protected by God. I understood the visions and dreams came from God but found it noteworthy that these are protected by God. His messages to us are protected by Him.

VISION, Thursday, 9/15, AM
While driving to work today, a logging truck passed by traveling in the opposite direction on the divided highway. I lifted prayers for protection for the driver, other drivers on the road around the truck, for the load to ride securely, and for safe delivery and unloading of the logs. I was driving, so my eyes were open while I was praying, when I received a vision.

I see a man wearing a blue plaid flannel shirt unbuttoned over a white t-shirt and blue jeans. I did not see his face or the faces of the other men. The man in the flannel shirt is helping unload the logs. Though not sure what to do, he trusts that the other men will lead and guide the process. Chains are used to secure a log and lift it off the truck. Suddenly a chain snaps and the log falls on someone who is killed. This man blames himself for the death. He accepts the guilt dumped from the enemy. He does not know how to process it, how to deal with it, and he allows the unresolved guilt to become the predominant focus in his life. He pushes away the people in his life who care about him. He rejects their love. He does not deserve to be loved or forgiven. The guilt has grown in layers and directs his decisions. He begins a relationship with a woman who does not love him, respect him, or want him. He stays with her and lets her use him and mistreat him and take everything from him that he can give, destroying ties with his family and friends and coworkers. He believes it is justified for the death of that man from the log. The condemnation from the enemy is accepted willingly and will be carried the rest of his life without divine intervention, believing he deserves to live in bondage. The destructive effect on the lives connected to this man is heartbreaking. No way out without Christ. No healing without Christ. No freedom without Christ.

Tears started flowing at this point as God revealed the lies of the enemy binding people through guilt. I prayed over the issues attached to this vision, covering this man as well as people in general who are living in the bondage of guilt. I prayed for God to open eyes and hearts to the truth, for captives to be able to receive and believe the truth, for freedom and healing from guilt and shame. I was overwhelmed by this vision and the revelations. The details kept replaying in my mind. I asked the Holy Spirit to seal all my visions and dreams, the truths and revelations, so I would not forget them. I asked that He continue to teach me and reveal the hidden messages in the dreams.

Saturday, September 17, I planned to spend some time at a Wi-Fi café. I needed to finish the third Legacy file. There was difficulty connecting to the internet, and after repeated attempts I was finally able to access the websites I needed. The next day after church I returned to the café to finish my writing. As I turned into the parking lot, suddenly my hazard lights began flashing and my interior overhead lights came on. I was moving slow through the parking lot. The hazard lights stopped flashing after several seconds, but the interior lights remained on. Pushing the buttons had no effect; the lights remained on. Turning my headlights off and on had no effect. I parked and turned off the ignition. The lights remained on. I prayed and repeated the same steps, but the interior lights remained on. I had not eaten anything since breakfast, so I stopped for a sub sandwich. A nice young man prepared the food. He asked about Scott's class ring around my neck, and I shared my story. I chose a booth to sit down and eat my sandwich, and a single penny was resting on the tabletop.

Refreshed, I continued my drive home to the mountains with the interior lights still on. When I arrived home, Bob went through the same motions I had tried, to no avail. He removed the fuse that powered the overhead lights to protect my battery. The interior light covers were very hot to the touch. He planned to check the fuse again the next day since it was now dark. The next morning he placed the fuse, which was not blown, into its appropriate slot in the fuse box. The interior lights came on and would not turn off even with the ignition off. We decided to leave the fuse out for the time being. I was concerned about the possible expense involved in searching for the root cause and repair.

VISION, Sunday, 10/2

I was in my room, in quiet time with the Lord, when He began downloading a vision for my future. I wrote without stopping, filling a sheet of notebook paper, until the vision ended. I reread the written words in total amazement. I had no idea how this vision would come to pass. I believed God could do anything, and I was filled with the wonder of His power and majesty. One of Pastor King's messages in the "Destiny" series focused on identity. God would give us our identity. He talked about God's plans for our lives. He encouraged us to speak every day in faith whatever God had promised and to speak it out loud. I dwelt on those teachings and wrote at the top of my paper, "Speak Every Day In Faith." He gave us a declaration to say out loud over ourselves daily, "I refuse to doubt, and I will never be defeated!"

The Hubbards informed me that a relative would be moving in soon from out of state with his therapy dog. This person was going through difficult circumstances and needed to relocate. He would live in the other spare bedroom until he could get situated elsewhere in the area. They were excited to help him, and I accepted this change as part of the big picture. I met him shortly afterwards, and there was a resounding thud in my spirit as I listened to him talk. I reminded myself not to make a snap judgment and to allow the Holy Spirit to lead me in guidance. The atmosphere in the home changed with his arrival, and I was aware of that every time I entered the house. I fought the heaviness in my spirit with this change and found reasons to stay away as much as possible, sometimes only coming home just before bedtime. I struggled to remain grateful for my blessings.

God led me to read Psalm 90:11-17 NKJV, "Who knows the power of Your anger? For as the fear of You, *so is* Your wrath. [12] So teach *us* to number our days, that we may gain a heart of wisdom. [13] Return, O Lord! How long? And have compassion on Your servants. [14] Oh, satisfy us early with Your mercy, that we may rejoice and be glad all our days! [15] Make us glad according to the days *in which* You have afflicted us, the years *in which* we have seen evil. [16] Let Your work appear to Your servants, and Your glory to their children. [17] And let the beauty of the Lord our God be upon us, and establish the work of our hands for us; Yes, establish the work of our hands."

While questioning God about this season of my life, I was reminded of a project with Scott in 2008. Once we had settled into our home in Goshen, I was eager to hang the "Oak Arches" picture that he had given me for my birthday the previous year. We agreed the ideal spot would be the partial wall above the stairs leading down to the basement. The decision was the easy part. Hanging it required careful preparation. Methodical planning and the safe use of an extension ladder contributed to the successful outcome. After it was hung securely in place, we gazed at this very special picture in mutual satisfaction with gratitude for all the steps that had brought us together. The end result was worth the extra effort required to mount the special picture.

I spent the evening in prayer and conversation with the Lord. "Be patient with the preparation" was the instruction I received. God brought memories to mind as I reflected over this time of waiting. I wrote in my journal; *Though the current season seems endless, supernatural movement is taking place. The end result will far outweigh any sacrifice or discomfort at present. The waiting is necessary while God works behind the scenes. His plans are farther reaching than my human eye can see. His peace filled my soul as I laid all my burdens at His feet. God has brought love and freedom into my life, and through His wisdom and loving guidance I am developing into the woman He created me to be. He has done an amazing work in a relatively short time, as I did not truly know Him prior to losing Scott in 2011. I will wait for You, Lord, and praise You in the waiting.*

Psalm 130:5-6 NKJV, "I wait for the Lord, my soul waits, and in His word I do hope. My soul *waits* for the Lord more than those who watch for the morning—*Yes, more than* those who watch for the morning."

VISION, Wednesday, October 12, 3 AM
I was wide awake in bed, having just gone to the bathroom, when I received a vision. *I see a small travel trailer, the type that is pulled behind a vehicle, in vintage colors of turquoise and white. The trailer is parked alone in a field of tall brown grass similar to wheat. The small trailer is not rusty or rundown and is clean without damage. There is nothing else in the area as far as I can see. An oversized dark brown snake is moving up the side of the trailer. The size*

of the snake is out of proportion to the trailer, much larger, with a triangular head. I rebuked the enemy and quoted out loud II Corinthians 10:4-5. I laid back down and went to sleep.

Reflecting on the vision, I understood that snakes represent the enemy. Elkhart County, Indiana, has been referenced as the "RV Capital of the World" for decades. Goshen is located in that county. There was a small trailer sitting in the field of tall brown grass. I believe this dream is another indication that a return to Goshen is in my future.

DREAM, same day, 6 AM

I am riding in a car. A man is driving. I do not know him or how I got in the car. I am confused and alarmed. Have I been kidnapped? What is going on? I ask the man who he is and how did I get in this car. He looks at me still driving but does not answer. Menacing. He is a White male, blonde hair, blue eyes, medium build, full lips, wearing a gray suit. I am uneasy. I ask him again how I got into this car. I have no memory of getting in the car. We are driving along city streets. He does not speak. The car stops and he looms over me in the seat, but this is out of proportion to the interior space of the vehicle. He appears to fill the interior of the car as he looms over me. He does not touch me, but thoughts of rape or physical violence flashed in my mind. I am dreaming, but I can feel the effects of these thoughts. I start yelling, "JESUS, help me, JESUS, JESUS!" The street now looks different, and we are stopped at a red light. I get out of the car and run down the street asking people to help me, but they do not see me or look at me. The man in the car does not pursue me. I see strangers' faces with dead eyes. No one responds. No one is concerned. I enter a building, like a brownstone in the movies, and go down the steps under the street. I do not know this place. I see a well-lit hallway with closed doors on both sides. A woman appears and asks if I need help. She is wearing a white tunic with a short navy blue cape across her shoulders and a red cross embroidered on the cape. I start crying and ask if she is a priest. Then I woke up.

Later, I realized the woman was wearing a vintage nurse uniform. I lifted many prayers and asked for full interpretation of the dream. The kidnapper represented the enemy. I was exhausted and did not sleep well for the next few nights.

VISION, Thursday, October 13, 2016

I was reading and catching up on email messages when I received a vision of Jesus. *His appearance was the same as in my vision of Him on the road, mentioned earlier. I am sitting before Him and He is positioned just a little above me. He is feeding me what looks like smooth flat wafers, very pale in color, that dissolve as I swallow. He is placing the wafers in my mouth individually, and I am swallowing calmly, at peace. I am receiving and being fed by Him through trials and difficulties. He is smiling at me reassuringly. He understands all. He is taking care of me. Everything is for my good. Taste and see that He is good.*

Saturday morning I was standing in my bedroom, looking out the window. I heard Bob and his relative preparing to leave for the day. All of a sudden a pair of bluebirds landed on the birdbath situated outside my window. They began splashing in the water. Then a third bluebird appeared and landed on top of the yellow mums next to the birdbath. Two more bluebirds joined on the edge of the birdbath, for a total of five. A vibrant red cardinal appeared and landed on the edge of the birdbath for a few precious seconds. I watched in awe, thrilled with this special gift from Above. Later in the afternoon at the house Bob led a time of Bible study and the relative participated. I remained quiet. Bob informed me that they may be moving in a couple of months. He added that as a family I could go with them. I knew immediately this was not God's plan and declined.

I went to my room for time with the Lord. I had settled into a routine of sorts with the Hubbards, and now everything was going to change again. Where was I going to live? I thought of the bluebirds earlier in the morning. God was reassuring me that He knew this would happen and He would take care of me. *"Where am I going, Lord? I am keeping my eyes on You. I am holding onto Your Hand as we walk on this road. I am being fed by You through all of this uncertainty."*

I eventually shared the kidnapping dream and the vision of the snake on the trailer with Bob and Kathy. He believed the dream concerned my job and that God was sending someone in a low position to help me. Most of the time we would run up, but I went down, and he said that could signify a lower position, an unexpected place for help. He did not offer any guidance on the vision of the travel trailer, but I sensed he had revelation and did not want to speak about it at that time.

Earlier in the year, my vehicle had passed 170,000 miles and I wondered if it was time for a newer car. I had talked about this silently to God one day while I was walking through the parking lot towards the building where I worked. I was looking at the different vehicles and had no idea what type of vehicle I should purchase. I wondered what type of vehicle I would need. I was thinking to myself, "Would I be doing work for the Lord that would require a specific type of vehicle?" Many questions. Scott and I had bought the car I was currently driving in 2009, and he had chosen the make and model. I would need to trust God to guide in the next selection. I had noticed an SUV that was popular, in red and in black. I asked God about this vehicle but did not hear a response. A few days later while I was walking through the parking lot, I was compelled by the Holy Spirit to stop. I was standing next to a blue vehicle of a different make and model. I asked the Lord, "Is this the vehicle I will need?"

Sunday morning, October 16, was powerful at church. Pastor King and his wife gave several words—healing of a shoulder, restoration of a woman's life, healing of sciatica/pain down the leg. Then Pastor King said he had a word but did not know who it was for or what it meant, but he was instructed to give this word, "Choose the blue one." My eyes widened and my mouth fell open as I claimed that word for me by raising my hand. God had answered my question about my next vehicle; however, He did not instruct me to make a purchase at that time. There was a dealership for this brand of vehicle in the city close to where the Hubbards lived. I drove by every day to connect to the interstate. Sometimes at night I would stop and park on the shoulder, then walk around the lot looking at these cars. I believed I would have one of these vehicles in the future through God's provision.

Saturday morning, October 22, I struggled with the Lord. *My flesh wants to leave here and not look back. I am feeling the loss of everything—family, shelter, security. I do not know what I am doing. I sat at a fast food place last night for Wi-Fi and observed displaced people and felt like one of them. People do not love one another anymore unless an advantage is attached. I am burdened about the world and people. My soul aches for Jesus. There is an oppressive atmosphere in the house and it hurts. I feel the effects, and I am struggling not to react in the flesh, but I am weak in myself.* My prayer Friday night was for God to help me, over and over. It was the same prayer this morning. I had plans for the day and looked forward to being out of the house.

I attended church the next morning. After service I headed for a Wi-Fi café in Clinton to work on files. As I was getting ready to leave that evening, I received revelation in my spirit, "You were supposed to stay with the Hubbards. They invited (the relative) to move in because of his perceived wealth. That was not from me." I lifted many prayers and thanked God for His blessings. I will continue to look to Him for my care.

Wednesday, October 26, I was leaving the office after work and rode down the elevator to the first floor as usual. I walked through the lobby area, and a woman was walking hurriedly from the corridor that connects to the hospital. She appeared frantic in her search for a charging station for her phone. She said other hospitals had charging stations for phones. I explained that I was not aware of any. I spotted a man from environmental services nearby, and he confirmed there were no charging stations.

The woman said that her son was in the ER with severe abdominal pain and needed to undergo emergency surgery. A CT scan had been performed, and the medical staff said he had appendicitis, but she told them that his appendix was removed years ago. She said they must have seen some type of mass or abnormality and were prepping for surgery. I asked if I could pray with her for her son, and she agreed. She told me his name as we joined hands. She was crying when I opened my eyes, and she hugged me warmly. She said I had no idea how much that meant to her, and she turned to go back to the ER. I continued to cover her son and all involved with his care and his mother and family in prayer as I walked to my car. The opportunity to pray for someone and offer a moment of comfort lifted my spirits tremendously and renewed my hope.

I was turning into traffic from the parking lot when the idea popped in my mind to bring beignets to the office in the morning. I ignored the idea at first, thinking this was just my imagination. The suggestion came again with more emphasis, so I drove to the local restaurant nearby that specialized in fresh cooked food and baked desserts. The owners worked in their restaurant and prepared the food themselves. I talked to the woman at the counter about ordering beignets to take to work in the morning. She said they probably would not be any good by then. Her husband came out of the kitchen and explained that they were best hot and fresh and would not be any good by tomorrow morning. She asked what time I needed them in the morning. When I replied at 9 AM, they agreed to make them fresh and have them ready to pick up at that time. I was happily surprised at their kindness and ordered three batches. She would not let me pay for them in advance and said they would have the beignets ready.

I left the house at 7:30 in order to get to their restaurant on time. Driving from the mountains in Morgan County was a long commute down to Knoxville and the interstate traffic flow could be unpredictable during morning rush hour. I arrived a couple minutes after 9, and the owners were there with the fresh beignets. I could feel the warmth of the hot pastries through the bag. Excitement was rising in me about this treat, but I did not know why exactly. There had been an atmosphere of tension in the office since Tuesday after I returned from lunch. Though the office administrator knew where I was that day, he had gone to lunch as well. Apparently someone was looking for me at the time that I was not in the office.

I placed the beignets on a table in the kitchen and let the office staff know about the food. These quickly disappeared. Everyone was appreciative of the delicious treats, and there was a definite lift in the atmosphere. I believe the Holy Spirit moved through that food to restore peace. Now I understood the suggestion after work the day before and thanked Him for His goodness.

One night at home, during time with the Lord, I received deeper revelation. *People are hungry for God, for truth, the Light.* I teared up at this point. *He is going to feed, save, and rescue the lost, malnourished, bound prisoners. His presence will be known. His Hand is going to open the door to set them free.* I sat quietly in awe of God's desire to teach and to show His heart and power.

The following Monday, I went to the usual Wi-Fi café after work to edit a long file I had not finished yet and this was due the next day. I had been working maybe 45 minutes when I noticed a police officer two tables over from where I was sitting. He was watching one of the TVs on the wall across from the area where we were seated. The TVs stayed on closed captioning and were muted, requiring the viewer to look at the screen to read the dialogue. I continued working until I sensed a soft nudge to speak to this man. As he was finishing his dinner, I spoke to him from where I was seated and said, "Excuse me, sir." He turned his head in my direction with a guarded expression. I shared my appreciation for his service and added that I prayed for the men and women in uniform regularly. He looked back at his food and said, "Thank you, but pray for those serving in the inner cities because that's a whole different ballgame."

We began a conversation that covered God, America, politics, Memphis, crime, et cetera. He quoted scripture and talked about different passages in the Bible and men of the Bible. I wondered if he noticed my eyes widening in surprise. He talked about his mom and her faith. He said he might still be in some bondage even though he was saved. I made a mental note of the last name on his badge to cover him in prayer. I could not see the first name initial as we were not sitting close in proximity. Throughout our conversation, he had maintained the same distance, sitting and then standing. He was fit for his age, well-groomed, uniform neat and clean in appearance. During our conversation, he talked about previous areas of service in East Tennessee.

He asked if I was traveling through the area. I explained that I was staying with friends in Morgan County and worked in Knoxville. "I come to this fast food restaurant for the Wi-Fi as my friends do not have internet service in the mountains." We talked at least 45 minutes until I realized the need to complete the unfinished file. Later that evening I drove home in prayer for the police officer, for healing and freedom, for protection, for forgiveness and restoration of any brokenness, for softening of any hardness from his line of duty. I also covered his request for the officers in the inner cities. It was almost 11 PM by the time I got home that night, but I was at peace and uplifted by this unexpected encounter. I continued to work at this particular Wi-Fi café on the Legacy files but never saw the officer again. He remained in my prayers as led by the Holy Spirit.

I signed up to participate in the Women's Expo at a local church in Lenoir City in November 2016. Each vendor was asked to donate a door prize. I had forgotten about it until I received an email reminder the day prior to the event from the coordinator. I spent a few hours after work gathering items to place in a special container, including a signed copy of my book, as a door prize that I would be happy to win. I was pleased with the final result and headed home.

Agitation rose once again last night while rearranging the stuff in my car in order to accommodate the books and items needed for the upcoming book signing. Odd bags and items in the front seat rested on top of what was already stored there, that I barely had room to drive, and I cried out loud, "God help me." Stress increased, and I said, "God, please help me because I do not have the patience for this. I can hardly bear this chaos. Please give me the strength." As I drove through Oliver Springs and turned onto highway 62, I began to calm down. I had no place to work on anything. I had stuff in storage and in my car. Traveling to a Wi-Fi café almost every day to work on files and my own writing was exhausting. I had to load the things I needed to use at the café and then bring these back to the house. There was no stationary desk or spot to work in the bedroom where I stayed, and I had to continually shuffle things back and forth from my car to the house and back again to Wi-Fi cafes.

Tonight I was overwhelmed with the situation, and I cried out in frustration. Life seemed so difficult, like I was swimming upstream constantly. Nothing was settled, and the losses from Scott's death washed over me with the ferocity of a tsunami. I collapsed into bed soon after I arrived at the house. How long was I going to be in this wilderness? I prayed to see the Lord move in some way soon.

Some days I felt like I was keeping on to keep on keeping on. I had a moment from God where I saw myself, and I was not happy with the view. I was responding to anxiety in an unhealthy way and felt inadequate to handle my situation. I recognized my deep constant need for God's strength, help, and guidance to move through this season. I also suffered physically. Multiple boils on my body came and went like a revolving door. As soon as one healed, another one appeared in a different area. I wanted relief that lasted.

The idea to drive to Pigeon Forge started a few days before the weekend in mid-November. Church began that Sunday with inspiring praise and worship, followed by a moving message. Prayers were lifted across the congregation for lost family members at the end of the service. This powerful morning provided the perfect beginning for a special day. I concentrated on the drive for the next hour, choosing the long route from Knoxville on this pleasant sunny afternoon. Driving through Maryville, Townsend, and across 321 to Pigeon Forge, I noted the local tourist attractions, billboards advertising hotels and cabin rentals, and craft/gift shops scattered along the highway. Some businesses were for sale, while new construction was underway in other spots. The sharp curves on the mountain road ensured slow cautious driving, while I mentally compared the passing scenery to previous trips to the area.

Many trips had been made to Gatlinburg during the 1980s to early 1990s. The landscape was different with less development, Dollywood was brand new, and the skyline was uncluttered. Once I arrived in Pigeon Forge, I cruised the parkway. Tall buildings of entertainment filled the horizon. Digital screens displaying moving scenes of the venues offered inside were situated in a dizzying row along the street. I hardly noticed the mini golf courses and pancake houses that once stood out prominently on the parkway. Very busy, very eye catching, very entertaining. People come here to have fun and enjoy time away from work and school schedules. Six lanes of pavement now supported the boom to the local economy.

I stopped at a once favorite shopping destination and walked through several stores linked together, browsing through the merchandise and enjoying the sights and sounds of activity. I eventually moved outside and sat on one of the benches in the courtyard. Parents waited in line with their children for a visit with Santa. I watched people on their phones and heard passing conversations. I noticed the flow of traffic on the nearby street and the lowering of the sun in the afternoon sky. Christmas lights outlining the buildings and landscaping shone dimly in the remnant of daylight.

As I sat quietly, questions rose in my spirit, "What about Me? Am I a part of the vacation, the weekend, the fun, the celebration? Do you leave Me behind, leave Me out, and forget to include Me in your plans? What happens when the lights go out, the doors are locked, and it is time to go home? Will your enjoyment of the day last through the night? Will it satisfy you a week from now, a month from now, next year?"

In reflection, I walked to the parking lot. God's words lingered as I drove past shopping centers and restaurants, people and traffic in continuous motion. Were they thinking of the Savior? Had they talked to Him today? The world is full of bright lights and bustling movement with enticing lures in the noise and activity, but there has to be more than the pursuit of visual stimulation and temporary pleasure for contentment and satisfaction in the soul. Awareness and desire for the Lord's presence brings a deeper need for what is good, righteous, holy, just, and true. Anything less is shallow and pales in comparison.

I turned onto I-40 for my return to Knoxville. The drive was filled with many prayers with the Lord, in gratitude for our special time together. I listened to music and sang Christmas carols as I continued north towards Morgan County.

The next day I shared with Kathy about time recently spent with the Lord. I shared what He had impressed through the Spirit about a woman who held a special place in Kathy's heart. I had met this woman previously at the family cookout at the Nemo Campground. She had gone through tremendous health issues in recent years and had been covered in prayer by many. I repeated to Kathy what the Lord had revealed. *She is opposing God with her daughter. She has allowed her guilt, whether real or perceived, to drive her decisions and behavior with her daughter. She is not letting God work according to His will. She is a stumbling block and in His way. She is disobedient, and the enemy is using it against her in her health, her marriage, and her life.* When

God revealed this the day prior, I had lifted many prayers in response, asking for His mercy and to give this woman the strength to face the truth. Kathy and I prayed together that God would prepare this woman to receive, accept, and comply. She explained that God gave me these words to repeat to her friend, and she would take me to her the next day. I was somewhat taken aback at Kathy's words, as I had expected her to relay the words to her friend, but she insisted that I needed to relay the divine message.

The woman was lying in bed in the hospital when we arrived. I had prayed in advance of our visit, and now repeated the words I had received from God with nothing added. She confessed that the words were true and seemed relieved to know the truth about these issues. We prayed over her and with her before leaving the hospital. This was a new and different experience for me, and I followed Kathy's leading in the situation.

Every time I hear or feel an unexpected thump while driving, I automatically look in my rear view mirror and wonder if something just happened to a tire. I do not know why I look in the mirror as I cannot see my tires there, but it seems to be an automatic response. I went through a season of tire failures, flats, patches, and used tires, in the dark days of the late 1990s. When I think there is a problem with a tire, I experience that same sense of dread. There have been cycles where my tires looked low, and I would check several times to make sure the pressure was adequate. Scott had kept a handy gauge in the car door pocket, and I used it frequently.

My tires had looked low for several days, and my vehicle was not handling as well. I sighed in dread. I did not like to air my tires. I rarely get them aired up enough for the indicator light to remain off. I have a fear of overinflating the tires, with visions of an explosion or some other damage running through my head while trying to pump more air in than I am letting out with the air hose. I checked them with the tire gauge, and they were definitely in need of air.

I had come through Oak Ridge driving home from work, so I drove onto Oliver Springs. The new gas station had opened recently with an air tank that accepted a credit card for payment. This made it so much easier than finding an ATM to draw out $20 and breaking the bill for enough quarters to use the air hose. I had stopped here previously and the machine worked great.

I parked in front of the air tank and removed the caps from the tire stems before swiping my card to save time on the timer. When I swiped my card, it did not register. I tried again and the card still did not register. My mind was processing the dreaded ATM alternative when I heard a voice call out, "Do you need some help?" I turned around, and a young man in his 30s was walking across the parking lot. He set his gallon of milk on top of the tank, and I explained that my card was not processing. He swiped the card, and the tank turned on. He took the hose and proceeded to air up my tires. I thanked him several times while he was filling each tire.

When he got to the fourth tire the time expired on the tank. He said, "I might have four quarters" as he reached into his pocket. I said, "Oh no, I'll pay," and walked back to the air tank. I swiped the card, and it would not register. He followed me, and tried the card with success. I was dumbfounded. I had swiped the card fast the first time, but after watching him slide it slowly, I did it slow too; however, that had not worked for me. He filled up my last tire. I just stood there somewhat in awe at this blessing. I was not sure what the expression was on my face, but he gave me a soft hug and said, "Oh, it's ok. We help each other around here." He said his name was "Davy" and he was going to take his son to look at Christmas lights. I thanked him several times. When I started my car to leave, the low tire indicator light went off and stayed off. My car rode much better as I traveled down the highway, and I thanked God for His unexpected gift of kindness from this pleasant stranger. I prayed blessings over the young man and his family. Only God knew how much I dreaded airing my tires, and I teared up at His compassion and mercy. A timely reminder from Him that He knows our needs as well as our preferences.

Prior to church Sunday morning on November 20, I was sitting in the parking lot at a fast food restaurant on my phone because I had arrived too early. I heard a tap on my car. Surprised, I looked up to my left and a young man was standing at a safe distance from my vehicle, not close to the window. We spoke through the glass. I noticed that he was clean and his clothes were clean. He showed me some quarters and said he had just gotten out of rehab and needed three dollars to get to someone's house for the night. He shared the details, but I did not record them in my journal. I knew I had some ones in my wallet, so I pulled out three and rolled the window down far enough to give him the money. I told him I did not know if he was telling the truth but that he was not accountable to me if he was lying. He said, "I'm accountable to the Lord Jesus Christ." He turned away and walked over to a car and got in. I did not know if he was legit. I did not get the sense that he was an angel or a test, but I was aware of that possibility. It seemed odd that he only asked for three dollars, but I had peace about it and turned my attention to the time as I drove to church. Pastor King had completed the series on "Destiny" and now was teaching on "Faith For The Journey". This was a longer series, and there was much more to learn.

Sunday evening I returned to Redemption for movie night at church. I enjoyed the popcorn and treats served in the foyer prior to the movie, "Miracles From Heaven". This was a wonderful feature based on a true story of miraculous healing. I focused on the events of the lives represented in the movie, and I was refreshed.

On Wednesday I traveled to Memphis for Thanksgiving and the holiday weekend with my daughter and grandson. I was thrilled to see them again and the days passed too quickly. My daughter prepared many delicious meals, and Thanksgiving dinner was extra special. We went to Zoo Lights one evening. We spent some time shopping and then decorated the Christmas tree. We worked on craft projects, played games, snacked, laughed and made good memories. My son joined us for Thanksgiving dinner, and that was a blessed day. This trip was Christmas for me, and I loved every minute.

I drove back to East Tennessee on Sunday and did not know where I was going to stay. My time had come to an end at the Hubbards' home. God had not given me a lead on where to go next. I had been praying about this change since He revealed the alteration in His plans. I was in conversation with the Lord during this trip. I stayed in a hotel that night and Monday night, continuing in prayer. I did not have enough money for a third night, and payday was on Thursday. There was no word or movement from God, yet, in answer to my prayers. I slept in my car Tuesday night in a hospital parking lot. Severe thunderstorms raged that night with repeated lightning flashes. There was no fear and no doubt. In spite of these undesirable circumstances, I knew God was with me. I slept through the night.

I used a public restroom early the next morning to change clothes and put on makeup. Same routine Wednesday night and Thursday morning. Silence continued from God. Wednesday night after work, a woman was standing next to the parking lot entrance that was adjacent to Walmart. There was a ping in my spirit so I turned around to hand her the ten-dollar bill in my wallet. I told the woman that it hurt to give it to her because this was all the money I had but hoped it would help her. My heart was heavy. *God, why are you being so quiet when my need is urgent?*

Friday after work I stopped in Oak Ridge for a bite to eat and to relax in spite of this extremely uncomfortable waiting period. While eating dinner, I received the idea to send out a text to my small circle of friends and ask for prayer about a place to stay. Immediately a woman I had met in a bible study at church responded and told me to come to her house. I could stay there for a week while her roommate was out of town. Then, another friend I had met at the Campbell County Church campus in 2014 messaged an invite to come to her home. I was almost in tears as I thanked God for the blessings of these friends. The first woman who responded was a very interesting person and loved animals. She lived a full life and remained active. She actually maintained a mini farm on her property, and a large bird occupied the space downstairs in the walkout basement. I never saw him, but he was able to make his presence known. The week passed quickly, and I thanked her for opening her home to me for those few days.

The following Friday, December 9, I moved into my friends' home in Scott County. "Al and Judi" lived in a country setting outside the nearby town. The area was quiet and scenic. They were very accommodating and welcomed me warmly. I was overwhelmed at their friendly hospitality.

We spent many hours talking and prayed together when we shared meals. Her husband traveled out of town frequently, and she was busy with projects and maintaining her home. I came and went according to my work schedule and the ongoing work on the Legacy Project at church, typically only being home at night to sleep. I continued to use various Wi-Fi cafes for the internet, and my commute to and from Knoxville followed a different route. I remained at Redemption Church in Knoxville, while my friends attended a local church closer to their home. The bedroom where I stayed had its own private bathroom. I expressed my gratitude for their generosity and kindness to them and to God.

DREAM, Sunday, December 18, 2016, 4 AM

I am in a large city, and I am going to be on a television program by a popular host. I am riding in the back of a cab and looking out the windows at the tall buildings in the skyline. I am calm, not excited, and not nervous. I am here on mission, for purpose. I can "see" in my mind's eye while riding in the taxi the people sitting in the studio audience. I am casually wondering about wardrobe, makeup, and other small details. I see myself sitting on a stage, face to face with this host, talking about the book/the love story. God will be there and work according to His purpose.

When I woke, I sat up in bed and relived those images over and over, as though they were being sealed definitely into my mind and spirit. I finally laid down to sleep and woke feeling refreshed. Later that night I reflected on the kidnapping dream. A change in employment was coming soon.

I was struck by the realization that obedience to God would propel me forward and upward, while life around me would be business as usual. Two simultaneous realities. Great steps go unnoticed while God is moving in a profound way. I absorbed this in wonder.

I stopped at a local popular barbecue spot in Oak Ridge for their weekly special on December 20. As usual on Tuesday nights, the line was backed up to the door. I squeezed in and then became aware of a man behind me who had managed to enter the door as well. Since the line was long, I decided to check my phone. There was a prayer need posted by a friend's husband with an update on her condition. Prayers went up in alarm. I was processing this information when the man behind me started talking about an elderly man who had just fallen in the parking lot. Apparently he had hit his forehead and a woman was taking paper towels out to the man.

I turned to look, and an elderly man was on the ground in the drive-thru lane. The man standing behind me walked outside to help, and I approached the counter to tell the young man at the register what had happened. He walked to the door and looked outside, and then disappeared into the kitchen, supposedly to tell someone in management, but no one came out to assist. I walked out the door and by this time the elderly man was on his feet and walking to his car held by his wife with the man who had been behind me in line. I went back inside, and the man entered again as well. The young man from the register came to the door, and we informed him that the elderly man and his wife were now in their car.

The dining room was adequate, but tonight there appeared to be more people than available tables. I was assessing the situation while moving in line and mentally considering the possibility of carrying the food home to eat, which was not appealing as I had 45 minutes to an hour travel time still remaining. At that moment, the man behind me suggested that we share a table, and I accepted, relieved at this alternative. We carried our trays to the only available table and sat down. I introduced myself, and he shared his name, adding that he was retired and lived in Oak Ridge. I told him I was going to pray over the meal. He sort of nodded and remained silent. I guessed his age to be mid-70s. He began talking about activities in college (Memphis State and UT), and shared fun memories from those days. He was originally from Kentucky, but his family moved to California for several years when he was a young child. He shared a few scattered details of earlier adult years, and I sensed loneliness in his present life.

He then spoke of a young man, "CJ", who had barely escaped with his wife and family from the horrendous fires earlier that month that had destroyed or damaged more than 2000 homes and buildings in Sevier County. Fourteen people had died and at least 200 were injured in the fires that burned more than 17,000 acres in the Great Smoky Mountains

National Park. Those who had managed to get off the mountain described the experience as escaping death through walls of fire. Tears rolled down the man's cheeks as he spoke, and his hand shook as he lifted the fork to his mouth. The fires had been extinguished in the beginning of December, but the tragedy was still fresh. His eyes were focused on his plate while he talked. I let him speak uninterrupted and studied his face as he spoke. I told him I would cover this young family in prayer for their needs with the loss of their home and possessions, and I made a mental note to pray for this man as well. I then shared my story of meeting Jesus through the death of my husband and the ways this had changed my life. He lifted his eyes when I began talking and listened.

We finished our meal, and he left first. We did not exchange any personal information. I never saw him again though I continued to stop at the restaurant occasionally on Tuesday nights for the dinner special. A few months later my job radically changed, my driving route was altered, and I did not pass this way again.

Driving home through the mountains towards Scott County, I prayed over the results of the fires and further extensions of those issues as led by the Holy Spirit. I prayed for the people of Sevier County and all who were affected by the fire and the aftermath. I thanked God for prompting me to stop tonight at the restaurant. My friends were leaving town in the morning for the Christmas holidays. I had planned to get home early in case there were any special instructions I needed to know. The miles passed with prayers and praises lifted into the atmosphere.

I drove to work Friday morning thinking about my light workload and how I was going to enjoy the day. Maybe the office would close early as part of the holiday weekend. I turned into the parking lot singing aloud with the Christmas music on the radio. I had my choice of spots as the lot was half empty. A bundle of red cellophane lying on the ground in the adjacent parking space caught my attention. Had someone dropped a gift? Curious, I picked it up. There was some wrapped candy scattered on the asphalt around the paper. A handwritten note, penned in green and red ink, was taped to the red cellophane that read, "Just want you to know

Jesus loves you!" A pretty silver bow was attached. There was more of the same candy inside the wrapping and an empty cardboard holder for a mug. The recipient had taken the mug and thrown the rest of the package on the ground. The paper and bow were fresh and clean, and had not been crushed by tires, so this had happened a short time earlier.

I looked at the note and thought about the heart that had given this gift. Was this a gesture of concern for a coworker or friend? Was the gift a token of encouragement to a hurting soul that God cared? I thought about the heart that had rejected it as well. She did not want the note. She did not want to hear that Jesus loved her. She did not want to take any of this gift home with her except the mug, which could be used or re-gifted.

I set the opened package on the ground where I had found it, in hopes that the receiver would come back and pick up the rest of her gift. I prayed that she would accept the love and concern behind the gift. I prayed that the giver would not be discouraged if she learned that her gift had been rejected.

Later in the afternoon I left work in anticipation of the Christmas weekend. As I approached my vehicle, I was sad to see the package. Someone had stepped on the candy pieces outside of the cellophane, but no one had claimed the discarded gift.

My thoughts turned to God and His love. He created us in love. He gave His son as an atoning sacrifice for our sin to restore relationship with Him. A free gift, available to all, if we will accept it. My heart was heavy as I lifted prayers for those who have rejected God and thrown down His gift in anger, rebellion, resentment, disappointment, despair, bitterness, unwilling or unable to believe and receive. I asked God to work in the lives of those who have not yet recognized their need of Him. The greatest gift of all remains ready to be picked up by a willing heart.

On Saturday, Christmas Eve, I stopped at a local store and then at a fast food restaurant in the afternoon. A woman was at the counter placing an order. She handed the cashier a gift card to cover the cost. This was declined with an available balance of only $1.12. He tried scanning the card twice with the same results. The woman turned and left without the food. I could have paid the $19.42, but I did not say anything. I did not look to see which vehicle she was in or if she was alone. I do not know why I remained silent. Had I just failed another test? I drove to a Wi-Fi café when I left there, located just off the interstate. This was a large fast food restaurant with much out of town traffic. A woman approached me in the parking lot and asked for five dollars. I listened as she spoke and offered to buy her food as I did not have any cash to give. This did not feel the same. Later, as I was leaving I observed her approaching someone else for money and used the donation to purchase a large coffee drink. The woman earlier had genuinely needed help. Though I had this second chance to pay, it did not help the woman earlier and did not cancel that missed opportunity.

I attended a friend's church that night as her son was being baptized after service. I focused on the message and celebrated this young man's decision. I came home and spent time with the Lord and in the Word. I talked to Him about the incident earlier with the woman and the gift card. I was concerned that I had failed another test. I asked God for forgiveness for my hesitation, doubt, and selfishness. I prayed for God to give me boldness and discernment.

Christmas Day was quiet and peaceful. I was blessed through conversations with my family on the phone and enjoyed the beauty of my surroundings. The Lord was ever present, and I thanked Him for the gift of our Savior, His only Son, Jesus. I reflected on the steps that had led to this moment, and I thanked Him for my family, my children, and my grandson. I thanked Him for pursuing me with His love and for the love I shared with Scott. I thanked Him for the goodness of friends and prayed blessings over those who had been kind to me. I prayed blessings over my family.

The next day I woke up with a phone number in my mind. There was no area code; only a seven digit number. This was not a familiar number to me personally. I checked the internet, and there were two listings associated with the number. One listing was in Florida, and the other was in Alabama. I prayed over both listings. I received no revelation from God about the number and simply made a note in my journal.

CHAPTER SIX

2017

Wednesday, January 4, 2017, I woke up with the impression that my next employment would be as a caregiver. This was strong in my spirit, and there was no doubt that I had to make this change. I cannot say I was thrilled. The correlation to "going down under the street" in my dream was clear. I would be stepping down from my current position to a lower pay scale into a job that is not as desirable in the world's eyes, but God was directing my steps for His purpose, for my good, and for the good of others who would be impacted by my obedience. The people who work in that capacity (the nurse in my dream) care for those who need help. I recognized this was an important step and I must obey.

The next day at work I battled chaotic turmoil in my spirit and mind with uncertainty about job change leading. That night my daughter called. She said my grandson told her, "Let's call Grandma!" I so loved seeing their smiling faces and hearing their voices. This was a wonderful gift of love and reassurance.

DREAM, Friday, 1/13/2017, 7:45 AM
I am in a beautiful place that resembles a resort located on top of a mountain overlooking the blue ocean below. There is green grass where I am standing. It is a beautiful day with bright sunshine and blue sky. People are moving around me socially. In the foreground of this scene, almost like a photo added at the

bottom of my field of vision, separate from the resort area, is a head and chest shot of a man. His eyes are hooded by his eyebrows as he seems to be facing the sunlight. He is wearing a black and white small check sport coat with a white shirt underneath, and I can feel his discomfort. His arms feel bound in the jacket. His hair is somewhat messy, not combed, as though ruffled by a breeze. I do not know who he is or who he represents. He does not resemble Scott. He is not a part of the scene. Different women are telling me, "He really loves you." As I am moving through the people, four different women speak to me stating the same words. They pass by me saying the same sentence. A different word in the sentence is emphasized by each woman when spoken.
"HE really loves you."
"He REALLY loves you."
"He really LOVES you."
"He really loves YOU."
I am overwhelmed by the truth of this love. Then I woke up.

Though I no longer resided with the Hubbards, I continued to communicate with them by phone. I still considered them my spiritual parents. They had counseled me while I was in their home, and I missed our prayers together and their spiritual guidance. I shared the details of this latest dream with both of them over the phone. Bob explained that the face I saw in the foreground was from God. Sometimes God or a messenger appears different than what we expect. When God comes the attire is different. He is clothed in flesh to come to us in human form. God is speaking to me about His love for me and relationship. Other people see His love for me more than I can see it. God meets people on the mountains, the high places.

I was planning a book giveaway on social media for "Showered By Grace" and started shopping for various items to include as a total package. My first stop was the florist in Oak Ridge that I had previously visited a few years prior. At that time, the leader of the widows' group had suggested an outing following our Saturday morning meeting. We were introduced to the owner by our group leader, who was her personal friend, and we browsed through her shop. She was a beautiful younger woman truly gifted in floral arranging. The displays were striking, and the blooms were fresh and vibrant. I spotted a primitive angel on the corner of a shelf and picked it up for a closer look. The body appeared to be a wooden spindle with glass wings attached. There was no price on the angel, so I carried her to the counter and expressed my interested in purchasing the piece. The owner said the angel was not priced because she was missing her halo, and she gave me the item free of charge, to my surprised delight.

The owner offered a friendly greeting when I entered her shop on Tuesday, January 12, 2017. She asked if I needed any help, and I explained about my book and planned giveaway. I shared how my love story with Scott had morphed into greater love with Jesus. I showed her the class ring I was wearing around my neck and explained the miraculous return of the ring following my husband's death. She was amazed. I told her that I was trying to promote the book the best I could on social media. We talked at length. She explained that she had some free advertising with a local radio station and she wanted to donate that to me to promote the book. She felt this was a powerful story that needed to be brought to the attention of the public. We talked about this for a while. I paid for the gift items I had selected for my book giveaway, and the owner said she would contact the advertising sales representative at the radio station to further discuss her idea. I was excited! Could this be the breakthrough I had been hoping and praying for since the book was published?

I received a call from the sales representative the following week, and we had a lengthy discussion about the donation of the florist's radio advertising. The representative proposed several ideas to plan in the spring season, and I was in agreement. I would meet this man in person with the station manager of their sister station, which was a Southern Gospel radio station. The manager was on vacation at that time, and he explained that he would discuss all the plans further when the manager returned and then contact me in two weeks. The call ended, and I jumped up and praised God for His blessings through this florist.

Surprisingly, a special lady called me the next evening just to catch up. I held this woman in high regard. I had met her at the first church I attended in Knoxville when I moved to Tennessee. I was happy as I shared with her the good news of my upcoming book promotion through the radio advertising donated by the florist. She was quiet and did not say much in response. She asked me to keep her informed about the plans. I was still celebrating in my spirit.

There was no phone call from the station after two weeks. I called and left a voicemail but did not receive a return call. I waited a few more days and then sent an email to the station representative, but there was no response to my message. My spirit registered a resounding thud, and I recognized that something had happened during this time frame. I started crying and went to God in tears. I had been warned previously about trusting the wrong people, and I felt the pain of betrayal pass through my heart. I seemed to be learning the hard way.

I eventually learned through the florist that the station did not feel the book would be a good fit for their Gospel station format and the station manager was not interested in promoting the book. All plans were canceled, and there was no further communication with either the station or the florist. I was heartbroken. What had happened to change their minds? I spent time with the Lord with tears, questions, prayers, and finally acceptance of this closed door. Breakthrough would come at a later time. This triggered reflection of the pain and losses of my life, the revelation in 2005, the love with Scott, the loss of Scott, the love in Jesus, and the changes in my daily life. I thanked God for His love and grace as He continued to work in and through me. I would trust God to bring to pass His plans for me in His timing.

God saved my life Friday morning, January 27. Literally. I mentioned earlier about my disdain for airing the tires. Since the young man had aired them a month prior at the gas station, I had needed to add air to my left front tire a few times. The low tire indicator light came on again Thursday evening. I had worked on a file in a Wi-Fi café after work, and by the time I reached the interstate exit to head home it was almost 10 PM. Tired, I decided I would wait and air the tire in the morning.

Friday morning I stopped at a truck stop at the I-75 Huntsville/Oneida exit for gas and coffee and air. When I unscrewed the cap to inflate the tire, the top of the stem broke off inside the cap and air started rushing out of the tire. Quickly, I put the cap back on. I did not hear any sound of air, and I prayed the cap would hold until I reached the auto center I had recently discovered in Oak Ridge. I drove South on the interstate to the Clinton exit, then across to the Oak Ridge Turnpike, about 30 miles. I tried to keep my speed down to 60 on the interstate and 45 on the other roads.

By my description, the mechanic said I had probably pulled the core out of the valve stem and that is a common thing that can happen. However, after inspecting the tire, he told me I was "extremely, extremely lucky". He said the top of the tire sensor had actually broken off into the cap and that somehow when I put the cap back on, it seated just right to stay in place while I drove. I explained that I had driven from the I-75 exit at Huntsville, and he was stunned. He shook his head back and forth several times. He explained further that if the cap had blown off while I was driving, the tire would have gone totally flat in a matter of seconds. His words brought an image to mind with an unpleasant outcome, especially driving through the construction zone on I-75 with narrow lanes and concrete barriers. My eyes swelled with tears as the realization registered that God had brought me safely to this shop.

While my car was being serviced, I talked to other people in the waiting area who had come in behind me with different needs. Their words were reassuring about the mechanics and the service they had received on their vehicles previously. The mechanic working on my vehicle then entered the waiting area and showed me the break of the stem on the tire sensor. I asked if I could have it, and he left it with me as he went to finish the job. I looked at the sensor in wonder. I shared with the other customers what had happened, and we all agreed that God had kept my vehicle safe.

The mechanic and I talked as he printed the receipts and processed my payment. He remarked again how lucky I was to have driven that distance safely without any mishap. I told him it was not luck but God alone who had protected me.

I sat in my vehicle for a few minutes looking at the broken sensor in my hand before driving onto work, still somewhat shaken, in overwhelming gratitude to God for His protection. He alone is my provider, protector, refuge, and strength. He is my all in all.

Psalm 71:15-16 NKJV: "¹⁵ My mouth shall tell of Your righteousness *And* Your salvation all the day, For I do not know *their* limits. ¹⁶ I will go in the strength of the Lord God; I will make mention of Your righteousness, of Yours only."

Driving in Scott County on highway 63, frequently I would see water running over rocks. God had blessed East Tennessee with refreshing rain and it was wonderful to see the water flowing. Every time I saw the wet rocks I would thank God for His goodness. He is the Living Water.

During quiet time one evening in February, I reviewed the kidnapping dream once again. Interestingly, Pastor King made the statement in a recent sermon concerning destiny and faith for the journey that in order to go up, you must go down. The idea of working as a caregiver returned to mind, and I believed I should apply. Though the idea was scary, I applied online to several job postings. My efforts produced only one screening phone call a few days later. Since I had no experience in this field, the company was not interested. Uncertain of what to do, I prayed again for interpretation. Eventually I called Mrs. Hubbard in mid-February, and we discussed my impressions. She told me how I minister to people is how I minister to Jesus. She suggested I was trying to protect myself and reminded me that fear is not in me, it is from outside, and to rebuke the spirit of fear. I then asked her if there is power or effect on surroundings with the presence of a saint. She confirmed, "Absolutely."

On Tuesday, I was happy to see "JG" driving the golf cart shuttle when I arrived at work. He spotted me as I was walking from my car and gave me a quick ride to the front door of the building. I told him it was good to see him again, and he explained that he had been sick but was back now and feeling better. I first met him when I started working at this office in the fall of 2015. He gave me a ride one day, and a conversation started. I learned that he was retired, originally from Chicago, and he volunteered at several places to keep busy. He was a very interesting person, and during subsequent rides I shared about my love story with Scott and with Jesus. He was surprised and said he would read the book. A few weeks later he opened our conversation about the book. He had read it and was amazed that I was the author. We discussed many topics from the book. He was always smiling and pleasant, and I enjoyed the friendly banter.

I continued to seek God's direction about "going down to go up." The message on Sunday focused on increasing our faith. I wrote in my journal these words from the sermon, "Using faith at our current level and building faith as God develops us. Our authority/dominion increases with our faith."

My prayers on Sunday night included asking God for help and to bless my life, and I asked for provision. Because of the change in my living situation, I was driving further to work and further to church. The majority of my income covered gas expenses and food expenses since I was out of the house most of the time through the week. I needed to work on Legacy files after work, and it would be too late to eat if I waited until I made the long drive back to Scott County. I reminded the Lord of these details, though I knew He was aware. Morgan County had been a long distance, and Scott County was even further away from West Knoxville.

Friday after work I stopped in Oak Ridge for dinner. I then headed north on the interstate towards the exit for highway 63. I crossed the Scott County line and passed through an area with houses and a few commercial buildings. I noticed the security lights on the highway and across the landscape looked like star angels. Even the red lights on the airplane towers had the same appearance. I was filled with a mixture of amazement and calm simultaneously. Was this supernatural, or did I just want it to be supernatural? Was something going on with my eyes or vision? I blinked my eyes quickly and wiped each eye. Every light looked like star angels even after I arrived at the house and looked out my bedroom window. I stood gazing in awed wonder.

DREAM, Monday, 3/20/2017, 7:15 AM
I had been praying for God to help me and to bless my life before I went to bed. I woke up from this dream.

I am sitting on a couch and I am asking God to help me. I am rebuking the enemy. Suddenly there is a baby on the couch next to me. I am shocked. The baby is lying on its back and looking at me. The baby appears to be talking and the only words I remember are, "You know." The baby disappears. A white fluffy puppy comes to me across the floor. I am praying, confused. The puppy comes again, now grown, and then turns away. Another puppy, black and white, comes to me. I resume praying, then I turn around and the puppy is gone. I am holding my bible in my lap. There is a tract inside with a declaration I read. As I am looking at it, the center of a face appears that is evil. Dark eyes, black around the teeth and lips. Mouth is moving and appears to be saying something. The expression is angry and agitated. I feel horrified looking at it. What is going on? I try to rebuke the enemy with words, but I cannot move my mouth. I am straining to open my lips and speak. I am desperately trying to say, "JESUS!" The scene changes. I am in a public place that looks like an office building, and I see a friend I recognize. She is happy to see me and is smiling. I want to tell her what just happened, but she does not understand the seriousness of what I am saying. I keep telling her this is different from anything I have seen or encountered previously. She seems to listen but does not comprehend the depth of what I am sharing. What does all this mean? I am alarmed. I woke up with my heart racing at 7:15 AM. I prayed about what I had seen while writing the details on my notepad beside the bed.

The Hubbards believed the baby represented the abortion at age 16. This was confessed to God again after Scott died, and I have been forgiven by Jesus. The black equals curse. The face is evil. The puppies represent distractions. The enemy will attempt to distract me. When I try to give revelations to people, they will not be able to grasp the vision from God. They warned me that people will not see what I see. The enemy will try to attack through things or people that are close to me. As with every dream or vision, they encouraged me to keep seeking further interpretation from God. They ministered to me and prayed over me before we ended the call. There was much to review with the Lord later that night.

In March, I once again prayed about employment as a caregiver. I responded to a few new ads but received no response. I went to the Lord in prayer and reminded Him that I was seeking employment as a caregiver at His leading. Where was I supposed to work? I was off on Friday, March 17. I received a job alert from a different company that I had not seen in the previous listings. The ad stated a caregiver was needed for one specific client, 20 hours a week. I completed an application on the website and attached an updated resume. On Monday, the office contacted me, and I was scheduled for an interview on Wednesday, March 22. I completed the necessary forms for background checks and entrusted the process to God. The office contacted me on Friday and offered me the job. I accepted, because I already knew this was God's will. Orientation would be on Monday and I needed to bring my SS card. There was no work to be done at my regular job, so I took my car for a long overdue oil change, which was not good, but there had been no extra funds to pay for this service. The mechanic informed me that there was very little oil left in my car and warned me strongly to check the oil regularly. I humbly thanked God for protection over my vehicle. I stopped for a much needed haircut in Oak Ridge, stopped for lunch, and stayed at a Wi-Fi café for a few hours to work on the latest Legacy files I had received.

I went to the storage unit on Saturday to dig out my box of files for my Social Security card. I had a vague idea where the box was located, but when I opened the unit and looked at the contents, I had no idea where to find the box. No option but to start removing stuff out of the unit until I could access the boxes. I was not a happy camper as I stacked items in order to repack after I found the one box I needed. Finally, I found the box marked "Files" and pulled it out. Overstuffed and heavy, I managed to set it down without dropping it onto the floor. Thankfully the folder I needed was on top inside the box. I attempted to repack the unit in better order. I needed to pay my car insurance and take those cards to the office as well for proof of full coverage insurance. I prayed for connection with the client according to God's plan. Fatigue and exhaustion washed over me that afternoon, and I sat outside for a couple of hours in peace.

Pastor King delivered a great message on forgiveness at church Sunday morning. He explained how forgiveness keeps love in our heart and fuels our faith. His teaching was thorough, and I jotted some notes in my journal; "Unforgiveness prevents faith from working. You must forgive, but do not forget. Be smart, not naïve." I prayed for forgiveness and to forgive those who had hurt me on any level. I prayed, "Lord, let no root or seed of unforgiveness remain in my heart."

DREAM, Saturday, 3/25/2017, AM

I see two dogs. One is a black German Shepherd sitting up on his hind legs. His ears are up and his tongue is hanging out like he is panting. A larger brown dog is facing the black dog and I can only see this dog from the back and a little to the side. The brown dog appears to be cleaning the underside of the black dog and the color of the exposed skin is light pink. I see a bone sticking out on one side, straight out to the right. The black dog is awake and eyes are open while the brown dog works. I am wondering why the black dog is allowing this larger dog to do this. What is going to happen to this dog? The dog does not seem concerned and seems at ease. Meanwhile, a man is making arrangements to have some alterations made on his property. He wants two column structures moved to another site and something else built. I am not really paying attention because I keep thinking about the dogs. Now I see the dogs again. The black German Shepherd looks weak and ill. The brown dog has eaten into the flesh and the black dog is being hollowed out. The underside is now dark red and much flesh is gone. From the outside the dog looks intact, but the inside continues to be eaten out. In the first view of the black dog the eyes are still alive. In the second view, the eyes are dull. No light, no life. The dog seems to have accepted the inevitable. It is almost dead. The brown dog continues feeding. It is painful to see. I woke up disturbed by the images of the black dog.

Monday, 3/27/2017, 8:30 AM

Driving to work on Melton Lake Road through Oak Ridge, I received a download in my spirit. *There are men and women who have proven themselves faithful and steadfast through the past several decades in their obedience and service to God. They know the Lord. They understand and utilize the Kingdom principles in the Word. He has blessed their service and their lives through their relationship with Him. They are comfortable in their present lives, living on the fruit of blessing, but He is going to call them out for a new assignment. God is going to call on these men and woman for something new. They will know His voice because they are already familiar with Him through relationship and years of walking with Him. Do not doubt His voice or His call. Do not be afraid to stand up and obey this new directive. He will not contradict His Word. This new assignment will be different from how they have served previously. Trust Him. Seek His will. Follow His instruction.* This message was not directed at me as I have only followed God a short few years. I understood that I was to pray for the called--for courage, unity, clarity, clear direction. I am to pray against doubt, fear, hesitation, seeking man's approval or understanding. God will call and speak to His chosen. Faithful servants will step up as brave soldiers in the age old battle.

I went to the home care agency office later in the afternoon for orientation. The client assigned to me was an elderly woman with severe macular degeneration. The hours were 12:30-4:30 PM Monday through Friday. I was offered the job, and I accepted. I had very little work at my regular job today and had none last Friday. I was in need of funds to pay my car insurance in order to get the proof of insurance letter for the agency. Later in the afternoon I realized I had not asked about my salary. My mind was all over the map that morning, and I was intensely focused on the information I was receiving. Since I had never worked as a caregiver, I did not know what types of questions to ask. I was given a manual to read containing pertinent information regarding company policy during my employment. During my time with the Lord in the evening, I prayed for provision and for His help to remember all the rules and instructions on this new job. I asked Him to help me serve this lady with love. The Holy Spirit impressed on me His command to pray for His plans.

Wednesday morning I met my prayer friend for coffee. We caught up on each other's lives between sips. It was good to see her and have more than a few minutes to talk. I then shared the dream about the dogs. I was not prepared for her response. She said, "Iris, the black dog is you." I started crying in shock as a definite punch registered in my gut. I thought I was progressing and getting stronger, but she said that I was the dog that was being hollowed out. I felt deflated, knocked back to the starting line. I was disgusted, hurt, and angry all at the same time. Everything seemed pointless in that moment. She said she was not allowed to say anything else and that God would reveal to me. She left soon afterwards. I was numb at this revelation, and I was hurt that she offered no prayer and no encouragement. She simply dropped the hammer, as though on assignment. All of the pleasure of reconnecting over coffee was gone. I drove to work in pain and confusion, longing to understand. The dog images churned in my thoughts all day. Was God going to take my life soon? Had I failed? Would my destiny be fulfilled that God had shown me in 2016? I calmed down and reminded myself to take all of it to God in prayer.

On my way home, driving through Clinton, I was listening to the radio. I heard a siren and turned down the radio. I looked to the left and to the right, checking the rear-view mirror for flashing lights. There were none. I started praying for God to help anyone in need. I asked Him to send angels to minister to those who needed help. A few seconds later a news alert came on my phone that a bus had crashed in Texas with fatalities. Prayers continued.

The next day, March 30, I drove to the client's home in West Knoxville for the first meeting. Someone from the agency would be there to show me what I needed to know in her care. I was extremely nervous about this responsibility. The woman from the office showed me the recipes I would need to prepare for the client and informed me of her preferences and many other details. There was much to remember. I left the house in dread of the next day. The shocking words spoken about the dog dream were replaying in my mind. Fatigue settled on me like a heavy blanket as I made the long drive back to Scott County. I was informed that my wage would be almost half of what I made in my office job. I felt like I was getting knocked down. Nothing in my life made sense. What was happening to me?

Later that night I repented of my fear and doubt. This new job was God's will, and I wanted to obey. Emotions are not a gauge of truth, and I settled down as I read the Word. I had no doubt of God's love for me. He would guide me and help me do all that was expected in this position. There was no further revelation concerning the dog dream.

Fighting negative thoughts and asking Jesus for help, I drove to my client's home in Farragut from Scott County. The day was different than I had anticipated, though I did not know what to expect. My first day was on Friday, and the client was sitting in her living room when I arrived. This elderly widow had severe macular degeneration that medical treatment could not improve, and I would serve as her eyes, so to speak. She gave instructions on housekeeping, laundry, cooking, her weekly schedule, and her dog. She then asked me to read her two stories. The first was a true story she had written and was published in 1992 in the "Doll Reader" magazine. The second was her Elvis story.

I worked four hours a day, five days a week, and I continued to work part-time for my previous employer. The days and weeks passed in a mostly routine pattern. I drove the client to the hair salon on Wednesdays and afterwards to the neighborhood grocery store. She rode the electric cart and knew where every item was located on her shopping list, the aisle and the shelf. I was somewhat amazed as I walked with her through the store. After a couple of months, she declared she would remain in the car while I did the shopping.

I drove her and the dog to the groomer every other week. She was a small dog with long white hair, and she had fresh bows in her hair when we left the groomer. She rode home in her owner's lap, sitting prettily, facing forward. Children in passing vehicles would wave or point. My client loved Elvis music. The CD player in her car held many recordings of her favorite songs, and these played continuously every time we rode in the vehicle. She was in a doll club that met monthly, and we drove to a different member's home for each meeting. We glided across I-40 in her Lincoln Town Car with Elvis rocking on the radio to doctor appointments, to the post office and the bank, to meetings, to Sonic on 50-cent corn dog days, to Wendy's for an occasional junior bacon cheeseburger, everywhere she desired.

DREAM, Tuesday, April 11, 2017, 7:45 AM
I am shopping alone. I am looking for some special earrings, either red or pink, and I cannot find what I am looking for. All I see are some cheap earrings. There are several tables to browse. Every pair looks the same on every table— small pink velvet stuffed balls with a small gold ribbon tied in a bow around the top. I am very frustrated and disappointed, almost agitated. The Eiffel

Tower is in the background, but I am not interested and I am not looking at it. I am searching tables and displays for these special earrings, but I cannot find them. My daughter called to talk and the phone ringing woke me. I had forgotten to set the alarm.

One of my client's instructions regarded her plants in the sunroom. She explained there was an orchid given to her by her son who had died two years prior, and she instructed me to put three ice cubes in the pot every week. I walked out in the sunroom to check her plants, looking for the orchid. This room was full of furniture and small items on tables. Large plants were in pots on the floor. I finally noticed a small short round pot, about three inches in diameter, on a table. There was a plastic pot inside with two dried sticks in the dirt, which had been secured with string to a small wooden support. The ends of the sticks were shriveled. This plant appeared completely dead. My heart sank as I picked it up and carried it to the client, to show her its condition. She repeated her instructions to give the plant three ice cubes once a week. I asked her if it had bloomed since she received the plant, and she did not answer. Sighing, I placed the orchid back on the table in the sunroom and placed three ice cubes in the pot every Tuesday.

My client had lived a fruitful life but was not a happy person at this stage. She had earned a Master's Degree in teaching and taught high school students for more than 25 years. Her husband was a retired engineer and a veteran, and had passed away several years prior after losing his sight. Her home was filled with antiques, but her failing vision no longer allowed her to enjoy them. She explained that she could see me but could not discern my features. She could not taste her food. She was disciplined to eat meals to maintain her health but no longer enjoyed dining in restaurants. She could not see well enough to read a menu or view a movie at a theater. She suffered with IBS, and this significantly limited her social life. Most of her family had passed. I sensed loneliness and depression, as well as a distrust of people in general. She had a large walk-in closet stuffed full of clothes she no longer wore and boxes of shoes from past style trends. She had been strong and healthy most of her life, but losing her husband, her son, and the decline in her health had taken a toll. Her body weight was appropriate, but she had lower back issues and could not stand up straight or walk very far even with her walker due to weakness.

Some days her countenance was bright, and she talked more than usual sharing stories from her years of teaching or fond memories from the past. These were always accompanied by laughter. She was charming on these days. Most days, however, she was quiet and reluctant to talk much beyond what was necessary. When I was hired, I had been instructed to engage the client in conversation. I spent the first two days desperately trying to make small talk, without success. She would only respond with "Yes" or "No" to questions, and there was a sharp tone to her voice when she spoke. We spent the majority of time in her bedroom. She sat in a recliner on one side of the bed, and I sat in a chair by the window across the room. The third day, while I was sitting in my chair looking out the window through the open blinds, I prayed and asked God for help. How could I start a conversation with this lady? The Holy Spirit provided guidance. "It is not necessary to talk; your presence is enough." I received those words with thankful relief and only asked questions that were in line with my duties. I responded when she initiated conversation, and the flow was much easier.

During the months of my employment, there were many days I spent in prayer, sitting in that chair, looking out the same window. I even prayed over the orchid. I asked God to spark life in that plant to bloom again for this lady. I believed it would cheer her heart to see the blossoms. She eventually shared the heartbreaking details of her son's death. Additionally, I learned about the private caregiver who had worked for her prior to my employment. The woman had been a close friend to the client. She had helped in the care of the client's husband for several years prior to his death and then became the client's caregiver. The woman was diagnosed with pneumonia and hospitalized. She was expected to recover and be discharged; however, she died unexpectedly on March 23. Her death necessitated the client's need for a caregiver. The client talked about the shock and pain of her friend's sudden death, and I listened in quiet awareness that God had sent me to fill that void.

One day while we driving in the car, the CD player suddenly stopped working. My client immediately became upset and insisted that I set it right. I tried every button, but there was no response. I removed the CDs and then reinserted to no avail. Turning the player off and back on did not work. The radio would not play either. When we arrived home, she instructed me to take her car to the dealership for any necessary repairs.

I entered the dealership and was directed to the service area. I explained the situation to the man behind the desk and gave him the keys. I waited in a lounge area where a man was trying to sell some type of insurance. A short time later a technician approached to tell me the car was ready and handed me the keys. I asked about the issue with the CD player. He replied that it was working perfectly. They could find no problem. Every function of the CD player and radio was operational. I was surprised. I asked for the invoice to pay, and he said there would be no charge. What?! He repeated that there was no charge. I returned to the client's home and explained all that had happened, and she was astonished. She mentioned it several times through the rest of the day, and I repeated the same scenario. She could not believe they did not charge her to check the CD player.

JOURNAL ENTRY, Saturday, April 29, 2017
I recognize in myself a growing dissatisfaction with pretense, performance based behavior, fluff without substance, junk, brokenness in society, and worldly structure. I am angry at the destruction, and it also breaks my heart. So many lost people. Too many believers walking in the shadows instead of the Light. Overwhelming sometimes. I was reminded this week of the baby Christians in a previous dream. I want more of You, God. I want great and mighty acts to be accomplished for Your Glory to impact Your Kingdom eternally.

I then received a vision. I see a room, just a portion, and I understand this is my future home. I see the wall color, the curtains covering part of a window. I see the arm of a sofa and a throw pillow on the cushion next to the arm rest. I love the colors, the style, the textures. I can feel the warmth, the pleasure, the peace of my home. God will be there, and all who enter will feel welcome. The home is beautiful and comfortable, a sanctuary. I want this. I praised God for the vision and thanked Him for my home.

On Tuesday, May 16, I found myself at the familiar crossroad of lack and need. God had changed my employment, and I had obeyed. My living situation was altered by others' decisions, and I was dealing with the consequences. The distance from where I was staying in Scott County to the home of my client was 63 miles each way. With the increased fuel need and cut in salary to serve as a caregiver in obedience to God's instruction, I did not consistently have enough money to cover my basic needs until the next payday. I only had five dollars in the bank and the fuel gauge registered a quarter of a tank. Payday was Thursday. I needed to drive to work and home again on Wednesday and Thursday morning. There was not enough fuel for all those miles. I prayed and declared scriptures as I drove. I stated out loud a declaration of faith to the Lord, remembering His words spoken to me and the details of the vision from October 2, 2016. My faith was strengthened as I connected to I-75 North. I did not know how, but God would provide.

I stopped at the truck stop just off the exit for Highway 63. I parked in front of the store and sat outside on the patio until almost 10 PM. Then, after sitting with the Lord, I pumped the balance of my checkbook, $3.79, into the gas tank. I headed out onto the highway trusting God in confidence, praising the Lord. I had quiet time with Him after I arrived at the house and went to bed. I woke up the next morning well rested. I visited with the Lord before I finished getting ready for work. I worshipped in quiet singing and read out loud some scriptures of praise, the Lord's Prayer, and Psalm 23. Amazing peace and strength filled me, and I knew exactly what to do. I also understood everything would happen as promised and God would guide me at the appropriate time. I drove on highway 63 towards I-75 filled with the Holy Spirit, very strong. I prophesied and prayed and bound the enemy and his plans, declaring victory in the Name of Jesus. I was confident, assured, and filled with purpose. Joy surged with sharpened focus. I went to the ATM in Lafollette and then to the nearby gas station. I drove onto Knoxville. This morning was incredibly powerful with God. Today was new, a higher level than I had experienced with God previously. Tears of joy flowed, and I praised Him for this wonder-filled time. I was aware of His presence all day. The peace was glorious.

One evening, I was sitting at the kitchen table at my friends' house in Scott County. I was eating a light supper while my laundry was in the washer. I became aware of what seemed to be spiritual downloading of God's plan. Not all the steps in detail, but assurance of all to come. I was amazed. This was happening quietly, while I was sitting at the kitchen table. I listened as I received. I said to the Lord, "I receive. Thank You, Lord." I noted in my journal, "God is kind to me, but He also takes care of business. I must, too. Help me, Holy Spirit, to obey promptly and completely. I love You, Lord."

The office called on a Friday afternoon with an urgent plea for coverage for a different client over the weekend. The regular caregiver for this particular woman had worked full-time for months without a break, and her husband wanted her to take off for the Memorial Day Weekend. The part-time and prn employees were already assigned for the holiday, leaving a need to cover the 12-hour shift on Saturday and on Sunday. I sighed. Deeply. Struggling to find a reason why I could not accept, while silently acknowledging no legitimate excuse, I sighed again in resignation as I heard myself agree to take the weekend shift. I drove home that evening mulling over the pertinent information provided. My regular job ended at 7:30 PM on Friday night, and then I stopped at a Wi-Fi café to complete two Legacy files. It was 11 PM when I finished, and I drove home apprehensive about the 5 AM alarm that would soon blare to wake me in the morning.

I arrived on time in East Knoxville, and we spent the first hour covering necessary care information. The client was frail and weak but continuing to function as much as possible with the known terminal diagnosis. Her husband of 60+ years remained by her side, overseeing her medications and encouraging her to eat. Apparently their words and responses were a familiar dialogue. I lifted her from the recliner onto her rollator and seated her at the kitchen table where they shared meals and discussed the news. He ensured that her medications were taken correctly while I cleared the dishes and cleaned the kitchen.

Assistance was required for the bathroom before returning to the den to rest in the recliner. We were both amazed that I was able to lift her up and down for every transfer as needed throughout the day, and I silently thanked God for the strength. She was petite and small in stature, and the effort was not overwhelming. She expressed gratitude for my ability to lift her in her weakened state. Once, she looked up at me and said, "You are an angel!" Smiling in response, I shook my head in denial and explained that God was helping me take care of her for the weekend.

She remained at the kitchen table after lunch for a while, gazing outside through the glass patio door. I remarked on the trees and the yard, and she spoke of her husband's efforts to maintain the lawn and the landscaping. She noticed something yellow in the flower box that was built above the ground, but she was unable to discern the type of flower. The bright green leaves obscured the blooms. Picking up my phone, I stepped outside to take a few pictures. I crossed the patio and walked around the raised brick flowerbed, happily surprised to see five beautiful yellow calla lilies in bloom. I snapped several pictures and walked back into the kitchen. I showed her the photos, and she explained that one of their sons had given her the flowers a few years ago. She was delighted to see the lilies were thriving.

I slept well that night and woke up the next morning feeling rested and better prepared. Sunday progressed according to the same pattern. We shared details from our personal lives, and I enjoyed listening to the stories about their families and life experiences. Though the hours were long, the weekend had not been difficult to cover, and they were kind in their remarks to me as I prepared to leave at the end of the shift on Sunday evening.

The trip home that evening would take at least an hour, and I decided to stop and eat on the way. Fatigue was settling in as I pulled into a local fast food place at the Powell exit. Thankfully the dining area was quiet and not busy. I chose a seat by the front windows and sank into my chair. There were only two other customers inside; an older couple in a booth and a young man who had chosen a stool at the Wi-Fi counter. He was busy on his phone as I turned back to my food.

Looking out the glass windows, I noticed a young mother outside with her toddler. The little girl was picking up small pieces of mulch in the landscaping and handing them to her mother, who graciously accepted and then placed them back onto the ground. This continued for a few minutes while the mother sat on the curb around the landscaped area. She did not have the appearance of homelessness, but I wondered if she or her daughter might be hungry. I watched them for a couple of minutes before deciding to walk outside.

I spoke to the mother and asked if they were hungry or needed anything. The young woman smiled brightly and explained that they were waiting on her husband inside to get off work. The little girl was getting restless so she had brought her outside to wait. She smiled again and thanked me for offering.

Upon returning to my seat, I noticed a bright new penny was gleaming on the dark metal window sill next to the table. I looked around and then sat down, suddenly refreshed without a trace of fatigue. I studied the penny to check the year, stamped 2017. I barely noticed the departure of the young man from the counter nearby in my stunned state of mind. The penny was not on the window sill before I went outside. Tears pricked my eyes as I gazed at the penny in my hand in wonder.

I finished my meal in peace and drove home safely, grateful for God's guidance and blessings throughout the weekend, grateful for His presence and the blooms that brightened the wife's face, humbled by His kindness and tenderness.

The following Sunday I attended church as usual that morning. After lunch, I visited my favorite spot in Clinton until it was time to return to church for movie night. I was driving on Clinton Highway when my tire indicator light started flashing and an alarm was chiming. This had never happened before, and I was scared. The flashing light and sounding alarm continued, and I spotted a tire center ahead on the right. I pulled in and parked my vehicle. I turned off the engine and then restarted it. The indicator light started flashing and the alarm was chiming again. I checked the pressure in the tires and the left front was only a little low. I went inside and explained the issues. Perhaps I had a slow leak in that tire.

A short time later the mechanics checked the tires and said they could find nothing wrong. I was told that my tires were worn out and needed replacing. I explained that I was not prepared to purchase new tires at that time. When my name was called to check out, the man behind the counter simply handed me my keys and wished me a nice day. He gave me a copy of the safety checklist showing the inspection findings and called it a courtesy check, free of charge. I smiled at him with a hearty, "Thank you! God bless you!" I walked out to my car not quite understanding the situation. I thanked God for His protection and for the check of my vehicle and tires. When I cranked the engine, there was no alarm and the indicator light was no longer flashing. I asked God what had just happened but received no answer. I was confused but thankful as I drove towards church. I lifted prayers over the hands that had performed the inspection and the man behind the counter who did not charge for the service.

The clock showed 5 PM, which was too early for church, so I went to a nearby fast food place. I would get a small drink and browse on my phone to wait out the next 30 minutes. I stopped at the restroom first. A woman was washing her hands. She smiled warmly and commented on my purse, and we started talking as we left the restroom. She shared that she was in town for her father's funeral after a time of illness. She was anxious and uncertain about her future. She had just gone through a divorce. There was much brokenness. I told her some of my story and said I would like to pray for her. By this time we were outside in the parking lot. She followed me to my car, and I gave her a copy of my book. She was surprised and commented about our chance meeting. I signed the book and then prayed for her and her son. I prayed for her travel, as she would be driving back to Nashville, and for her future. She returned to the restaurant, and I drove onto church.

On Sunday, June 4, I was driving on the interstate to church in Knoxville. I was listening to the radio on a preset station at 89.1, and it started jumping to 88.9 and then to 89.3 repeatedly. Even when I pressed the station button for 89.1, it would jump. I wondered about this. It continued for several miles and then stopped. The next day the same thing happened. I was driving on highway 63 when the radio started jumping from 89.1 to 88.9 or to 89.3 repeatedly. Pressing the preset button did not prevent it from jumping stations. This only occurred those two days and did not happen again. I laughed and thought of the Holy Spirit confirming His presence by doing a thing twice exactly alike.

I became close to one of the couples I sat with at church on Sunday mornings. They lived further east of Knoxville and drove in for service every week. He was a minister, and they had recently relocated in obedience. His wife was a sweet woman and they were a close couple. I enjoyed our conversations about the issues in society and spiritual matters. We shared prayer requests and prayed for one another after service. On this particular Sunday I shared with them the vision God had given me in October 2016, and I shared the dog dream from March 2017. The husband had much to say and then gave me a word of knowledge, "God is reprogramming you." I gave his wife a copy of my book after a prompting from the Holy Spirit. I prayed for God to move in their lives in a powerful way.

During the next week in June, God laid a special woman on my heart named Diann. I had met her initially at the church I attended in 2013 after I moved to Knoxville. She was a delight to be around. Most recently she had attended the Perry Stone conference at Redemption Church with our mutual friend, Brenda, and we had enjoyed the teachings and the fellowship with much laughter and the warmth of friendship. In our conversation I learned she had recently purchased and moved into a new home. We rejoiced over her good fortune! Driving home from church that evening, God began directing me to make some purchases for her as a house warming gift. This seemed a little strange, as I did not know her very well, but I trusted God to obey.

I visited a few stores that sold home décor and allowed Him to guide the purchases. The first item was a nice large rectangular decorative pillow, cream in color, with small gold sequins sewed on that spelled "DREAM" in cursive script. I found a beautiful cross nightlight and added a set of gold heart measuring spoons. I spotted a white coffee cup with a pearlescent finish and pink interior. Gold lettering on the outside of the cup read, "Be Awesome!" The last item was a beautiful angel of glass. I bought a shopping bag large enough to hold the items, and the bag was printed with words related to wishes and dreams. I wrapped each gift individually. I selected an appropriate card and wrote His inspired words inside. As I was cutting strips of gold curling ribbon, I heard the words, "LAVISH LOVE." I could feel His love for her in my heart as I cut the ribbon and fashioned the 12 long strands into a bow. My heart was overflowing with joy when I finished, and I could hardly wait to present this bag of love gifts to Diann. I contacted her on Saturday and simply said that I had a special gift to deliver. We agreed on a time to meet at her home after church on Sunday.

I arrived the next day around 2 o'clock carrying the large bag. She turned on the coffee and then showed me her home. This was an older home that was well preserved, very spacious, and comfortable. She had been busy unpacking, organizing, and decorating. As we settled in the kitchen with the fresh coffee, she shared the details of all the blessings associated with the house purchase. She was still rejoicing every day in how God had worked on her behalf in favor. I then focused her attention on the bag and explained how God had led me to bring her this gift. She was very surprised and excited. I told her He had chosen the gifts. She opened each gift with tearful joy. I watched her express delight with each item, in awe of God and these gifts from His heart. I shared with her the message of "Lavish Love" when I had fashioned the 12 strands of gold ribbon into a bow. She was speechless as she read the card.

She prepared lunch for us, and we talked for the next few hours, sharing God moments and blessings. We had not been a part of each other's daily life, and we were both astonished that God had directed me to bring her these gifts. We prayed together in conversation at the kitchen table. I left her home around eight that evening. This mission from God was fantastic. I loved the entire experience—shopping for the gifts, wrapping each item, selecting and writing the card, tying the 12 strands of ribbon, and then being with her as she unwrapped and discovered each gift of love in the large shopping bag. Every moment was a special blessing from the Lord.

JOURNAL NOTE, Wednesday, 6/14/2017, 11:45 PM
"My heart jumps for joy at the Master's voice! Reassurance in my spirit from God. Thank You, Lord." I thought about the face of the man on the interstate in May 2014.

JOURNAL ENTRY, Friday, 6/16/2017, PM
I wish I could describe how God has worked in my heart and mind over these past months. Many things I have not shared or written—just held onto in my spirit with God. I treasure everything He reveals, teaches, and corrects. It is ALL love. I have shared prayer requests, but the beautiful moments from God I have cherished within my heart. Sometimes I did not understand everything in the moment, but it was drenched in His presence, and I lifted praise and gratitude in response. I am not the same woman who moved to Tennessee in November 2012.

I am burdened for marriages and relationships everywhere. I am not sure why this is on my radar, but I follow God's promptings in prayer and His teaching. This I know for certain—my marriage to Scott was more astounding than I ever imaged while I was living out the thrill of our time together. I appreciate more every day the love God gave us for those few short years. I can see Jesus in Scott's place solidly, and this has grown exponentially since the vision in Morgan County.

DREAM, June 24, 2017, Saturday AM
I am with a woman I knew previously from the widows' small group. We are on a gravel road coming into a local fair. Lots of people are here. I am trying to make conversation. She is not talking. We get separated in the crowd. I am trying to find her. I think she is in line to look at an exhibit. The line is moving slow. I finally make my way to the line, but I do not see her. I walk by the next few exhibits. No sign of her. I go back to the exhibit where I started. There is a counter, like a diner, and a man is sitting on one of the stools in front of the counter. He is dressed in 1940s attire, drinking a cup of coffee, facing the opposite direction. I receive the idea to use my cell phone to call my friend. As I am pulling my phone out to call, a guy walks up and starts to tell a corny joke. I am trying to type her name into my phone, but I keep misspelling her name. This guy is annoying and is holding an ink pen and the end lights up—part of his joke. He is talking loud enough that the people at the counter can hear him, but no one is laughing. I had the impression during the dream that my friend had ditched me and left me at this place. I had made a negative comment just before she disappeared and I wondered if that was the reason she had left. The man in the 1940s attire never turned and looked at me, but I was aware of

him and wondered. *The first exhibit was a white house on a hill, like an old white clapboard house. People were lined up waiting to go inside. I wanted to go in. I climbed the small grassy hill, but there was a short wall of rocks around it. I could not find an opening. Feeling a little frustrated, I moved onto the next sight. There were two large box cages with wood trim, painted green, and large leaf ivy growing in the wire. These were positioned on stands on the grass beside the concrete walkway the crowd was walking on. There was a metal handrail next to the steps leading down this hill. I did not see inside the cages or walk by them, but I sensed they held butterflies. Still looking for my friend. The next exhibits were on level ground.* I woke up in confusion and lifted prayers for interpretation as I wrote down the details.

Later that morning, I went into the kitchen to visit with my friends. There was a definite change in the atmosphere. There was no conversation between them. The spirit of the Lord impressed upon me to prepare dinner. There had been an undercurrent of tension in the house recently. I was gone most of the time, but I had prayed after sensing this shift. God instructed me to cook chicken and dumplings today. Joy surged in my heart in response, and I was suddenly filled with the desire to prepare this meal. I drove to a nearby grocery store and bought what I needed to prepare the food. I worked in the kitchen through the afternoon. They watched TV together, but their conversation centered only on the program they were viewing. He left for a men's gathering that afternoon at their church. I prayed with both of them before he left. She ate dinner with me and was congenial as usual. I was aware that God's love, ushered in through the cooking and the meal, had changed the atmosphere. This continued the rest of the day and evening. When I came home Sunday night after church, the atmosphere had reverted back to heaviness. He did not eat any of the food, and I finished the leftovers. I thanked God for teaching me through this unusual assignment. He revealed to me that this was a picture of God's love and how people respond when they do not perceive His gift. Many people cannot recognize the love of God because they do not perceive the deeper things of the Spirit. They respond in the flesh. He had completely rejected the food, while his wife had shared one meal with me. My heart hurt for their confusion about my motives. I did not explain any of this to them and trusted that God would reveal more in their relationship with

Him. I loved my friends. They had been so kind to me while I was staying in their house. They had opened their home and their hearts to welcome me. We had shared many prayers and meals through the months, and I was blessed by their generous friendship. I prayed for them regularly and asked God to bless them abundantly.

Tuesday morning while I was driving to work, I received a vision. The man who had been standing on the interstate on Mother's day in 2014 was now riding next to me in the car. He was in the passenger seat, smiling at me, extending His Hand for me to hold, and I saw the hole. It was a quick vision and lifted me above my concerns about money for gas and food. Doubt tried to crowd into my thoughts, but I had seen the hole in His Hand. Oh, how I longed for more of Him. My focus remained on Jesus the rest of the day.

The next day I battled restlessness and an unsettled feeling. I refused to entertain the negative thoughts and emotions. I was down to my last five dollars and a quarter tank of gas. Again. Would it be enough to drive home tonight and drive to the gas station in the morning? Same question I had faced over and over. I determined in my mind I would trust God to provide. He would not leave me stranded unsafely. I declared, "God is my Source!" and claimed scriptures for provision. I quoted II Corinthians 10:4-5 out loud and refused to follow negative thought patterns, with the help of the Holy Spirit. I made it home without using much gas. The needle had barely dropped. I had enough to drive to the gas station in the morning before work. "Thank You, Lord, for the supernatural gas mileage."

Thursday night was spent in prayer with God. There were irritations during the day with my shoes. The buckles had broken, and I was using large safety pins in their place until I could buy a new pair. This day was especially frustrating as the safety pins would not remain fastened. I had to stop and refasten the pins every few steps. That night I asked God for new shoes. I reestablished my desire to be completely yielded and surrendered to Him.

Saturday morning I was able to sleep late and catch up on rest. I moved at a leisurely pace as I prepared for the day. I spent some time at a Wi-Fi café writing a new blog. Satisfied with the result after editing, I gathered my laptop to leave. Then the idea occurred to me to stop at the store where I had purchased the shoes I was wearing. This was a local close-out store, and more than a year had passed since my previous purchase. I prayed as I drove in that direction.

There were several people browsing in the Hammer's store in Wartburg when I arrived. I walked to the shoe section and was thrilled to find a similar pair of shoes in my size and reasonably priced. I noticed a younger mother with her two daughters browsing in the store. I walked through the store looking at different items, grateful for the new pair of shoes. While looking at some items on display close to the cashiers, I overheard the mother scolding the oldest daughter. Apparently the young girl had laid her money down in the store while looking at merchandise. She was in tears looking for the money, to no avail. My heart was touched when I heard the young girl speak negative words about herself out loud. I wanted to do something. I heard the manager at the register ask about the money, and the mother explained her daughter had lost a ten dollar bill. A larger group of shoppers had made their purchases and left the store. I remembered I had some cash in my purse. While the mother and her two daughters continued to search, I paid for my shoes and handed the cashier a ten. I asked her to wait until I had left the store before giving the money to the mother and her daughter. I could only imagine the delight on the daughter's face and the relief of the mother. I wanted the daughter to stop berating herself. The cashier was happily surprised and agreed. I lifted prayers for the mother and her children as I drove home. The rain had stopped, and the sky was painted with incredible colors from the Master Artist. God had answered my prayer, and I wore my new shoes home! "Happy feet, happy Iris! Thank You, Lord!"

Kathy called and invited me to meet her for dinner Monday evening after work. We had a nice meal and conversation, and then we sat in her vehicle for a time of prayer. She shared that Bob's relative had moved out of their home. His stay initially promised to be much more rewarding, but had turned unpleasant, and they were relieved when he moved elsewhere. They had come through a difficult season. Prayers were lifted for this man and for Bob. The time we spent together that night was special.

I received a text message from her on Friday, inviting me to meet on the following Monday night for dinner, dessert, and prayer. We ate at one place, drove to another for dessert, and then spent some time in her vehicle in prayer. I enjoyed the evening, two Mondays in a row, with good food and many prayers. She shared with me that last Monday night while she was praying for me, God had showed her a large silver coin in my hand. She prayed about that provision and told me the coin represented much more than a single coin. I arrived back in Scott County around 11 PM, and Judi was still up. Her husband was out of town. She shared with me that eight teens from their church in Lafollette had just returned from Perry Stone's Warrior Fest where they had received the baptism of the Holy Spirit. The anointing had remained on them during their travel back to Campbell County. We rejoiced over this powerful move of God in these young people!

Kathy invited me to attend a women's meeting at a local church in Morgan County on Saturday night, July 22. This was going to be a reunion for the women of the church with a potluck dinner. She had prepared several dishes and told me not to worry about bringing any food. I prayed for God's presence and blessing over the evening as I drove to the church to meet Kathy. Women of different ages had come together for the evening at the small Pentecostal church. The leader opened in prayer and gave a warm welcome. We enjoyed delicious food and then we received communion together. Afterwards we walked over to the sanctuary and sang many songs. One woman accompanied on a guitar. The worship was beautifully simple. The leader gave a message about "The Well". She then put oil on her hands and touched every woman's hands in the group. Some fell out on the floor. I heard tongues being spoken during the praise songs. The leader prayed over many needs. She took my hands and prophesied over me. She said many things that confirmed the dreams and visions I had received previously from God. She told me there was an anointing on me and I could not see it but others could. We were all seated and then she said she wanted to hear my testimony.

I was amazed at how calm I was, as I walked up to the front of the group. The women were seated on the first few rows of pews. I did not stand behind a podium; rather, I sat in a chair facing the group. This was an intimate setting. Before I shared my story, I spoke what the Holy Spirit had laid on my heart to say to these women, "Be kind to each other and to those around you, because your connection to one another matters." Then I began sharing my story. Surprise registered on their faces and in their eyes. I observed tears and smiles. Happiness surged in the awareness of God's gift to share His love story. When I finished speaking, Kathy told them about my book. I had brought a copy, so I signed it and handed it to one of the women in the group. She said she would read it and pass it onto the others when she finished reading. Kathy and I stood in the parking lot after everyone had gone. We talked about the women, the church, the evening, Bob, and we prayed many prayers. This was a wonderful night. A short time later I received a personal message from one of the women, "Margaret." She had finished the book and shared that it had touched her profoundly. Glory to God.

Sunday, July 23, was the beginning of a time of prayer and fasting at Redemption Church. The pastor's message that morning focused on the power of fasting. The church would be participating in corporate prayer in groups during the week as well. My sister invited me for lunch that afternoon. We had coffee following the good meal she had prepared, and we walked outside to look at the yard and her flowers. We prayed together before parting, and I returned to church that evening for an hour of praise and prayer.

Pastor King was prophesying over the church body, and I experienced a quickening in my spirit as he spoke. "The things lost in the past can be restored. Time lost in the past can be returned." I listened in silent awe. He said the things we have seen God do, the times He has worked in our lives, will be replaced by new and bigger movements of God. He specifically said, "Your life will be more than a story in a book." There will be greater things than we have seen, greater works and moves of God, more revelations and growth in things of God. My spirit was stirred at these words as I left church that night.

I stopped at a Wi-Fi café in Clinton to work on a Legacy file. I finished editing one file at 9:20 PM and decided to head home. Lightning was flashing across the sky as I entered I-75 North. The strikes appeared high up in the night sky, spread out like a blanket in the clouds. Sudden torrential rain poured down with strong winds. I began praying Psalm 91. I put on the spiritual armor in Ephesians chapter 6, and then I started singing. The traffic had slowed to about 40 mph, crawling on the interstate from 75-80 mph. Wipers racing on high could not keep the windshield clear of the rain, and the wind continued to buffet my vehicle. My voice rose louder. When I crossed from Anderson County into Campbell County, the lightning changed.

Now thin white spindly lines, in vertical bundles, resembling twisted tree branches, were flashing ferociously in front of my hood and along the sides of my vehicle as I drove. They were so intense that I was ducking at times or flinching at the constant lightning flashes that appeared close enough to strike my vehicle. I began to pray the Lord's Prayer out loud repetitively, and I was emboldened as I prayed. I pictured myself at home. I prayed loudly without stopping, while this fierce storm raged around me for many miles. I could almost sense the adversary throwing darts at me through this weather. When the intensity increased, my prayers got louder. I was strengthened as I rebuked the enemy and continued praising the Lord. It was as though I was pushing steadily onward through enemy territory as I drove. I received an inward assurance from the Holy Spirit that no harm would come to me or my vehicle.

This battle intensity persisted through Campbell County, until I crossed the Scott County line on highway 63. I let out several shouts of joyful triumph to God and continued singing praise songs until I arrived home. The storm had passed, and only soft rain fell on the remainder of the journey. I was bursting with glee from God's protection and love, and I wanted to yell from the mountaintop what God had done, like I had just slain a giant! The Lord's presence through the storm strengthened my faith and my trust in Him. God is faithful. He is holy. He is righteous. His Word is true. His character will never change.

Friday night I drove home in the rain. God had painted countless masterpieces in the sky on these drives through the mountains. The moon had glowed many nights illuminating the winding road to Bob and Kathy's home in Morgan County. Tonight, the sky maintained a measure of light even with the storm clouds, and the moon appeared over highway 63. I rounded a curve at one point and the light shone on two deer on the grass next to the highway. They remained still while I passed. Another night I was approaching the curve on the highway where Campbell County ends and Scott County begins. The headlights from other vehicles revealed a tree down across my side of the highway. I was able to move over into the opposing lane to clear the tree safely. I called TDOT when I arrived home to report the fallen tree.

I-40 and I-75 were heavily traveled interstates consistently. I listened closely to traffic reports on the radio every morning and every evening to hopefully avoid being caught in traffic back-ups due to accidents or other calamities. One evening after work I was driving on I-75 North when the radio reported a severe accident involving an overturned semi just past the Lafollette exit. I knew from past experience the traffic would stack up quickly, so I exited at Clinton and drove on the old highway up to Lafollette. I had not driven the secondary highway from this point up to highway 63 at night, so I prayed and followed a stream of other drivers with the same thought. The old paved road was used in the past when coal mining was operational in the area. There were no street lights, and no lines were painted on the old asphalt. The lights at the interstate exit faded out of sight in my rear-view mirror and the night was pitch black. I could only see what my headlights illuminated. Two cars in front of me pulled over and stopped. I did not want to lead, but there was no place to turn around, so in prayer I drove onward, and the other vehicles followed behind. There were unmarked curves and three separate single-lane bridges to cross, so driving was slow. After what seemed an eternity, we reached the connection to highway 63 straight out of the woods. I had not realized how tense I was until I saw that highway and the headlights of other vehicles. I was thankful for safety over the vehicles and drivers behind me, as we waited to turn onto this main highway. Exhaustion settled on me when I reached the house.

One day I walked to the mailbox center to check my client's box after a rain shower, and I noticed the raindrops on the nearby pine branches. Tiny drops of water glistened in the sunshine peeking out from the clouds. I snapped a photo with my phone. Most days I would have just collected the mail and walked back to my client's home, but today I paused and noticed this simple beauty. God provides refreshing moments throughout the day to remind us of His presence in creation.

In the mornings when I drove to work, the traffic was heavier and I used that long commute for time with God in praise and prayer. The miles were tiresome at times, but I was strengthened spiritually during the travel day after day. Paycheck to paycheck. Praise to prayer. Repeated cycle through this season in the mountains. God's love was the driving force that enabled me to endure.

God showed up in church on Sunday morning, July 30. Service started in the usual manner, and we waited in anticipation for Pastor King to walk up on the stage; however, on this morning he remained on the floor level. He shared a dream and said the Lord had impressed upon him to offer an altar call for the baptism of the Holy Spirit. At this invitation, I went forward, along with many other people. We were lined up across the front of the stage, and the pastor and his wife passed by in front of us while he spoke. He prayed over us, and I started sobbing. I bent over in sobs. Tears were streaming down my face. The sobs were loud, and I could not control the volume. Both the pastor and his wife touched me, but I did not speak in tongues. I cried more, and eventually we were dismissed to return to our seats. We were at the front of the church about 20 minutes. I walked slowly back to my seat, shaking. I continued to cry softly during the remainder of the morning service, and I was jittery. Some dear friends, who previously had prophesied over me, reassured me that I was okay and the Spirit was upon me. I wondered to myself what this meant and what, if anything, I was supposed to do.

My client asked if I would be interested in working an extra two to three hours every day, a total of seven hours daily, five days a week, and I began this new schedule on August 3. I discussed this change with my office employer. He would allow me to continue to work in the office around this schedule change. I worked a few hours every morning at the office, then left to work for my client, which was only a short distance away, and worked there until 7:30 PM. I then returned to the office for a few hours in the evening. If needed, I worked at the office on Saturday. This did not prove to be optimal for the office. Records were needed during the day, and I was not there to complete reports until evening. I submitted my notice of resignation to the office administrator on September 15. I was very uneasy about the drastic decrease in income, but I believed that if I obeyed God, He would take care of my needs. I enjoyed the office job and I liked the work. I was comfortable with those responsibilities, but I believed I had to let go completely to pursue this new path. The caregiving assignment was from the Lord, and I wanted to honor that commitment to Him.

It was during this time that the orchid began to bloom. I could scarcely believe my eyes. First one bloom, then another, then another, until seven blooms appeared on what had appeared to be a dead stick. The day the seventh bloom opened, I carried the small pot into her bedroom to show my client. She was speechless as she gazed at the beautiful blooms through her special glasses. The petals were white and the edges were tinged with purple. I was delighted with God's blessing and her happy reaction.

From our conversations, I learned that my client had grown up in church and had attended as an adult. Her husband's failing health changed their routine, and her physical limitations prevented church attendance in person for several years. Occasionally we talked about God. One day in October she shared about "images in front of her eyes." We discussed the problem, and I asked if she prayed for healing. She answered almost in a whisper, "Every night." I told her I would pray, too. I continued to pray for peace in her mind and heart. A few days later I prayed with her before I left for the evening, following a prompt from the Holy Spirit, and there were tears in her eyes when I closed the prayer.

One night during quiet time with the Lord, I was seeking a word from Him. He had been silent, though active, in many ways connected to my life. I was grateful but wanted more of Him. Softly, I heard, "Love heals," in my spirit.

DREAM, Sunday, 8/6/2017 AM

I am driving my car to a local store. I need to pay for something that I have been carrying around. I turn into the parking lot. Now I am at the checkout. The cashier has to carry something out for a customer and leaves the register. I decide I can check myself out because I only have one or two items to pay for. My cart is suddenly full. I begin to look through it, and all of this is my personal stuff…a pillow, papers, folders. I thought I had something I needed to pay for, but I cannot find anything new. I do see an unused sheet of carbon paper. I stand up, expecting people to be lined up behind me waiting in line, but strangely, now I am in a field standing next to my parked vehicle. There are people coming to this field, walking. There are young people, dressed in different attire. The men seem to be dressed in Amish style pants and shirts; however, the women's dresses are off the shoulder and deep V-neck. I am surprised. What happened to the store and parking lot? I see a concrete cut in on the curb, and I back out of the edge of the field and drive down the street. I enter an office building, and I am standing in front of a door to an office suite. I open the door to look inside, and I see the Amish-appearing people in the field vaguely, but the supposed leader is the focus. He is a young man wearing Amish style pants, suspenders, striped long-sleeve shirt, and a hat, with a reddish brown beard. I turned my head sideways, and the people were still there in the field. I bent over to the left (not sure why I did this?), and they are still there. Why am I seeing these people and field inside this office door?

Several days passed before I was able to share the details with my spiritual parents. The store, the office building, and the field represent the world. God is calling people to Himself, all kinds of people, all ages, all manner of dress and appearance. The devil is very active in the world, but God is very active, too. He has a wide open place to come to. God has given me things that are mine, yet the world is trying to make me pay for it, even though it is already mine. The devil wants me to think I have to pay for what God has already paid for me to have. The office buildings are a mission field. My presence, prayers, and witness affect change. I am not a part of the buildings I have entered. I have a prophetic call to minister to people. He advised me to continue to pray; if I get an opening, witness to them. Prayers and presence make a difference and things change. Only God has the power to defeat the enemy. Jesus is always there in the field calling them to come to Him. He stressed continued prayer.

I was driving on highway 63 two days later, headed to work, when suddenly an old memory from the early 2004 replayed in my mind. The recall was vivid, and I caught my breath in shock. This flash image from the past was an expression of deep despair and pain. I was crying out from my heart, out loud, outside. "Does anyone hear me? Does God care?" I did not recognize myself in the moment that this occurred. My voice was raw, begging, crying for love and acceptance. I went inside my apartment and sobbed in shame and embarrassment at my outburst. What was wrong with me? God brought revelation this morning on August 8, 2017. I understood this was a deep soul cry for love. God heard the cries of my heart way back, before the revelation in October 2005. God is love. God loves me. He is the only One who can satisfy the deepest longings of my heart. I had forgotten that night from so many years ago. God had not forgotten, and He chose this morning to remind me of His great love for me before I knew Him. I had not shared that memory with anyone, and only God knew of that night. God brought His love through Scott in September of 2006 when our paths crossed in the question and answer forum that led to our eventual physical meeting in 2007. The devil tried to destroy me just before I met Scott, but God did not withhold His love. He never will.

VISION, Wednesday, 8/9/2017, PM

I was in my bedroom spending some time with the Lord when I received a vision, a single image. *There are thousands of hands and arms in the air, in worship, towards a lighted stage. I see a sea of hands in the air, and I see light shining from the left side but I cannot see what or who is on the stage. I have the impression of someone sitting on a throne and the light is bright. It is dark over the crowd except for the light illuminating the uplifted hands. I do not have a good feeling. I am concerned and alarmed and grieved. Who is being worshipped? O Lord, how I pray for the lost captives to believe and receive Your love.* The image remained vivid in my mind. Jesus alone is worthy of all praise and worship. Many prayers.

Friday was a challenging day. There was tension at the office and then with my client who was stressed about family coming for a visit over the weekend. She kept me busy with extra chores and details she wanted in place before I left at the end of my shift. Days of this nature kept me in prayer as I worked, for wisdom and understanding to meet the needs of my client and to communicate effectively. I prayed for her inner peace and calm so she would enjoy her family and not stress over any troubling thoughts or worries.

The next Friday I received a disturbing vision concerning my employer at the office. The dark and ominous vision occurred while I was working at my desk. Alarmed, I began praying and then messaged my spiritual parents and prayer friend to cover him as well. I thanked God for alerting me to the need for prayer. I kept my employer covered in extra prayer for days.

On August 16, Redemption Church met at the World's Fair Park for an evening of prayer. The pastor and his wife felt we should pray for Knoxville in the heart of the city. This was an open air arena with a partial roof and graduated seating. The praise and worship team ushered in a spiritually intimate atmosphere for the gathering. We sang, we prayed, and we declared scriptural truth, closing the evening with candlelight and praise to our God. This was a powerful night for all who attended.

I met a nice couple in the parking lot. We had actually arrived and parked at the same time. Conversation began as we walked over to the park before service started. I delighted in meeting fellow believers in a surprising way. They invited me to attend an event on Friday night, the lighting of the Henley Street Bridge in blue to support law enforcement. I arrived late, but I saw the blue lights on the bridge, and prayers were lifted for all law enforcement officers. We joined up at Market Square later for dinner and to get to know one another better. This was a large group, and I was somewhat timid as an unknown guest to all but the hosts. The husband was a candidate in an upcoming local election. They were hosting a night at "Painting With A Twist" in Farragut and invited me to come. I declined due to a lack of funds, but she explained there was an extra ticket available. A supporter was not going to be able to attend and had donated her ticket to be used by someone else. I graciously accepted this unexpected opportunity.

I had painted one picture a few years prior and was excited to paint again. This turned out to be a fun night. A large number of people filled many tables. The sample painting did not appear too difficult, and I worked diligently to paint a replica. Food and drink were provided, but I was seriously concentrating on my efforts and wanted to finish on time. A nice young teacher was seated next to me, and we exchanged stories as we worked on our canvases. I relaxed some as we talked and painted. The evening was wonderful, and I enjoyed the camaraderie, but definitely needed practice to improve my artistic efforts.

During 2014 to 2015 I had participated in several bible studies, and three were led by a special woman at church. We had not seen each other after I began attending Redemption Church in 2016. She messaged me with an invitation to meet her for breakfast on Saturday morning, August 26. We agreed on a restaurant in Rocky Top, sort of halfway for both of us, since I would be driving south from Scott County and she would be traveling north from Anderson County. Breakfast tasted extra special as we caught up on each other's lives. We moved outside to the rocking chairs on the porch after finishing our meal and talked for a few hours. Our time of reconnection was refreshing and inspiring.

I drove down to Oak Ridge with the idea to stop at an auto parts store to check my fuse. I texted Kathy to ask Bob a question about my fuse box and learned that he was in the hospital. I drove the short distance to the hospital and spent some time with them. I joined Kathy in prayers over Bob before leaving the hospital room. She had not eaten anything and asked me to go with her to a local spot for a late lunch. After lunch, I went to work for the rest of the afternoon.

Days passed, some in calm, some in turmoil, always in prayer. I could sense the living situation in Scott County was drawing to a close, and I would be relocating soon. My friends were out of town over the weekend before I left. I sat outside on Saturday afternoon in the swing in the back yard. Their cat joined me and I provided a soft blanket for her to lie on next to me. This tuxedo cat usually stayed outside, but on cold nights she would come in the house. During the winter months she had started showing me affection, which surprised me. I had never owned a cat as a pet and was not familiar with their behavior. However, on several nights she jumped up in my lap and curled up to sleep. She rested one of her paws on my chest--so sweet. Many nights when I arrived at the house after work, she would be sitting in the driveway and allowed me to pet her when I got out of the car. I had quickly grown attached to this cat. Now we were sitting on the swing outside, and my heart was heavy at the thought of leaving her. She was squinting up at me because the sun was behind us, and I thanked God for the love from this little bundle. A hummingbird hovered in front of us for a few precious seconds. I reflected over the days I had been strengthened in focus and purpose, as well as the difficult days battling defeat. I could not provide adequate answers to questions regarding my future or my next step, because I was walking daily by faith holding onto God's promises by His grace. God had provided sweet affection through this cat, and I was strengthened by His attention.

I received an email from my friend I had met for lunch two days ago. She sent a special message on Monday, August 28. "I cannot stop thinking how blessed Saturday was seeing you and discussing everything, including 'finding and defining what Freedom in Christ is and means'. *You are my flower, Iris, and I love the way your face turns to the Son.'* This is from the Lord, girl. It has been burning a hole in my brain until I could get this email off." She then invited me to an upcoming community event she was planning and shared the details. In spite of all the chaos and turmoil, God was reminding me He sees me and He loves me. Stay focused on Him.

Kathy messaged an invite to meet her for an early dinner. She was tired but felt in her spirit that we needed to meet. She encouraged me to step out in faith about leaving Scott County. She said it was past time for me to leave there, and I received a quiet acknowledgement of truth as she spoke. The wife was going to have surgery soon, and I could not remain in my friends' house with her in the hospital. There was clarity in my spirit after we parted, and her words were strongly reassuring. This was not an emotional adrenaline response, but a consistent firm calmness, and I trusted the conviction.

After church on Sunday, September 10, I drove to Scott County and began loading my car. I only had clothing, books, and personal items to pack. My friends arrived home while I was working. She helped me carry out my clothes on hangers and laid them in the back of my vehicle. I said goodbye to the cat, already missing her. Her husband did not speak and stayed out of sight while I was preparing to leave. I returned the door key and the garage door opener. She seemed a little surprised, and I explained that God had let me know it was time to leave their home. I thanked her for all the goodness they had provided and the nights of prayer and fellowship. As I drove out of the driveway I prayed for God to bless them in their growing relationship with Him.

I returned to church for evening service. I stopped at the restroom before entering the sanctuary. I ate one of my breath mints and coughed a little. As I was washing my hands, I choked and could not breathe. No wheezing. Blocked. I could get no air into my mouth. Two women came over to me and laid hands on my back. I was praying silently, "Jesus help me. God help me". As the women started praying out loud, I felt my throat open and I could breathe without any restriction. When my throat closed, it was as though something was holding my throat shut, but oddly I did not panic. Though I could not breathe, I was not afraid. I was thinking to myself, "What is going on? I am not going to die. God's purpose has not been fulfilled." The women stayed with me until they could see I was ok. Another woman had gone looking for help, and a nurse was outside the door when we emerged. I explained that I did not understand why I was choking, but when the women prayed for me, my throat opened and I was breathing again normally. I recognized one of the women. She was the golf cart driver who had given me a ride on my first Sunday at Redemption Church in May 2016, and her name was "Jane."

I texted Kathy about this strange occurrence, and she instructed me to come to their house after church. I shared the details of the choking incident and the prayers that stopped the choking on the church social media page. I gave God the glory but wanted to acknowledge these special women who had not hesitated to lay hands on me and pray in that moment. After service, I stopped at a convenience store for a bottle of water and gazed up at the sky in wonder and gratitude. I watched as the colors and intensity were changing and snapped a few pictures with my phone. A revelation God had given me one Saturday while I was driving in Morgan

County came to mind. The sky was especially beautiful on that particular evening, and I could not stop to take any photos. There was no shoulder on the winding road and no place to pull off the highway. I was expressing my frustration inwardly, when God ministered to my spirit, *"Some things are to be enjoyed in the moment with Me. To try to capture it or preserve it is to corrupt it."* The dream of the cross tower and the people with cameras then replayed in my mind. I was convicted. Enjoy the beauty with God and be thankful for His gift in the sky. He paints new pictures every day. Be with Him in the moment.

The following Saturday my special friend, Brenda, from Campbell County invited me to her home for the afternoon. It was wonderful to see her again. She was an excellent cook and had prepared a delicious meal for us to enjoy while we watched a DVD. She provided homemade brownies and fresh coffee for dessert. We caught up on each other and our families and our walk with God, and then spent some time in prayer before I left that evening. These visits with special friends strengthened me and encouraged me in my walk with God. They may not have understood everything I was doing, but they supported me in prayer and kindness, which were priceless gifts of love from the heart of the Father.

The next week held days of constant battle in my mind affecting my attitude and disturbing my peace. I received a phone call from an acquaintance that lasted about an hour and then she had to get off the phone. This was always the pattern with this particular person. Communication was on her terms only. That interruption disrupted my entire day and lingered through the remainder of the weekend. I struggled to shake it off even in prayer. I talked to God about the phone call and the person. I worked on Legacy files at a Wi-Fi café on Saturday and Sunday, and the effort to concentrate was challenging. The oppression lifted briefly while at church and soon returned when service ended. With more prayer, there was a lift but not complete removal.

My last week of employment in the office was unpleasant and turned into a battle week spiritually. I had given a two-week notice in order to move forward with God towards my destiny. The kidnapping dream stayed on my mind during these days, and I believed leaving would break me free to pursue my next. I was willing to let go of the little I was holding onto in order to receive the greater from God. I experienced rejection with difficult interactions and unwanted questions from another employee that I would not answer. I knew she would not understand and there was no need to try to explain. The last night of employment, I returned to the office as usual after leaving my client's home at 7:30. I finished the work that was pending and gathered the few things on my desk. I placed my ID badge and key in an envelope for the office administrator and placed it where he had instructed. I had enjoyed my job here. The work was pleasant and I liked the people, but it was time to leave. I wanted what was before me more than anything I was leaving behind.

There were adjustments with my schedule change now that I was no longer working in the mornings. My client's schedule remained the same, 12:30 to 7:30 PM Monday through Friday. I had to adjust my time so that I would be in the area prior to starting my shift and find things to do before work. In mid-October my spiritual parents instructed me to take my vehicle to a specific tire place and gave me money for a set of new tires. Bob had negotiated the cost and the shop was expecting me. I drove to Harriman for the work, so thankful to God for this surprising provision. I knew my tires were almost bald and needed replacing, but I had not mentioned this to them, only to God in prayer. Thankful tears fell in gratitude to God once again for provision and protection. I thanked Him all the way back to the house. The car rode so much better, like a new vehicle, on the fresh tires.

Something unusual happened at church on Sunday morning during praise and worship. While performing the first or second song, the musicians received an anointing and their music was raised to a professional level on stage. The atmosphere was electrified the moment it changed—profoundly amazing. The wisdom in Pastor King's teaching was of the same anointing. This was a new experience, and I rejoiced in the profound presence of the Holy Spirit. I remained in awe of the entire morning. I prayed God would continue the work He had started. I returned to service that evening and drove home in the rain, praising God for His presence at church.

DREAM, Wednesday, 10/18/2017 AM

The details remained vivid after I awoke from this dream. *There was one single image—the face of a stranger. His light blue eyes were focused directly at me. I studied his features. His skin was pale. I could not see any hair and assumed he was bald. The lips were regular shaped, not smiling but not frowning. His head was tilted slightly to the right, and his gaze was steady and unblinking. There were no events in the dream, no words, no actions—only the face.* The image was prominent in my thoughts throughout the remainder of the day. I prayed for revelation to understand this message from God. There were no unusual occurrences in the days and weeks following, and I continued to consider this face in the back of my mind. God had impressed this so strongly in my spirit that it must be significant.

Wednesday night of the following week, I was relaxing in the glider rocker in my bedroom situated beside a window. While reading the Word, I nodded off. I heard a voice call my name. It sounded loud and somewhat firm. My head jerked up in response. It seemed important in that moment that I wake up. Nothing else happened.

The next day while I was driving to work I received inspiration for a new blog through the replay of a memory with Scott in 2008. The recall was vivid in detail. *"We were gathered with Scott's family at his parents' lake cottage in Michigan in late spring of 2008. This was my first visit to the lake following my move to Goshen. He had grown up visiting the cozy cottage every summer, and his excitement had faded through familiarity over the years.*

Standing off to the side of the room at one point, I observed Scott as he interacted with his brothers and their father in conversation. I smiled as I looked at him sitting casually on a stool, wearing his favorite shorts and sandals, talking and laughing at ease. Overwhelming love began surging through me. Loving care for my husband flooded through my entire being, and I was compelled to communicate my heart to Scott at that divine moment. The love was pure, untainted by lust, protective and healing, a touch from heaven.

Without hesitation I walked over to Scott and kissed him full on the mouth. In front of everyone. Without speaking a word. Our eyes met briefly before I stepped back from that intimate circle. My boldness in front of his family was startling. I had not experienced anything remotely comparable previous to my relationship with Scott. My heart was close to exploding with the fullness of love as I stood in awed silence.

Those unexpected moments of awareness between us in our short time together were powerful, stopping us in our tracks, as we gazed at one another in amazement. We did not understand why, but we knew it came from God. Together, we experienced love, shared love, and expressed love.

Discovering God's love for me alone after Scott's move to heaven has been transforming. He has cleared the extra clutter out of my life, my thoughts, and my emotions, with sharper focus and purpose. He has given me dreams and visions with a view of my future. He has taught me much about Him, much about the Kingdom, and much about life and people. Every revelation I have received from Above comes with the realization that there is vastly more to learn with an increasing hunger to go higher and deeper in God.

He continues to lead and teach me in loving guidance, and I embrace His divine pruning as I move forward in His precious love. Life renewed."

As the memory played like a video in my mind, words came tumbling that I would write later after work. I thanked God once again for the love, and I asked Him to help me remember all that I was receiving in my spirit.

DREAM, Tuesday, 10/31, AM
Woke up at 4 AM and went to the bathroom, then laid back down and fell asleep. I woke up at 9:30 AM from a dream. *I am looking at the ground. I see a small or young snake. It is white, clean, with a brown diamond pattern clearly stamped on the body. I can see the head and the eye, and I put my foot down on the lower part of the head. There are dried brown leaves on the ground, and I can see part of a larger snake close by. I cannot see the head or tail—only a section of the body uncovered by leaves. Same white body with brown diamond pattern on the skin.* I prayed when I woke up. I later shared with Kathy, and she will ask Bob. We are praying for revelation. I am thankful God spoke to me. I believe it is a warning.

On Wednesday, November 1, after I arrived at my client's house, I discovered she had a flat tire. I called and rescheduled her salon appointment, then called her insurance company that provided roadside assistance. ETA was 90 minutes, but the tech arrived in 20 minutes and quickly changed her tire. My client instructed me to take her car to Matlock's for the tire repair. Though they were very busy, my wait time was relatively short. When the car was ready, I went to the counter to pay, and surprisingly there was no charge for the repair. From there I drove onto the grocery store for the few things she wanted and returned home. I then drove her to the hospital for a scheduled MRI in evaluation of her back. We arrived at 4:15. Valet parking took care of the vehicle while I helped her inside to get registered. We then moved to the outpatient waiting area. The MRI tech transported her to the scanner just before 5. The waiting room was empty, and the desk staff had gone for the day. I was alone, when an elderly woman pushing a young man in a wheelchair entered the room. He was holding registration paperwork for a test.

We started talking. She told me her name (which was same first name as my client) and explained the young man, "Travis," was her grandson. He was diagnosed with MS at age 19 and was now 38 (he appeared much younger). She was a widow in her 80s. Her husband had died eight years prior from cancer, and they had been married 55 years. She said "Travis" had been engaged when he received the MS diagnosis. His girlfriend wrote him a note and broke off the relationship. He had a 3-year-old dog that he loved, and "Travis" shared some photos and a video. I mentioned that my husband had a nephew with MS diagnosed in his 20s who lived in Bristol, Indiana. That led to talking about Scott, our love story, and the love of God. "Travis" was listening though not looking at me. The tech then arrived to take him for his scan.

His grandmother shared more about the girlfriend and her grandson. I offered to pray with her and moved into the seat next to her. We held hands and prayed for "Travis" and his life and healing and other issues. We talked about our churches and families. She had lost three sisters in a 14-month time period and was grieving over those losses as well.

My client was not finished until 7:40 PM. I had phoned the office earlier and received approval to stay with her until she was settled at home. During the drive to her house, we talked about the events of the day. She was amazed that the tire shop did not charge for the repair. I reminded her that the Word says every good and perfect gift comes from above and blessings come from God. I said that I was thankful the flat happened in the garage and not while we were driving. She agreed and added she was thankful for a couple of blessings I was not aware of. Praise God! Later that night I thanked God for this good day, full of His goodness and presence, encouraging and strengthening for others and for me.

I was talking to Kathy one evening, reviewing many incidents that had happened and other dreams I had received during this time. I shared with her that I was in awe of God and how much He has done in my life already and I am still in the wilderness. I said, "I believe, trust, and declare in faith all of God's promises to me and for me in His Word." Overwhelmed by the goodness of God, I then asked her if God does this much for everyone. She reminded me that my first and most important ministry is to God. My relationship to Him comes first always. Ministry to others flows from that.

I attended "Christmas in December" at Bridgewater Place, hosted by Redemption Church, on November 4. A sweet friend from church invited me to attend and provided a ticket. Judy Jacobs would be the featured speaker. I met my friend in Clinton, and she drove us to the event venue. The tables and chairs were elegantly decorated for Christmas. Each table celebrated the season with a different theme and elaborate creative centerpieces, a feast for the eyes. We chose to sit at the table that was draped in vintage pink Christmas décor. Everything was sparkly and pink, strikingly beautiful. The pastor's wife welcomed the women and opened the evening in prayer. My back was to the stage and our table was located just beyond the halfway point of the large room. My head was bowed with my eyes closed while the prayer was being lifted. In the Spirit I received a vision of a column of golden glittering haze in front of and to the left of our table, extending from the floor to the vaulted ceiling. I did not open my eyes until the prayer was over. Judy Jacobs led the praise and worship and then delivered a powerful message, "The Time Is Now!" Her words were empowering, strengthening, and uplifting. She stressed to the audience that our voice represents our authority, and we repeated that after her several times, "My Voice Represents My Authority!"

We enjoyed delicious food served in the festive atmosphere, chatting with other women at our table. After eating we visited the other tables to see the unique decorations. We voted on our favorites, and the table design winners received a special prize at the end of the evening. This was a fantastic day of spiritual nourishment, celebration, and fellowship. I talked to a woman who sang with the praise and worship team at church, and I asked her about the anointing on the stage a couple of weeks prior. She said that the anointing fell on them during rehearsal, also, and they were all aware. I asked God to bless my special friend who invited me to share in this powerful fun day. What a glorious gift of joy and love! Later, I talked to Kathy about the evening and she explained that I had seen the Shekinah Glory of God. I tried to wrap my mind around that revelation while my mind dwelled on the image.

A few days later was another battle day regarding financial lack. I had read a praise bulletin by Merlin Carothers about victory and declared out loud boldly, "I believe I have Victory in every area of my life. I do have Victory." On Thursday I drove down to Knoxville to my client's home knowing I did not have enough gas to make the return trip back to Morgan County after work. I proclaimed victory over lack and believed victory in my heart. My head argued, while I kept proclaiming victory. I trusted God. The gas gauge needle was just above "E" when I arrived at work. I refused to worry or doubt. A thought came in about a loan, and I quickly rebuked that suggestion. I declared confidently out loud, "God is my Source". I prayed and asked God what to do in the afternoon. Do I start driving until I run out of gas? Do I ask for gas money? Do I wait on the side of the highway for help? I received the impression of my bank, a location close to my client's home. This was the answer to my prayer. I went to the ATM and withdrew some cash, then went to the closest gas station, only a block from the bank. As I pumped the gas, I thanked God for His provision. Peace, joy, and lightness moved through my spirit. I declared, "I am victorious in this provision hurdle by the grace of God!" My drive home was filled with praise and conversation with the Lord.

On Sunday Pastor King shared that he had been asking God about the word for the church for 2018. God spoke to him during the service that it would be "Resurrection of Lost Dreams." I started crying while he was talking, in release. All will come to pass as promised; lost years and forgotten dreams restored by God. My sister had invited me for dinner after church for a home-cooked meal. We enjoyed fresh coffee afterwards and visited for a few hours. We prayed together before I left to drive back to Morgan County. I spent the late evening hours reflecting on the weekend and the message at church that morning. God had worked incredibly in my heart and life; yet, I remain in the "wilderness." I declared my trust in God and faith in His promises for me in His Word.

Wednesday morning I stopped at a fast food restaurant to work on a Legacy file. I ordered a breakfast sandwich with coffee, and my card was declined. I sighed and instructed the young man to cancel my order. I went to my usual table to set up my laptop. To my great surprise, the young man brought my order to the table and said it was on the house. My mouth fell open in surprise, and I exclaimed, "Thank you! God bless you!" The food and coffee were so good, and I deeply appreciated this unexpected blessing. I worked two hours and then packed up to head to Knoxville for work. I was arranging all my stuff on my car seat when someone rapped on my window. I turned my head to see who and my heart sank. A woman was asking me to buy her a biscuit. I explained to her that I did not have any money, not even a dollar in my purse, and I was not able to buy any food for myself. My mind was circling on the fact that I had received free food and I was unable to pay it forward in this moment.

Monday was a very difficult day with my client and not her typical behavior. She was dozing in her chair when I arrived. I placed my food in the fridge as usual for dinner later and started the housework. I noticed she had not eaten much over the weekend and wondered if she was feeling sick. She did not want anything when I asked and did not engage in conversation. I went to the mailbox center to check her mail and the mail carrier had just arrived and was filling the boxes. I walked back to her home and informed her that I would check again after the boxes were filled. She took her rollator to the kitchen and opened the fridge. She opened my sandwich and then halfway closed the foil and placed it back on the shelf. That was strange. I always brought my own food for the evening meal and she never touched it. She then removed her favorite pie from the freezer and carried it to the bedroom. There was one large single slice left in the pan. Her demeanor was hostile and angry. I carried the empty pan back to the kitchen. She laid down in bed and slept until almost 5 PM. She had not exhibited this behavior previously while I was with her, and I wondered what had triggered this change. I warmed up some stew for her dinner later, and she offered a thank-you but no other conversation. I prayed for her as I drove away from her home that evening.

I was driving to work one morning before Thanksgiving, and I noticed with dismay the message displayed on the digital sign in front of the Wi-Fi café I visited most often, "Drive-Thru Open." There were service vehicles parked close to the entrance, and yellow tape blocked the door, indicating the lobby was closed. I prayed against the alarming idea that the interior was being remodeled. This had been my favorite Wi-Fi spot over the past 18 months. I came to this location frequently on weekends and most weeknights to work on Legacy files and to use the internet. Different seating areas offered a measure of privacy and barriers to contain noise. TVs were positioned to view sports or news. There were two regular employees who kept the floors swept, the tables and chairs clean, the trash emptied, and the drink station in order. One was an older woman who would smile in greeting but did not talk. She had a quiet manner and stayed busy. The other employee was an older handicapped gentleman who worked steadily through his shift. He shared that he had worked at that location for many years and liked his job. I appreciated his efforts and his friendly demeanor.

The clientele changed with the time of day. Seniors gathered in mornings for breakfast and fellowship. Locals who knew the area before development had changed the landscape greeted one another warmly with smiles and shared their latest news. In the afternoons and evenings, parents and coaches brought sports teams of young people, hectically trying to keep track of everyone and regroup before leaving. There were assorted travelers who stopped just long enough to eat or visit the restroom. There was a woman who came alone frequently in the evenings and always read a book while eating. We would exchange a smile in the familiarity of recognition, but there was no conversation. I observed over the course of many weeks different young men who came in later at night, usually alone. In the coldest weather, they would be without a coat or jacket, walking around, almost pacing, and sweating. They would sit down for a few minutes, then get up and move around, always on their cell phones. I prayed as I watched them. Had they just used drugs? Were they looking for a place to sleep, for money? I prayed as I worked. Eventually they would walk outside and disappear into the night.

An elderly man of slight build came in one evening and chose a booth across the room. I spotted an empty fry box on his tray and watched him pull two cans of Vienna sausages from his small backpack. He removed a bottle and filled it at the water fountain. When he finished his food, I saw him count some change. He was dressed adequately but was thin and of slight build. I approached his table and spoke in greeting. He smiled in response but declined my offer of food. Once he finished eating, he filled his bottle once again, put on his backpack, and disappeared into the night. More prayers.

I had been at the Wi-Fi café three days in a row, Saturday, Sunday afternoon, and Monday morning. I needed to upload the completed file I had worked on over the weekend, so I stopped quickly before work to email the file. I noticed a man sitting in a booth, reading the newspaper. This was the third day in a row I had seen the guy. He was dressed in the green fatigue jacket, buttoned, without a visible shirt underneath, that he had been wearing the previous two days. He was clean. His hair was cut, his eyes were clear, and he was adequately groomed. I had heard him talking to a woman on Saturday night. Apparently she had asked for directions, and he was attempting to describe the I-40/75 interchange. She was worried because her cell phone was almost dead. He spoke to me briefly to ask if I had a phone charger. I barely looked up as I answered that I did not have one. I thought he was being very patient with her, as I concentrated on my work. She eventually left, and he settled back into his booth. I finished my work and went home that night, forgetting about the incident. But this morning, he was here once again.

I walked over to his table and asked him if he would like some breakfast. He smiled brightly and said, "Sure!" We walked towards the counter. He explained that he had been living in the woods and was trying to find a job. He had gone to a local thrift store and found a pair of black pants. When he told the clerk that he had a job interview that afternoon, she kindly gave him the pants for free. He spoke well, he was at ease, and he was polite. He was not inappropriate in any way and did not ask for anything. I paid for his breakfast and told him I would pray for him and wished him well with his employment. He expressed his gratitude, and I left for work. As I drove towards Knoxville, I received an impression in my spirit about the man. "You saw this man twice but did not pray for him." I felt a punch of conviction as I realized the truth of those words. I typically prayed for people I met in random encounters either during or immediately following our conversation. Why had I not lifted prayers for him until the third day? I was so focused on the work I was doing over the weekend and the desire to complete it promptly that I failed to notice this person in need. The next time I stopped at that café, he was not there, and I did not see him again.

The day finally came when the words on the digital sign were changed to read, "Now Open". With some trepidation I pulled into the parking lot, dreading what I would discover. I walked inside and looked around in disbelief. The entire restaurant had been remodeled. All of the previous décor was gone, replaced with endless gray tile and plastic chairs. I chose a seat in the area where I had sat previously, fighting back tears from the shock. The heaviness in my heart felt like grief. The entire dining area was now wide open, with no intimacy or warmth. The TVs had been removed, and there were no barriers to buffer noise or conversations. The lights were bright and glaring. It looked like a utilitarian facility, not a place to gather. The previous atmosphere had been destroyed. I heard from one of the staff that the remodel was a corporate decision. Though I visited a few times after the construction was completed, the place remained uncomfortable. Devoid of its own uniqueness, there was no incentive to return. What was once there was gone.

My friends in Scott County invited me to join them for Thanksgiving Dinner at their house. One of her brothers and wife were in town, and a couple from their church came. The home was beautifully decorated for the season, and the atmosphere was warm and inviting. She had prepared a scrumptious meal, and we gathered around the table in the dining room in anticipation. Before praying over the food, she asked each one of us to share something that we were thankful for during the past year. Her husband started and mentioned his knee surgery. I said, "God's love that has filled all the voids in my heart." Then my friend said, "Iris!" She said God had brought me into their lives for her husband's needed surgery. This was a complicated scenario that began several years prior. My sister was working for an orthopedic surgeon who had agreed to review the case and past medical records, and subsequently had accepted her husband as a patient. I quickly stated that it was all God and that my sister had presented the information to the doctor. She believed that God had worked through me to help them. I was frankly shocked to hear her words on the matter. I had not viewed my time with them from that perspective, and I pondered over this through the rest of the evening.

Sunday morning I spoke in faith about a tank of gas at a station in Powell. I was very calm, matter of fact in my request, and believed it would be done. Though my balance was less than the cost, my card was approved for the full tank. After church on Sunday, I went to a different Wi-Fi location in an office building to work on a new blog. I brought some food from home to eat as a late lunch and a bottle of water. I had just started typing when a woman approached looking for a place to change a five-dollar bill into single ones to use in a vending machine. She appeared tired and frustrated. We started talking, and she sat down in a chair across from me. She lived out of town and had been staying at the hospital since Friday night with a friend. She talked about her friend's condition and her children. We talked about church and God. I shared my story of discovering God's love through the death of my husband.

I offered to pray for her. She told me her name and that she lived in Athens. I prayed for her over many issues, and then our conversation continued. She shared a painful experience at church with leadership. I prayed for her in the situation and for future opportunities to serve. She hugged me and said she needed to go as her friend would need help with her supper tray. When I shared about my book and how God had guided the entire process, she made the statement that I would write many books. We had talked almost an hour, and I was amazed at this unexpected encounter. We hugged before she left with smiles and tears, and I prayed for her again later that night.

I realized on my lowest days, God sent someone across my path for me to encourage and in so doing, I was lifted and strengthened. Precious love from Above. There were times when I was weary of the hassle of having to sit in cafes to use the internet, wishing I had internet where I lived, and I had shared that desire with the Lord. When I left the café that Sunday evening, I heard this question, "How could you have ministered to her at home on your private internet?" I cannot help others when I am tucked away in safe huddles and closed circles. The goal is not to get comfortable, but to continue to serve.

On Sunday Dr. King spoke further on "Faith For The Journey." This was a powerful series that followed the "Destiny" messages, and I had taken notes every week. He taught how faith comes by hearing and hearing and hearing the Word of God. He explained that we do not hear it once and get it; faith comes by hearing the Word over and over and over. We believe what we say more than what other people say, so it is important to speak the Word out loud, and speak it every day until the Word becomes a part of us. I listened and started reading in the Book of Ephesians over myself out loud during my quiet time with the Lord. It felt strange at first, but gradually I could feel the Word strengthening me and anchoring me in its truth. I added more scriptures in Colossians, until I could identify with what the Word said about me. My identity was not tied to who I once was or to the negative words spoken over me in the past. My identity was not tied to how people viewed me or reacted to my story. My identity was found in Christ.

My sister had made chili and invited me for lunch after church. She unexpectedly gave me her Christmas bonus. I did not want to take the money and resisted her offer, but she kept insisting because she was not going to travel over the holidays. She knew I was going to Memphis and would need gas money. I asked God to bless her for her generosity. We talked a while, and I prayed over us before returning to church for evening service.

Ringing the bell for the Salvation Army had been a secret desire for many years. During the Christmas Season, whenever I dropped money in a red kettle, I would think about serving as a bell ringer. I finally decided to follow-through and signed up this year. I attended an information meeting and was given many papers to complete. I thought it strange that this paperwork was needed to volunteer, but I complied and turned in the forms. The woman at the desk reviewed my information and informed me that due to my low income, I qualified to be paid as a bell ringer. I was surprised. I did not know anyone got paid for that and marveled at this unexpected blessing of extra income.

Over the course of five Saturdays, each at a different location, I was blessed by interactions with people. I enjoyed the children dropping coins into the kettle. Some were shy about approaching and held onto the accompanying adult's hand. Countless people came and went continuously throughout the day at the different stores. Some prayer needs were readily apparent, while others were more subtle. One woman's eyes, as she spoke of her daughter who once enjoyed putting money in the kettle, prompted silent prayer as she walked to her car. A man's voice trembled with emotion as he spoke of prayer for his mother. Another woman was facing a family crisis. A woman with dire health issues was in distress, struggling to find transportation home. A trucker shared that he and his wife with their dogs were stuck in a hotel locally, after his semi broke down on the interstate, and repairs were estimated to take a week. A man talked about taking care of his friend who was dying of cancer and the losses in his life. I observed numerous needs unspoken. People everywhere starving for love. God's divine love. His miraculous, conquering, healing, restoring love. Love without measure or motive.

I smiled at a pair of little girls skipping to the kettle, their ponytails bobbing in unison. I smiled at little voices asking questions such as "Who is that lady?" "Why is she ringing that bell?" "What is the Salvation Army?" One mother asked me to share with her son what the organization does with the money. I smiled at precious little ones saying "Merry Christmas!" I waved back at the hands waving from car windows as they drove by. Miles of smiles! Moments of simple pleasures strung together, creating wonderful memories of bell ringing. The opportunity to serve and experience such joy was a beautiful gift of Christmas.

December 9 was a special day of bell ringing. Because of my work schedule during the week, I was only able to ring on the weekend. I served every Saturday, 10 AM to 8 PM, during the Christmas season that year. The bell ringers gathered at the main office downtown and then were transported by vans to their designated locations. The vans returned at the end of the shift to collect the kettles and carry us back to the main office where we had parked our vehicles. On this particular day I was assigned to a grocery store on Cedar Bluff at Kingston Pike. I wore three shirts, two pair of pants, two pair of socks, gloves, ear warmers, Santa hat, Christmas scarf, blinking necklace and earrings, my winter coat, and added the traditional red apron at the kettle. Before starting my shift, I prayed over all the kettles and asked God to bless the Salvation Army's fundraising efforts, to bless the givers and their generosity, and to bless every bell ringer. Foot traffic was consistently busy throughout the day, with many shoppers dropping donations into the kettle.

Time had passed comfortably into the late afternoon. Suddenly I became aware of the temperature dropping as the sun was setting. The cold descended on me like a blanket. I noticed it in my arms first and then throughout my body. I was surprised, because the clothing I was wearing typically kept me warm on cold nights. And then I remembered a previous conversation with another bell ringer. Our initial meeting at the beginning of the season was held at the main office. The large room was filled with rows of tables and chairs. People chose a seat at random as they entered the room before the information meeting started. An older bell ringer sitting nearby spoke in greeting and shared that she had been ringing every Christmas season for many years. We talked a bit, and she shared some information with me as a new ringer. She said sometimes people would buy her hot coffee on cold days and it was acceptable to receive food or a beverage as a gift. She reminded me that we were not allowed to accept any money, which was covered in the rules at the meeting.

I was almost shivering as the woman's kind words replayed in my mind. I had no cash on me; indeed, my paycheck was in my pocket, and I would need to cash it for gas before driving home later in the evening. I lifted my head and looked up at the night sky. I prayed silently, sharing my situation and the other volunteer's words, and then asked for divine help. God had become my source in the years since Scott's move to heaven, and I trusted His care of my needs. Before long, a young woman came out of the store and brought me a small hot chocolate. I thanked her profusely and then thanked God. I knew this was from Him! The hot chocolate disappeared quickly, and I could feel the warmth beginning to spread as I finished the last sip. Soon afterwards, an older gentleman stopped at the kettle and said he would like to buy me something hot to drink. I replied that a small hot chocolate or coffee, whichever was cheaper, would be nice. "Humph!" was his response as he turned and walked into the store. He returned shortly carrying a tall cup and said he had brought me something special--a snickerdoodle hot chocolate with whipped cream. My delight was evident as I accepted the cup. I thanked him repeatedly, and he smiled at my response. Then I looked up and thanked God. Laughter was beginning to bubble up inside. I was thawing out and felt much better. A short time later, a young family brought me a small coffee. Their young children were wide-eyed at my appearance with the blinking lights as I accepted the very kind gift. I was completely warm by now and in awe of God's answer to my prayer. Unbelievably, a fourth person stopped and asked if they could buy me something hot to drink. I politely refused and explained that someone had just given me some coffee. Laughing, I thanked God once again and asked Him to bless every kind heart that had provided hot refreshment. I finished my shift wrapped in the warmth of God's love.

The van returned to pick me up a few minutes after eight. The driver unlocked the kettle from the stand and as he lifted it off the hook, he remarked on the weight of the kettle. Glory to God! The other ringers were already on board for the ride back to the main office. Once I reached my vehicle, I drove back to the grocery store to cash my check, continuing to thank God. The customer service clerk explained that earlier in the day the system had not allowed her to cash other Salvation Army checks but that she would try again with mine. I prayed silently while she completed the process. We were both excited when the transaction was approved! Now I had gas money for the long drive ahead, and another day's needs were met. The ride home was filled with tears as I sang to God in praise and gratitude.

Later that night, I noted these words in my journal: *"His praise brought givers and donations to the kettle. His kindness provided the warm drinks. His love translated into favor to cash the check for my needs. God is faithful."*

One day in December while sitting with my client in a waiting room for an appointment, she began to share some painful history between her, one of her sons, a grandson, and her husband while he was still alive. I listened in silence while she aired her thoughts and memories. Many prayers were lifted later in the evening, and I realized God was working in her heart.

A week before Christmas her son was admitted to the hospital with a collapsed lung. She was beside herself with worry. He called her that afternoon and told her he would be having a CT scan and then surgery the next day. I offered to take her to the hospital, but she declined at that time. I prayed with her before I left for the day. I drove to the hospital following a prompt from the Holy Spirit to go and pray over her son. I refused to engage any thoughts of doubt as I made my way to his room. He was definitely surprised to see me. I explained that I had come to pray for him and asked if he was agreeable. He nodded his head, and I held his hand as I prayed for healing and his situation. He wiped his eyes afterwards. The Holy Spirit was present. When I left the hospital, I thanked God for His courage. Conflicting thoughts had tried to discourage me, but peace came with obedience.

The next day my client wanted to visit her son in the hospital. He had undergone surgery early in the morning and apparently this went well. He was trying to sleep in spite of pain. She could not hear him when he spoke, and I repeated to her what he said after every sentence. She was beginning to weaken after the long walk inside the building and the extended standing. On the drive home, she told me she was unable to see her son clearly and that caused her great anxiety. I told her the room was dimly lit and the blinds were closed which probably contributed. She was exhausted by the time we got home and fell asleep as soon as she sat down in her chair. Her son improved and was discharged a week later. Prayers of gratitude were lifted.

VISION, Tuesday, 12/12/2017 AM
I woke up earlier than the alarm and went to the restroom. I laid down but was wide awake so I spent time in prayer. I received a vision. *I was cleaning scales from white skin. Suddenly a snake head turned and bit me on the back of my hand.* I immediately spoke the Blood of Jesus over myself. I put on my armor and prayed Psalm 91. I was angry at the bite in the vision and believed I had received a warning from God.

I drove to work and stopped at a bank to cash a small refund check from the car insurance company in Indiana. I was almost to the front door when I tripped over a curb and fell flat on the concrete, breaking my glasses and scraping my right hand. I was stunned, then angry and upset. A man was coming out of the bank and helped me up. I had shared the vision of the snake bite with Bob and Kathy that morning, and they had prayed with me before I left their house. Bob had said that I was cleaning scales off the snake that was revealing of what was hidden. The vision was a warning. I believed I was safe because of the prayers. Anger was simmering when I got into my car. I prayed protection over my family, my friends, and myself. By the end of the day my wrist was swollen and tender.

I talked to my spiritual parents again that evening about the fall. I could not understand why our prayers did not prevent the accident. Kathy explained that she had suffered a severe fall several years prior in which she broke her arm and her hip, and she was covered in prayer on the day she fell. I realized I needed to be grateful, much more grateful. My fall was minor compared to what Kathy had endured, and I was convicted about my attitude. I thanked God for His divine protection as my minor injury could have been much more serious. The broken glasses were the greatest loss. My insurance coverage ended when Scott died, and these glasses had been expensive even with his insurance. The lenses were okay but the frames were broken around the lenses and could not be repaired. I settled for regular readers and used those for reading small print.

DREAM, Thursday, 12/14/2017, 6 AM

I am in a house, sitting on a couch, watching a movie on TV. I do not recognize this house. I ask myself, "Whose house is this?" I sense that my son is with me in the living room. A small dog appears, white with large tan spots. He seems a little shy and then jumps on the couch next to me. I pet it, and then it jumps off the couch and leaves the room. The movie ends, and I get up to change the DVD, but the next one is already loaded and starts to play. I walk to the refrigerator. There is a wide shallow tray full of water. I am thinking I need to empty it. I prop open the storm door on the back porch so I can carry the tray outside. The sky looks unusual. I run through the house to the front door and grab my phone. I go outside in the front yard. Now I have an elevated view and I can see across countless neighborhoods. I see people coming outside from their homes. Everyone is looking up at the sky. Huge, enormous, 3D snowflakes are forming and spinning in a blue sky. It is not winter. People are wearing regular clothes without coats and the grass is green. These ginormous snowflakes are beautiful and spectacular. They are distinctly different. I have the impression that there are many. There is no noise. Everyone is standing still, wide-eyed, open-mouthed, looking up at these larger than life snowflakes suspended and spinning in the sky overhead. One of them appears to freeze as it explodes in color, similar to a spectacular firework display. They are disproportionate in scale to things on the ground.

I stopped at Walmart before church Sunday morning to pick up a few things as it was too early to arrive at church. The door greeter spoke to me, and I told him I was getting ready to go to church. After I checked out, the same greeter asked for prayer at church for a specific name for health issues. I assured him prayers would be lifted and smiled at him in response as I touched his arm. I prayed as I drove onto church and again that evening.

Sunday evening was movie night, and the feature was "It's A Wonderful Life." I had not seen the film in a few years, and I watched the classic film with fresh eyes and a deeper appreciation for the timeless story. The church had set up a beautiful holiday photo prop in the foyer for people to take a selfie or a group picture. I asked a young woman standing nearby if she would take my picture as I was not good at selfies. She snapped several pics and asked how long I had been attending the church. That started a conversation, and I shared my love story. I thanked her for taking the pictures and then started the long drive home in misty fog. God protected my vehicle and me, and we arrived safely in Morgan County.

The next afternoon my client mostly dozed in her chair with her dog in her lap. My mind was busy with writing ideas, and I started jotting down notes to remember for later. I went to the usual Wi-Fi café after work and finished one Legacy file. I then wrote and posted a new blog. It was 10:30 when I finished, and I arrived back at the house at 11. I sat in quietness with the Lord before bed, and I received a revelation in my spirit about the writing. It is not about approval or attention; rather, it is about conviction to love people, to love others with the love of Jesus. Not all of my writing will be popular. My writing is for the Lord and His purpose.

DREAM, Tuesday, 12/27/2017, 4:06 AM
I am walking on the sidewalk of a five-lane road, residential. There is a suited man walking a little distance ahead of me wearing a sports jacket and dark gray pants with black dress shoes. We round the corner and then turn right again on the first street marked "Dead End." It is a short street. I stop and watch the man, who I understand to be a cop, approach a house and knock on the front door. He sees me and motions with his hand. Is he telling me to go or to come? He motions again, and I move forward on the sidewalk toward the house. A thin blonde-haired young man has followed me. The cop disappears into the house. I turn around and speak to the young man. Suddenly he pulls out a handgun and takes a firing posture. He slides the hammer twice, and I squat looking at that gun. It is a light colored metal. The gun does not fire. I know I am going to be ok. He tries to fire again and the trigger will not pull. He is frustrated as he attempts to slide the top of the gun. I am safe and stand up.

I have another dream directly behind this one, completely different. *I see myself getting out of bed. I am trying to straighten the shade on a lamp on the table. I am really puzzled about it, and I can feel this in my dream. I hear*

Bob get up and move by the door. Our bedrooms are on a hallway across from each other. We seem to be in a conference center or hotel and not a house. Bob stops at my doorway and asks what I am doing. I tell him I am trying to fix the lamp. Something about the shade—is it upside down? The body of the lamp is loose and needs tightening. I turn around, and both Bob and Kathy are in my room. I share about a dream. They are both encouraging and positive in response. Then I woke up. I wrote the details on my bedside notepad.

Later, I shared the first dream with Bob and Kathy. He said the five-lane street is the broad way. I am following authority – God. He is leading me. He motions me to follow Him when I stop, unsure. The enemy will try to come against me, but God will protect me. Keep following Him.

CHAPTER SEVEN

JANUARY – MARCH 2018

Tuesday morning, January 2, I was driving to work when I heard in my spirit, *"I am not impressed with how much people know but how well they love."* God is looking at hearts.

I drove to the Salvation Army office in Knoxville the next day to turn in my apron and bell and to retrieve my final paycheck. I had prayed for God to move on my behalf to help me get this check. A woman I recognized from the day I signed up to be a bell ringer just happened to be at the door when I walked up to the entrance. I pushed the apron through the opening in the glass door, and she allowed me to enter the building. I told her about my paycheck and that the commander had said he would mail it. She asked me to wait while she searched for it. She returned with an older woman, and they went to look in the safe. They returned with my check in their hands. I signed for it and thanked both of them for their help. I praised God all the way to the bank.

I recalled a vision from two years prior where Jesus was looking down over Goshen. I was standing in an empty loft upstairs in a Downtown building with light streaming in the windows. The people I had known previously from Goshen were standing together opposite of where I was standing, and we were facing each other. I started praying about this recall. I received an impression to sell the remainder of the large items stored in the garage at the house in Knoxville. Kathy had shared with me previously that she believed I would be returning to Goshen for a period of time and that God would be with me. She did not know how long I would be there, but it would be temporary. She sensed unfinished business in Goshen. Now I was recalling the vision and her words with this impression. "Is it time to move, Lord?"

At this time my client's son was rehospitalized with a collapsed lung on the same side at a different hospital. There were some complications with treatment. CT scan and surgery were scheduled. I prayed with my client that evening before leaving for the day and then stopped at the hospital to visit her son. I sat beside the bed and talked with him. I held his hand and prayed for him. There was peace and calm. His recovery and healing took longer, but he was discharged home from the hospital on January 22. Glory to God. When I left her house Friday evening, she surprised me by saying, "If you have nothing better to do, give me a call tomorrow."

One morning before work, my spiritual parents were praying together with me. Bob led in prayer and while he was speaking, Goshen came to my mind, with an image of the Downtown view and the garage at the house in Knoxville. I believed this was the next step.

The Hubbards informed me that a young woman they considered a daughter, who was serving in the Philippines with her husband, was planning to come for a visit in the near future and would be staying in their home. I accepted this as another sign that God was going to position me somewhere else.

I drove to the usual Wi-Fi café in Harriman and had worked several hours when my laptop froze. There was no response to any commands, so I packed it up and drove to a local store for some needed items. I prayed over my computer in the car. I drove to another Wi-Fi spot and decided to check my laptop. There was technical gibberish flashing continuously on the screen. I texted a friend for advice. I went inside, and the only outlet available was on a wall where a long bench seat was situated. Several tables were spaced apart in front of the seat. I sat at the first table by the wall and plugged in my laptop. Some older men were sitting at the other tables and soon were joined by several other men and a few elderly couples. It was apparent they were friends and met here on a regular basis. I tried to keep my eyes on my screen and not focus on their conversations. I downloaded a program and then began to work on my files.

The large group began leaving around 9 PM. The last to walk by towards the door was a small elderly gentleman walking with a cane and assisted by a younger woman, his daughter. I smiled at his kind face as he passed by. He stopped and asked me what I was up to on my computer. I explained that I was working on a project for the church I attended. He shared that he had been a widower since 2009 and that he knew the Lord. I told him a short version of my story and how I had discovered God's love through the death of my husband. I told him that love comes from God. God is love and true love never dies. His eyes grew moist, and he smiled during our conversation. I handed him a book card and he asked if he could keep it. I sensed he wanted to talk longer and I would have enjoyed it, but his daughter was gently prodding him to leave. The sweetness of our conversation refreshed my spirits, and I drove home in gratitude. I had a wonderful time with the Lord in the Word and prayer. The short conversation with the elderly gentleman had lifted a burden off my heart, and I thanked God for that encounter. I woke up from a bad dream just a few hours after going to bed.

DREAM, Sunday, 1/7/2018, 5 AM

The room I was in began to change. A mottled gray swirling cloud was spinning around the room. It was on the walls extending up to the ceiling. I tried to rebuke it but could not speak. I opened my mouth, and it was as though my jaw froze. I strained to move my tongue, to form words, but could not. I then said the words of rebuke to the enemy silently. Immediately I could move my jaw. I was not afraid but angry and frustrated. Once I saw the effectiveness of my silent words, I relaxed and the gray swirling disappeared. I had no awareness of the enemy when I went to bed to sleep; this was only in the dream. I praised God that the enemy is defeated and I have victory in Christ.

Wednesday was salon day for my client. She was called back by her stylist, and I waited up front as usual. An older woman entered and checked in with the receptionist. She took a seat next to me and began a conversation. She was a little nervous about her overdue haircut. Someone had recommended this salon, and she was hoping for a good experience. I shared that my client had been a customer for several years and that the salon had been in business for many years. She noticed my name tag and asked me about my work. I shared some of my work history and that I was an author working as a caregiver. She perked up and said that her daughter was a writer in Southern California. She talked about her daughter's personal life and marriage, and her concerns about some recent changes in their lives. She mentioned that she had prayed for them for years, and she teared up as she spoke. She wanted to know about my book, and I shared my story. I talked about God's love and how that discovery had changed my life. I sensed her distress. I reached over and touched her hand and told her I would pray for her and for her daughter and husband. My heart hurt for her pain. My client was ready at this point, and I had to leave. I covered the woman and her family in my prayers for many days. I thanked God for this blessed divine encounter.

DREAM, Friday, 1/12/2018, 9:30 AM
I woke up from a strange dream. *I am looking at a section of crumpled red clay colored paper. It looks like an evil rendition of a wedding vow or something sacred. The words have been altered to exclude the Name of Christ; i.e. crite, with symbols and small drawings of animals, such as a bird with head down and small crosses above the words. I know this is evil. I want to tell my spiritual parents, so I walk into another room. I share this with the husband, but he seems distracted. I need God's interpretation. I overhear a personal conversation from another room and I am uncomfortable with what I hear.* I woke up disturbed and prayed for revelation.

Saturday was a wonderful day. Kathy had cooked delicious homemade biscuits and gravy. Bob was playing a worship DVD. The three of us were standing and singing with our hands in the air. The presence of the Holy Spirit was so sweet and loving. This was a precious day with the Lord. I spent some time in my bedroom relaxing and reading through the afternoon. Kathy prepared a roast with potatoes, green beans, slaw, and an apple cake later for dinner. Everything that day seemed to be touched by God's love. An incredible gift.

Pastor King's message the next day at church was enlightening and informative. I was a little unsettled because I missed my usual exit off I-75. In a moment of blankness, I drove by the exit and could not understand why that happened. I used the next exit and had breakfast at a different fast food restaurant before service. I spent the entire afternoon at a Wi-Fi café until time to return for evening service. I enjoyed a conversation with some special friends I had met previously at church. Though the day had been pleasant, an uneasiness persisted in my spirit. Prayers were lifted during the drive home.

Tuesday morning I was in Knoxville on Kingston Pike traveling in the direction of my client's home. Dairy Queen was just ahead on the right, and I was impressed to stop. I was reminded that I needed to pay back the young man who had recently covered my lack when I tried to pay for some ice cream. My card was declined that day, and he had already made the cone, so he told me just to take it anyway. I gave him what I had in my purse but was short about seventy cents. I pulled into the parking lot and went inside. The young man was there. I gave him a dollar bill and thanked him for his kindness. His eyes widened in surprise. Kathy had insisted that I accept $20 that morning for gas before I left the house. She said the Holy Spirit impressed upon her to give me the money. I put $19 in the gas tank after I left DQ, and I arrived at my client's home on time. Knoxville received heavy snowfall that afternoon, and my sister offered to let me stay at her house that night. The following night I drove back to the mountains, and the roads were clear. I was grateful for safety and many blessings.

Thursday morning I prayed for God's protection driving down the mountains. The temp was below freezing. I went into the kitchen to pour coffee into my travel mug before leaving for work, and Bob said a snowplow had just driven by the house. Kathy explained that the plows and salt trucks typically did not come up as far as where they lived, but today one truck came just as I was leaving. I gathered my things and drove down the mountain that morning following the salt truck, once again praising God for His divine protection.

DREAM, Monday, 1/22/2018, 7 AM
I woke up from a disturbing dream. At first I thought it was an attack of the enemy, but the Holy Spirit revealed the need to pray about the demonic influence on the porn industry and what it is producing. I am to pray against this destructive evil.

DREAM, Wednesday, 1/24/2018, AM
Another dream regarding pornography involving men, children, and women. Awareness of the pain, destruction, and evil. I am to pray for deliverance, healing, and mercy.

DREAM, Monday, 1/29/2018, 6 AM
There is an alligator in my bedroom wearing a felt mask that looks friendly, but I know its real face is ugly. The mask is like a kid friendly felt overlap with bright colors and harmless expression—a lie. I do not like it, and I want it out of my room. I take a shoe with a solid heel and strike it on the top of the head several times. It makes an attempt to bite me, unsuccessfully. I hit several more times but not sure if effective. The alligator seems to slump, but he is not dead. Someone is telling me he is harmless, but I say, "NO, get him out of my room." I want him out. The alligator is positioned under the bed with only part of the snout visible. This person is sticking their hand under the bed, as though to play with it, but I know the danger and they are going to get bitten. The alligator is small, not an adult size. I demand it be removed. They get it out from under the bed and carry it out of the room. I woke up at that point.

DREAM, Thursday, 2/8/2018, 6 AM
I am talking to people in a building, like an antique shop with windows and shelves. I am standing next to the front plate glass windows. Someone is asking about an item. I said, "It belongs to Grandma". Is Grandma's stuff being sold? I wonder if she is leaving soon. This is not my grandmother; rather, it is my children's grandmother on their father's side. Prayers lifted. I spoke to my daughter about the dream.

On Sunday, while at church, I could sense a detachment from Redemption. I wondered if this was related to prayer last night. The Hubbards and I had stood in a circle holding hands. Bob prayed over me and for direction for all of us. As soon as he started praying, "GOSHEN" came to my mind, a downtown view of Main Street, and the garage at my sister's house. Confirmation that this was my next step. I would continue to seek God in prayer.

Several hours remained before the start of evening service. I lived quite a distance from the church, and it was not feasible to drive back and forth between services. I made plans every Sunday for how I would spend the afternoon between the morning and evening service. One of my favorite places was a Wi-Fi café that provided a quiet setting to write or read. My bag contained a can of tuna and some crackers for lunch, and this is where I headed after morning service.

The room was empty when I arrived, and I chose a table that was positioned near an outlet. While I was setting up my laptop and getting situated, a man carrying a brown paper bag entered. He chose a table in the middle of the café and sat facing in a different direction. I barely noticed him as I began reading on my screen. I opened my tuna and ate while I scanned through the file. Usually this light lunch was satisfying, but that day I was still hungry. I refocused my thoughts away from the reality that it would be a few hours before I returned home and continued to work steadily.

A short time later the man rose from his chair, and, to my great surprise, walked over to my table and stopped. I noticed the bag in his hand was from Panera. I lifted my eyes to meet his while he spoke. He said he wanted to give me a cup of soup and some bread, and offered me the bag. My eyes widened as I looked up at him in astonishment. This was the face in my dream from four months ago. His skin was pale, his face was round, and his eyes were light blue. In the dream, I could not see any hair and now I understood. His hair was slick on his head, short and straight, light red in color. He stood about 6'3" and was very fit. Oddly, he was dressed in a white t-shirt and blue denim overalls. His clothes and white tennis shoes were very clean and neat. I stared at him without answering, processing these details, when he spoke again. I stammered, "Are you sure you don't want it?" He responded somewhat firmly, "I thought it would be nice for you to eat, rather than just a can of tuna. You are hungry, aren't you?"

Embarrassed at my hunger, I accepted his kindness and thanked him for the blessing. As he turned to walk away, I said, "God bless you." He did not speak in response or turn around. He simply walked to the door and turned the corner.

My heart had been heavy earlier in the morning. Before church I had stopped at the ATM to check my balance and discovered no funds were available to withdraw. I had brought my lunch of tuna and crackers, determined to be thankful, but God had provided a surprise, a gift of love and compassion from His heart. The soup was still warm and the bread was fresh. While I was enjoying the meal in deep gratitude, awareness unfolded that God was nourishing, encouraging, and strengthening me in my spirit. Recognition of the face from the dream months prior came with reassurance to trust and accept His provision today. The Lord has continued to build, to prepare, and to teach me in layers. Discovering hidden truths in the layers is part of the journey, which has perpetuated forward movement and growth with an increasing hunger for more of Him.

Monday morning I stopped at the ATM, and my balance was $9.04. I could not make a withdrawal. I drove to the gas station in prayer, to empty my funds into the gas tank. I set the handle to pump, expecting it to slow down close to the limit, but the gas kept pumping to a full $30.50 and the purchase was approved. I thanked God for provision.

DREAM, Wednesday, 2/14/2018 6 AM
I am walking towards what looks like a ride in an amusement park. I am walking with someone from the past. The ride is situated in the side of a mountain of black rock. There are at least three levels in the mountainside with openings. People are riding in individual cars over a roller coaster track in and out of the openings. As we are walking towards this, I look up and notice someone is riding in a single car along what looks like a power line overhead. This looks dangerous. We are getting in line, but the person I was with wanders off. I try to find this person, walking to different loading stations. I spot them on another level below. I catch up and they are talking to someone. We did not get on the ride. I woke up wondering why I was dreaming of someone from so long ago.

DREAM, Thursday, 2/15/2018 AM

I am standing in a house looking towards a window. All I see is a plain wall and a single window. A window shade is pulled down and covers one-quarter of the window. The sun had been shining. Suddenly I see blackness dropping over the light. It is moving quickly. I move to look out the window and I can see the edge of the darkness. It is solid, not hazy. Now the light is completely covered. The blackness is heavy and thick; cannot see anything through it. Next, I am walking in a mall store. I see a lot of Christmas merchandise on sale. I am wearing a vivid blue shirt and silver sequin pants. The sequins are large and dangly. I am aware that people are staring at my pants. Some even turn or stop to look. I keep walking, unconcerned with the people in the store. I am comfortable and at ease in spite of the attention and comments. I walk through a door, and now I am outdoors in a rural setting. A younger couple holds the door open. I start walking across the grassy uneven ground, expecting to meet someone, a man. This couple is following behind me. The man of the young couple asks me if I think the man is coming. I think so, but I am not sure. A few large dogs run into the scene, barking and noisy. Then more dogs keep coming. They are across a small pond from where I am standing and they notice me. The man I was expecting does not appear, and I am thinking he is not going to show. I am wondering where to go and what to do now. I wake up at this point. Who is the man I am seeking in the dream? Am I seeking Jesus?

The days with my client were up and down. We had good days mostly, but a day could turn sour for no apparent reason. Occasionally I would bring her a treat that I knew she liked. Sometimes she accepted it graciously, but there were times when she would not eat it and did not offer any expression of gratitude. I learned not to take anything personal with her behavior and knew whatever troubled her was inside her heart. She remained in my prayers daily. Friday, February 23, was very troubling. She was depressed and disinterested in everything. She was frustrated with her lack of energy and weak back. I was helping her write her checks, which was part of her normal routine, when she made a comment about the hopelessness of her physical situation. I talked to her about her words and prayed for her. She was more settled by the time I left that evening.

Saturday night I was awakened from sleep with a sudden onset of severe excruciating pain in my foot. I covered my mouth with my hand to keep from expressing the pain out loud. It gripped for several seconds and then was completely gone. What had triggered such pain? I had not experienced this previously.

The next morning at church the pastor interrupted the praise and worship to honor an impression upon him from God. He stated, "Anyone suffering nerve pain in their feet come to the altar." I was not hurting so I did not go down. Many people went forward. He then mentioned fibromyalgia. He laid hands on every person. That night, I started thinking I was supposed to have gone forward during service. That was the reason for the severe pain in my foot that woke me Saturday night. I missed a healing touch because I did not go forward. As the week passed I became more certain of the missed opportunity. I prayed for forgiveness with a heavy heart and asked God not to give up on me.

DREAM, week of 2/18/2018
I am walking across the room, and there is a white rumpled throw on the floor. As I walk by the throw, something tries to bite me. A baby gray snake snaps at my foot. The head is smooth and rounded and raised off the floor. The mouth is open and the jaws are full of small white teeth. I noticed the teeth right away. They look like baby teeth. Strange. I see a very small snake close by, and I sense there are more, but not visible. I woke up. I sensed a warning, but I was not sure how to interpret it. I prayed for revelation and protection.

I shared the visions and dreams with Bob and Kathy one Monday morning. He explained that the person from the past and the amusement ride represent flesh behind me. Let go of the flesh and seek the Spirit. The dream I experienced the next day of the window shade and darkness represents what is to come. The darkness is coming when the enemy will be trying to remove the Light. The mall store represents the world, making money, seeking wealth. The open door represents an escape to where God is, in His creation; the grass, the trees, the animals, the pond. The young couple will open the door of escape. Snakes represent the enemy.

JOURNAL ENTRY, 2/23/2018
"I continue to wait. But, sometimes I feel like a horse being brought into the corral to be broken for the first time. I trot around and snort a little nervously,

willing, I think, to yield. Then comes the bridle and bit. I start dancing around, running around the corral for short bursts, then standing still, snorting and shaking my head. I can do this, I think. Next comes the harness and saddle with a rider on my back. Oh NO. I begin bucking, jerking my head up and down, running around the corral, trying to get this authority off my back, snorting, stomping my front legs, rearing to throw off this rider. The reins tighten while I struggle to get comfortable in my yielding. Have Thy way, Lord." Philippians 1:6 NKJV: "being confident of this very thing, that He who has begun a good work in you will complete it until the day of Jesus Christ."

The details of the vision concerning my destiny from October 2016 remained in the back of my mind. I read the words almost daily and prayed over what God had revealed. I understood that God's timing is not ours, and we have to be patient and trust Him in the waiting. But I struggle at times with the waiting. He continues to teach me patience. I let out a deep sigh.

VISION, Sunday, 2/25/2018, after church
I am driving home from church when I receive a powerful vision. *I am standing backstage waiting to speak. This is a large venue. Featured artists have performed and speakers have spoken. The event promotor is anxiously standing nearby. He wants to be acknowledged as a major promotor. He is an ambitious, young, clean-cut man, greedy for recognition and advancement. He is monitoring all activity. He is not talking to me and does not notice me, but I am aware of these desires in his thoughts. I "see" a young man in a bathroom sitting on the floor, getting ready to shoot up. Instantly, the syringe and tourniquet disappear. This man is delivered from addiction. He jumps to his feet in awe. People in the building are being healed, delivered, and restored. I hear gasps of surprise as the Holy Spirit touches people. The power is quickly moving around the building. All sin, decay and disease of sin, are being removed. Sin cannot be where He is. The Lord shows me what is going to happen."* The vision ends.

This vision was extraordinary. I had seen a similar venue in a vision in 2015, but at that time no other details were provided. I prayed that I would be obedient to God and for understanding. I had prayed to be in alignment with His plans.

I shared this vision with Kathy first the next morning, and we both felt the presence of the Holy Spirit as I described the details. I was overwhelmed with emotion as I talked, and Kathy's face and eyes registered stunned wonder. Later, when I shared with Bob, his only remark was, "So be it."

Sunday morning service was anointed by the presence of the Holy Spirit. Pastor John Green was strongly impressed to offer the invitation before service. Our heads were bowed and eyes were closed, but I could hear many acknowledgements of hands raised. Wonderful to welcome new brothers and sisters into the Body of Christ! The pastor delivered a powerful message on spiritual maturity. I went to the Wi-Fi café after church and worked all afternoon into the evening. I finished the Legacy files I had been working on, wrote and posted a new blog, and caught up on emails and messages. I thanked the Lord for this good day and for the spiritual nourishment from the morning service.

DREAM, Tuesday, 3/6/2018, AM
I woke up from this dream when my phone rang. *I am at an event where there is a Christian speaker, music, and food. I see a table of corndogs stacked on a table and each one has mustard on it. But I am not interested. I wander into a shopping area/gift store. I see a friend from the past with her daughter and granddaughters. They are laughing and enjoying themselves, but I am not interested in the store. I spot a large green door on a back wall with heavy metal hinges and hardware. I want to open the door. Now I am standing in a natural habitat. There is a dirt road curving ahead. I see a large cage with an animal inside. A man is explaining about this particular animal, but I am looking at the road. I am thinking that Jesus is on up the road. I want to follow the road. I cannot see around the bend, but I want to keep moving. I want to find Jesus. I want to see Jesus.*

DREAM, Saturday, 3/10/2018 5:45 AM
I am sitting outside in a chair, on a farm. I am holding a baby on my lap. I am patting her on the back as though I am burping her. I think the baby is fine, but suddenly I realize she is choking. I am scared. I am patting harder. He eyes roll back, and her entire face turns dark red. She puts her hand to her neck. I start running with the baby, looking and yelling for help. I see some people nearby, and I run towards them. One of the women takes the baby

and asks her name. I do not know the baby's name. I hesitate to answer. I am thinking. I say her name is Betsy, but the name, "Elsie," is in my mind. The woman looks at me, black hair and brown eyes, and repeats the name as a question, "Betsy?" Now the baby seems to be ok. The three women are talking like everything is fine. I feel so relieved. Baby was not a newborn, maybe 3-6 months old, and she had a lot of straight hair.

When I arrived home that night, Bob and Kathy were still up. Bob was reading while Kathy was busy in the kitchen. He put his book down, and I shared the dream about the baby. He said the baby was my book. The book has been out for a while now and is not a new release, not an "infant". The book has been choked, but no more. The choking has been cleared, and the book is alive. Later in my room, I pondered over his words and spent some time in prayer.

VISION, Tuesday, 3/13/2018

I was reading the Word this morning in Hebrews. "Serving God" was the message I kept seeing repeatedly. Suddenly, I received another vision concerning Indiana. *I am standing in an upstairs room in Downtown Goshen with lots of windows. I am standing across from Sue and other familiar faces. I understood that God's provision would come through helping hands. Receive with gratitude to Him. Rejoice for those who help. Provision would come at time of need. I then started thinking about money for rent, utilities, et cetera, and there was no specific revelation about those expenses.* The vision ended when my thoughts turned to physical needs.

On Thursday I was talking on the phone with my daughter when my phone buzzed on vibrate. I looked at the phone but did not see any banner alerts. I kept on talking. The phone buzzed again, twice. I ended the call and checked. I had received a text a little after 8 AM from Kathy for prayers. Bob was in the OR. I began praying at that moment. As I was praying, I felt the love of God for Bob surge through me. This was unexpected and exhilarating. I was praying for God to flood Bob with His healing love. I lifted prayers for his surgery and recovery. I was overwhelmed by God's precious sweetness while I prayed. I thanked God in reverence and awe. The love for Bob from God was overpowering.

I composed a letter of resignation. God had impressed upon me about selling the large items remaining in the garage in Knoxville and using those funds for my return trip to Goshen. He would guide my steps upon arrival with provision for my needs. Whatever was next for me was in Goshen. I prayed over the letter, the upcoming sale, and the travel. I prayed over my sister and for my client and her issues, trusting God's divine hand on everything connected to this move.

DREAM, Friday, 3/16/2018
I am sitting outside looking at the horizon as the sky is getting dark. I see some brightly colored lights, and I am thinking I might get a picture. I walk in that direction. As I move closer, I see what appear to be transformers coming out of this area, like a cave or hidden entrance. Each one is bright in color—yellow, green, red, fully covered. Each has a different type of weaponry on their forearm. They appear to be marching single file somewhere. I move on. I am now sitting in an event. A preacher or leader is speaking. I see and hear a young woman talking. She is worried the man will say something wrong. I can see the fear in her face, and I can feel her tension.

Friday night, March 23, I was at Bob and Kathy's house reflecting on the events of the past week. Rain had canceled the planned yard sale and the week was difficult in many ways. My sister had paid for gas in my car and offered to let me stay at her house for a few nights as she was going out of town and her roommate was out of town as well. This saved on gas mileage, and I was thankful for those blessings.

I drove to the agency office on Friday morning, to submit my letter of resignation. I talked to the staff about my next move and the leading of the Lord back to Goshen. They were surprised but spoke words in support. I shared my story with them and how God had brought me to their company. I thanked them for the opportunity to serve during the past year.

My client was in high spirits when I arrived that afternoon. We had a good day, until I told her that I had submitted my letter of resignation earlier that day. She became angry and immediately called the office. She was demanding and stern the rest of the day. The atmosphere was tense. I had not expected her to react so strongly. She made several calls and had someone else lined up to take my place privately. She would not use the office for my replacement. I wished her well and planned to keep her in my prayers. I had peace that God would take care of her as she belonged to Him. He had decided now was the time to leave, and I trusted His wisdom.

Her birthday was the following week and I would not be with her, so I brought her a small chocolate cake to celebrate early on my last day, Friday, March 30. She expressed no interest in the cake and did not cut it while I was there. Her demeanor changed in the afternoon, and she became negative and demanding. I stayed busy and refused to respond to her in the same manner. I explained to her why I was leaving. God was calling me to return to Goshen, and I was following Him in obedience. I reminded her that He was the one who sent me to her a year ago. She could not believe I was going to move to Indiana in faith, without a job or shelter or any other plans in place. I told her about my faith journey with God since the death of Scott and how I had discovered God's love for me through my husband's move to heaven. God had carried me and directed me every step since that time, and I had learned I could trust Him. I believed His Word. The wind left her sails, so to speak, at that moment, and she let out a deep sigh. She told me to keep in touch, and I told her I would. When I left her house that evening, I had a flashback to the day Scott and I drove to Goshen back in 2008. I knew when we left my driveway that morning I would not pass that way again. The same feeling recurred now as I left her driveway for the last time.

I had rescheduled the yard sale for March 31 and advertised on social media market sites. I stayed at my sister's house Thursday and Friday night in preparation. The items were priced, and the signs were made. Everything was ready for the first customer who stopped just after 6 on Saturday morning. All of the large items were gone by 12:30. We boxed up the few small items remaining to donate to KARM, and we were ready to leave, when the garage door would not shut. We tried the remote control and the button on the wall inside the garage with no response. A truck pulled up in front of the house at that moment, and a man walked up the driveway. He had bought my clock earlier at the sale and had some questions about the buttons on the back. I explained about the clock and then asked him about the garage door. He was able to close it manually. I was so thankful and told my sister that God had answered our prayer for help. She would phone the landlord on Monday and report the situation for any needed repairs, but at least the garage door was closed and she could leave the house without worrying.

The next day, Easter Sunday, was my last day at Redemption Church. I met my dear friend, Brenda, in Jacksboro after church for dinner with her family. I shared details about my journey and my desire for more of God. I talked about my new life in walking with Him and how I was growing through service to others. We discussed many things after eating, and I was prompted to lead in prayer with the family. I began by thanking God for our blessings, our families, our friends. I prayed for churches and leaders to seek the Holy Spirit in decisions and solutions, for people to see and love with the heart and mind of Jesus. I prayed for blessings over their family, their home, their marriage, the granddaughter's future, Brenda's role as matriarch in the family, blessings for their faithfulness, friendship, encouragement, kindness, and generosity. I became aware while I was praying that they were in tears, and I broke as I closed the prayer with emotion. We were wiping our eyes. The Holy Spirit had touched each of us. We shared hugs as we said goodbye. My heart was filled with love for this special family.

I visited with Bob and Kathy that evening. They shared with me that God had revealed to them at the end of February that I would be leaving in April and they had received instructions to give me a specific amount of money just before I was ready to leave Tennessee. Kathy shared that I would not be staying in Goshen permanently, but something was unfinished there and I had to return for a while. They handed me a sealed envelope with the money and a card of scriptures to read later. I was happy to hear this confirmation about returning to Indiana. I understood this provision would cover the cost of travel and sustain me through the transition of settling in Goshen.

On Monday I returned my ID badge and employee manual to the home care office. I had a partial denture repair that was ready to pick up at the dentist's office. Next was an oil change, car wash, and laundry. Bob and Kathy invited me to meet them for dinner in Knoxville, and we revisited some of the dreams and events of our time together. I drove back to the house and loaded my vehicle. I cleaned the room I had been staying in as a guest in their home and then walked outside. I prayed over their property, for blessings and protection over them, and for a future buyer when they were ready to sell.

I thanked God for the beauty of the mountains where I had lived for the past five and a half years and for all the steps that had brought me to this point with Him. I thanked God for the blessings of family, my children and grandson, for Scott and the life we shared, and for my future with Him. I met Jesus in Goshen in 2011 and arrived in East Tennessee in November of 2012 with a raw heart and uncertainty about my future, knowing only that God loved me and would be with me wherever I lived. I had returned to Goshen for the weekend of July 4 in 2016, when God healed my heart of the pain from grief and losses of the past. I will return to Goshen tomorrow for His purpose. He will be with me whatever I face. I am ready to leave, secure in His love for me.

I settled down for bed and repeated the words I had spoken in response to the invitation from Jesus in 2016:

"Yes, Lord, I take your hand
I walk with you forever
Down this road
Not knowing where
In joy
In love
In intimate relationship
There is no greater bliss!"

This is the same invitation Jesus extends to everyone, to trust Him and to allow Him to lead and guide with His everlasting love.

Give God your hand, your heart, your life, and see what He can do with you, in you, and through you, to make an impact in this world for His glory. Allow God to craft a story through your life that will encourage and inspire others, and discover more about your true self in the process. Celebrate your victories. Confess your failures. If you have found yourself stuck on your spiritual journey, share your thoughts and desires with God. Pick up your cross and press on toward the prize that Paul spoke about in Philippians 3:12-14 (NKJV), "12 Not that I have already attained, or am already perfected; but I press on, that I may lay hold of that for which Christ Jesus has also laid hold of me. 13 Brethren, I do not count myself to have apprehended; but one thing *I do,* forgetting those things which are behind and reaching forward to those things which are ahead, 14 I press toward the goal for the prize of the upward call of God in Christ Jesus."

I had written a statement in my journal from one of Pastor Charles Stanley's sermons about the Holy Spirit, *"Walking in the Spirit is living moment by moment in dependence upon Him, sensitive to His voice, and in obedience to Him."* I am returning to Goshen in obedience to God. I pause to reflect on my progress, from where I started to where I am at this moment. I am pressing onward with my gaze on the horizon, anticipating the fulfillment of God's promises.

EPILOGUE

My first book, "Showered By Grace," detailed my life before Scott, the beautiful love we shared, and the greater story of falling in love with Jesus.

"Showered By God's Love" reveals the deepening intimacy I experienced with God as I walked through trials and adversity. He patiently guided me when I stumbled on the learning path orchestrated by my desire for more of Him. Through the difficulties, the lack, the uncertainty, I learned to trust God. I am humbled and thankful for the process and the outcome. This book chronicles the 5-1/2 years I spent in East Tennessee where I began an incredible wilderness season of healing and discovery. God alone provides the joy, the peace, and the love that we all desire. God's infinite love is the power that sustains.

My ongoing quest in the pursuit of Christlikeness will continue when I return to Goshen, Indiana, tomorrow in another stage of bloom. I encourage you, fellow sojourner, to take courage and press on. God is worthy of our sacrifices.

Printed in the United States
by Baker & Taylor Publisher Services